FOLIAGE PLANTS

Christopher Lloyd

FOLIAGE PLANTS

COLLINS
St James's Place, London

William Collins Sons & Co Ltd
London · Glasgow · Sydney · Auckland
Toronto · Johannesburg

First published 1973
© Christopher Lloyd 1973
ISBN 0 00 214044 6
Made and Printed in Great Britain by
William Collins Sons & Co Ltd Glasgow

Contents

*

Illustrations

Illustrations

Illustrations

All colour photographs are by the author

CHAPTER I

Foliage and the Reader

*

You have picked up my book and you have read the blurb on the flap (few reviewers go any farther than that). You have flipped through the pages to see what the pictures look like, how many are in colour and how unnatural the greens have turned out. Now you come to this bit where the author has to present and justify himself and his subject.

Like every other author who wishes to be read, I have to be and am thinking of you even harder than you are of me, and I'm trying to imagine what sort of person you are likely to be. You may simply be in Hatchard's on a Saturday morning where and when you make a habit of dipping into as many books as you can without the slightest intention of buying them. No matter; you must have some interest in gardening to have got even this far, and even if you're desperately hunting for Christmas presents, you will prefer to give something you would yourself like to receive. To be interested in gardening you must at some time in your life have done a bit.

And to find out what sort of gardener you are, or were, before you took to flat life, I can hardly do better than ask you how you react to foliage. Unfortunately I cannot hear your replies, so I shall have to make some up for you.

If you had been an 'I like colour' gardener, you would never have touched the book. If its title stimulated a thought, that thought would have been a disparaging 'Who wants foliage? Give me flowers', and some scarlet and yellow blobs would have jumped before your inward eye in a vision of salvias and marigolds.

Clearly you are not one of them, although you probably were once. We all were. For it is an indisputable fact that appreciation of foliage comes at a late stage in our education, if it comes at all. If we don't actually live among primitive people we can still recognise primitive reactions (supposing we have forgotten our own early state, as is usually the case) in children. They love bright colours above all things aesthetic.

But foliage is seldom bright or obvious; it is undoubtedly an acquired taste, one that grows on us. It provides a satisfying and sustaining diet.

Sustaining and sustained. One of the most obvious attributes of the average leaf is that it is with us for much longer than the flower. That is truest of the evergreen, whose every leaf remains on the plant for one to three years; true also, however, of the deciduous plant whose foliage probably lasts for 4, 5 or 6 months.

With the exception of a few freaks like the *Coleus blumei* hybrids, foliage colouring is seldom brilliant, but its quality is subtle and its shading changes with age and according to the season. Some leaves are at their most entrancing when young; others reach a brief climacteric as they are approaching death. Others, again, are quite different in winter from what they were in summer, changing from green to puce or purple.

But then a leaf is not just one colour at one moment in time and another at another. It may be several colours at one and the same time. Variegated. More often than not, this is an abnormal condition, a deviation from some plain and unremarkable norm.

People reacted strongly to variegation. Captain Collingwood Ingram ('Cherry' Ingram) who is a doyen among gardeners, an authority on rhododendrons, ornamental cherries and many other shrubs, told me flatly that he couldn't abide any variegation and would not allow a variegated plant in his garden. At 90 plus he is old enough to make such a statement baldly. Younger people (mostly male) would tend to qualify and excuse their dislike, knowing it to be unfashionable.

And it is unfashionable. Variegation has been popularised by the flower arranging movement which has been a notable social and (perhaps we might claim with such modesty as we can muster) artistic feature of post-war Britain. Variegated leaves have contributed importantly to the range of material available to the flower arranger, who saw more to them than had been apparent to the gardener, but who has induced the gardener to take another look at them and their role in the garden. Cross-fertilisation between the arts has always been productive.

Even the normal leaf is usually a different colour on its upper surface and on its lower. Perhaps green on top and grey beneath or green on top and fawn or rust beneath. And so we get a different impression of a plant according to whether we are seeing parts or all of it from above or from below. And our position, in this relationship, can be altered for us by the wind. Especially is this the case with trees having long leaf stalks resulting in exceptional mobility: with the grey and green of certain poplars; of the lime, *Tilia petiolaris*, and the maple, *Acer saccharinum*.

Leaves are two-faced because of the different finish on the upper and lower surfaces, which brings us to the sensuous subject of leaf texture. Sensuous because so many leaves seem to be inviting us to touch them: to feel their attractions through our finger tips. They may be waxy, woolly, silky, clammy or crinkly: these are all conditions requiring tactile recognition. And while some leaves, like a fully expanded banana frond as yet untorn by wind, may charm us by their fragility, others are no less fascinating for being thick and solid: my pet *Senecio reinoldii* (*S. rotundifolius*) comes to mind.

The shapes of leaves are almost as various as the shapes of flowers: not quite so, however, because the vast majority of leaves are thin and flat with a well defined top and bottom and none of the complex sexual paraphernalia located in the flower.

Within these limits, they are of all shapes and sizes. Even a very small leaf, like that of *Helichrysum microphyllum*, succeeds by sheer numbers and by their arrangement on the branches, in creating a mosaic pattern that beguiles the eye. Larger leaves like the palmate maples, the spears of yuccas, the nobly designed cardoon and the fans of *Fatsia japonica*, are thrilling to contemplate in tufts, rosettes, clouds and masses. They are impressive not merely in their substance but in their shadows – shadows cast one against another, shadows against a pavement even from some quite small and lowly plant like a cranesbill. Very often we notice the shadow before the leaf.

There is a band-wagon labelled Foliage. It has none of the rave appeal of those marked Roses, Ground Cover, The Labour-

Saving Garden, The No-Time Gardener. But it is modestly there, capitalising a demand. We had *Hardy Foliage Plants* from Richard Gorer in 1966; Sybil Emberton's *Garden Foliage for Flower Arrangement*, which I shall doubtless crib as I go along, is a favourite of mine; there was a book (probably more than one) devoted entirely to dwarf conifers; a thirsty circle of enthusiasts welcomed A. H. Lawson's *Bamboos* and very much the same group opened its arms to Reginald Kaye's *Hardy Ferns*. Latest of all and presented by my own publishers is Mrs Desmond Underwood's treatise on the Greys. If it emerges in print while I am at this book (and it must, because I can see myself taking two winters) I shall hardly know whether I dare read it, for fear of being unduly influenced, or dare not to read it in case of blunders that could hardly pass unnoticed, where comparisons are inevitable.

But it is not just, or even mainly, the band-wagon aspect that lures me into my subject. It is that my growing appreciation of foliage is something I want to share with you, the reader in Hatchard's, who has skipped all the last bit anatomising foliage in order to see what my last introductory flourishes will be. All addicts want to increase their circle of addicts.

My own particular pretensions or qualifications for writing on foliage are, first, in the Jack-of-all-trades-but-master-of-none category, that, having gardened all my life and specialised less than is normal in these days of specialisation, I can cover a wide field. This has advantages and drawbacks. The obvious drawback is that I shall be inaccurate and inadequate in discussing dwarf conifers, say, or bamboos. This may pass unnoticed by you, poor reader (I will soon have done with this maddening and archaic apostrophising) but will be only too obvious to the specialist in dwarf conifers or in bamboos. He would do my job much better in his own field. But perhaps he would feel slightly uncomfortable when he came to discussing annuals for foliage or one of the other facets of the subject that I intend to bring in.

Second credential. I am aware that plants in a garden have to be grown side by side. Also that a plant not only has a context but is liable to be seen in its context. And I find this business of juxtaposition and setting, which makes all the difference between a jumble and a picture, is one of the most absorbing aspects of gardening. So I shall harp on the theme of plant relationships, hoping that it is one that interests you too. Many of one's greatest successes in this department arise either by accidental associations – plants that have placed themselves – or from other gardeners' ideas. This is nothing to be ashamed of. The great thing is to be receptive to ideas, from wherever they may have sprung; from inside yourself or from outside. So if something has worked especially well for you in your garden, I hope you will come and tell me about it here in mine at Great Dixter in the village of Northiam, 8 miles from Rye in East Sussex, where we can swap lies about our children, as my mother would say, and enjoy ourselves hugely in the exchange (but you must allow me to carry on with my weeding while we chat).

As I am not much of a pigeon-holer, I shall try to mitigate the unavoidable categorising of my foliage plants as far as possible and also avoid divorcing them from flowering plants, merely for the convenience, as it would be, of organising my book. Where all this is going to take me I don't yet know, as I am writing this introductory chapter at the start of my book and not at the end (this being the wiser and commoner practice). But I hope we shall enjoy the journey.

CHAPTER 2

The Field

*

THE question of what is herein going to be defined as a foliage plant must be discussed and we can at the same time see how certain plants make the grade while others fail. Then, having come to the daunting conclusion that thousands more foliage plants exist than could be fitted into this book, even supposing I knew them all, I must define my frontiers and limitations.

The criterion that I shall aim at, in defining a foliage plant, is of one whose leaves are ornamental (there would be no point in describing and recommending couch grass) and of greater aesthetic importance to the gardener than its flowers. Nevertheless, many will be useful flowering plants in their season and I shall say why and how, as the occasion arises.

Certain groups of plants have particularly dull and dreary foliage, and depend 100% on their flowers to disguise the fact. Such are many of the composites – the daisy tribe. Think of the leaves of Michaelmas daisies, sunflowers, heleniums, rudbeckias and golden rods. The best you can hope of them is that they will remain unobtrusive. With few exceptions dahlias are little better and the type of large-flowered florist's chrysanthemum that wins prizes at flower shows has appallingly coarse and unappealing leaves. If you go back to these plants' prototypes you will often find that their leaves are unassuming and even mildly pleasing as it might be in *Aster ericoides* or in a cut-leaved, small single-flowered chrysanthemum. 'Improvement', i.e. enlargement and elaboration of the flower, or increase in 'flower power', invariably entails a coarsening of the leaf.

Among shrubs there are groups that are equally uninspiring leaf-wise. There are the deutzias and closely related *Philadelphus*. Whereas some *Escallonia* species have acceptable leaves, the hybrids such as Apple Blossom and Peach Blossom are a miserable crew. The Japanese quinces, derived from *Chaenomeles japonica* and *C. speciosa*, have nothing to recommend them beyond their flowers and fruits. The majority of winter and early spring flowering shrubs have the dullest leaves in summer: winter sweet, Chinese witch hazel, winter flowering honeysuckle (*Lonicera fragrantissima et al.*), forsythias, peaches, almonds, cherries. The beauty of naked trees and shrubs in flower provokes the revolutionary and (to my purpose) unhelpful reflection (with a wink towards the virtually leafless brooms) that it would be rather delightful and an aid to the better appreciation of their blossom, if we could do without leaves altogether. I must apply a firm heel to that thought.

It is obvious that the dull dogs among leaves will find no place herein. They have been summoned for the express purpose of immediate dismissal. There are other plants, however, in which the balance between leaf and flower is more delicate and less readily defined. *Camellia japonica* in many of its cultivars has a good leaf: dark, lustrous and ever-present, but it could hardly claim to greater weight than the blossom. Some of the cistuses have nice foliage. Particularly in winter, I enjoy the leaden hue of *Cistus cyprius* and the purple-tinted, wavy-margined leaves of *C. corbariensis*. These enhance; they do not outshine the flowers. I have grown a batch of Tige de Fer carnations from seed sown in April and transplanted to their flowering positions in the autumn. They have made large mounds of healthy glaucous foliage that gives me marked pleasure, in between bouts of snow causing their temporary disappearance. Yet the flowers next July are what I am undeniably waiting for. And those epimediums that one hears loudly acclaimed as ground cover in shade: the coppery tints and clearly cut outline of their young leaves is certainly an additional charm, if you took the necessary step of removing their disreputable old foliage just before their successors' appearance, but I should have no truck with them if denied their flowers.

Even the dullest leaf shape can be transformed into a rave success if it is prettily coloured or variegated. Many such will find a place in this book but I will take a few examples here. What duller than the oval form? How better epitomised than in hedging privet, *Ligustrum ovalifolium*? Yet the golden privet, if not exactly the latest hit, is an extremely popular foliage plant and was acclaimed by no less a gardener-artist than Gertrude Jekyll. She used it at the back of her principal border. 'This Golden Privet is one of the few shrubs that has a place in the flower border. Its clean, cheerful bright yellow gives a note of just the right colour all through the summer. It has a solidity of aspect that enhances by contrast the graceful lines of the foliage of a clump of the Japanese striped grass Eulalia, which stands within a few feet of it, seven feet high, shooting upright, but with the ends of the leaves recurved.'* Her Eulalia is the zebra grass, *Miscanthus sinensis* 'Zebrinus'.

Other oval leaves redeemed by variegation are those of the winter-flowering *Cornus mas,* of the red-barked dogwood, *Cornus alba,* of the laurustinus, *Viburnum tinus* and the Portugal laurel, *Prunus lusitanica.*

The laurels and, even worse, the spotted laurels, are still a much despised clan – among plantsmen, that is; not with flower arrangers (I am on the side of the angels, on these occasions). Even such an enthusiast as Vita Sackville-West couldn't abide anything with this kind of leaf. And she, in common with a number of gardeners I know, disliked all oval-leaved hebes, regardless of their flowers. But, oval or not, so often there are redeeming features to which these people seem blind. Just think, for instance, how the light green colouring and high polish on a cherry laurel's leaf set it on a plane way above the dim matt-ness of a hardy hybrid rhododendron such as Cynthia.

Most writers on foliage concentrate on hardy plants. Well, if they got mixed up with house and greenhouse plants, where would they be? Where should I? On the other hand I rather relish some of those lush tropical-looking subjects (or objects) that can be grown in the garden during our summers. A few of them will be given room.

I shall exclude most rock plants within the foliage definition, because I have no rock garden and rather dislike rock gardens as a genre. I like the plants but I'm not on intimate terms with them. For the same reason, that they are mainly used in rock gardens, I know few and grow fewer of the dwarf conifers – an extremely confusing group with a wild diversity of pseudonyms. But some,

* *Colour in the Flower Garden,* 1908.

like the low-growing and creeping junipers, are such valuable members of many a mixed team, that they must put in an appearance. Much the same with heathers. The colour in modern calluna plants does not for me redeem the bittiness of their foliage nor the squalor of their habit.

If a deciduous shrub or tree achieves distinction only, or almost only, by its capacity to colour up in autumn, I reckon it is not worth including in any but the largest gardens. Fothergillas, *Nyssa sylvatica* and *Photinia villosa* strike the note I want to sound, in this respect.

This leaves me, at a wild guess, with 600 plants with which I am, at the least, on nodding terms, and at best closely acquainted. I mean to take the trees on their own, first. That will leave the shrubs, herbaceous plants, annuals, biennials and tender perennials, any of which may be used in combination in our garden beds and borders or in plantings too large to be called beds or borders.

I shall describe and discuss some of the Principals in these groups, then suggest ways to set about using them. Finally (if I ever get there) I shall put forward other possibilities in the way of plants that would hardly be described as important in a general sense but could be made so if the gardener fancied any one of them and chose to concentrate on increasing his stock of it. The little liriope with variegated foliage, for instance. How many know it? Very few, and they probably have just one plant; a sample. But you might suddenly decide that it was the very thing to grow in a large patch next to autumn-flowering sternbergias. You would work up a stock and the plant, to you, would become as important as any mentioned in this book. So be it. We can do with more gardeners of that sort.

CHAPTER 3

Trees for Foliage

*

MOST gardens, more's the pity, are too cramped to allow the inclusion of many trees. The more important, then, that we should choose the right ones. So often the choice falls on a flowering crab or a flowering cherry and yet the majority of these have little to recommend them outside their blossoming time, and that lasts in average spring weather for a mere week or 10 days. Even those popular purple-leaved crabs, *Malus purpurea*, *M. aldenhamensis*, *M. eleyi* and *M. lemoinei*, begin to look sooty and tired soon after flowering, and their foliage is subject to scab disease the same as any fruiting apple's.

If we are choosing coniferous trees, there is a strong probability that it will be for their foliage, although it may be for the mechanical wind-protection this foliage provides rather than for its appearance. But evergreen conifers make splendid backgrounds and those with colourful foliage show to advantage against those that are more sombre. And there are at least three delightful conifers that are deciduous.

First in alphabetical order is the large and important genus *Acer* – the maples, which include the sycamore. Their leaves are nearly always palmate, the lobes making more or less sharp points, and this is a decorative outline. The exception is *A. negundo*, the box elder, whose leaves are pinnate, being divided into three or five leaflets. These are too broad and too few to lend much elegance to the leaf as a whole. The box elder would be dull indeed but for its several variegated forms. Some are supposed to have a broad white margin; in Aureo-marginata it is supposed to be yellow. I have seen groups of both types grown side by side on a nursery and the difference is so slight that you couldn't, at a distance, tell where one block ended and the other began, but that was in summer. In spring, there is a marked distinction. This maple makes a scraggy tree. It is seen at its best when treated as a shrub and pruned hard back every, or, better for the plant's long-term health, every other winter. Then it can look really rather striking.

Some acers make trees of the largest size. Suppose you had a park . . . I don't see why gardening authors should invariably aim their remarks at small-garden owners on the assumption that these people's minds are as small and their interests as narrow as their gardens. Parks do still exist and the small-gardener may even take pleasure in visiting those that are opened to him and enjoy their trees no less for not being able to plant them himself. Such is certainly my own case.

It is a great treat for me and for many another to visit Borde Hill in the middle of Sussex, let us say, and admire its magnificent park specimens and groups of *Acer saccharinum*, the Silver Maple, once *A. dasycarpum* yclept, which the more readily prevented confusion of its name with *A. saccharum*, the Sugar Maple, of Canadian fame.

The Silver Maple makes a great broad-headed tree, whose subsidiary branches sweep vertically to the ground, or to the cattle-chewing line, whichever comes first. Their five-pointed leaves are smooth and green on top but silky and white beneath and they make a memorable impression, when set in motion by a summer's breeze.

Two of the largest maples are *A. pseudoplatanus*, the Sycamore, and *A. platanoides*, the Norway Maple. The latter is the more distinguished because its leaves are not coarse-textured nor subject to disfiguration by tar-spotting, like the sycamore's, and their points are sharply etched. One of the Norway Maple's variants that I particularly covet is Drummondii. The leaf margin is bordered in white and is clearly separated from the green central area. This is a clone and is propagated true to type by grafting. Variegated sycamores, by contrast, are often seedlings and thus vary a good deal, but the general idea is of radiating streaks of mixed-up green and white. This is a comparatively messy arrangement but they do none the less contrive to make large and handsome trees.

There is a popular cultivar of the Norway Maple most commonly known as Goldsworth Purple but Crimson King and various other aliases are either the same or near as makes no odds. The leaves unfold coppery brown but are nearly black at maturity and would be too dark for effect but for their glossy sheen. It can make a handsome background to a large, light-coloured shrub such as the Golden Elder. *A. platanoides* 'Schwedleri' has quite bright reddish young leaves that change to uninteresting green at maturity. Grown as a tree, it flowers attractively in April. You can also keep it as a large shrub by cutting it hard back every other winter, in which case you will get none of its lime-green flowers, but the plant will continue extension growth and hence the production of bright young terminal leaves, right into August. I grow this at the back of my main mixed border and I like it without pretending it is a five-star plant.

Three sycamore cultivars called Nizetti, Brilliantissimum and Prinz Handjery are in a quite different category, being slow growing and at some pains to make trees at all. Their efforts are all expended on a thrilling and dramatic spring outburst. Brilliantissimum is shrimp pink; Prinz Handjery is yellow on top, purple beneath, and Nizetti, which I haven't seen, is said to be similar. So much early brilliance can only end in tears and mortification. These trees are hard put to it to manufacture any chlorophyll, the green pigment by which they grow. A little along the principal veins, but the rest changes to a pernicious-anaemic yellow by late spring and so remains. Still, if you planted them as bushes in a rather open bluebell glade (which wouldn't need to be visited except in spring) the effect could be ravishing.

I will deal with the Japanese maples as shrubs later on. Likewise the Tree of Heaven, *Ailanthus altissima*, treating this as a shrub for foliage effect.

Perhaps I might squeeze in a few kind words for two alders, in passing. Our native *Alnus glutinosa* is, after all, extremely useful for growing on boggy ground which we don't want to have to drain. Nothing could be more solid than its broadly rounded leaf, but *A.g. incisa* is deeply cut into narrow segments. *A.g.* 'Imperialis' is also cut up and makes a distinguished 30-ft. tree in Maurice Mason's garden where I saw it, but Bean* remarks 'often a thin, rather ungainly tree', so there you are.

* W. J. Bean, *Trees and Shrubs Hardy in the British Isles.*

1. The deciduous or swamp cypress, *Taxodium distichum*, in the Oxford Botanic Garden.

2. ABOVE, a squad of incense cedars, *Libocedrus* (*Calocedrus*) *decurrens* at Westonbirt arboretum in Gloucestershire.　BELOW, the golden foliage of *Robinia pseudoacacia* 'Frisia' retains a wonderful luminosity throughout its season.

Amelanchiers flare up in autumn but their leaves are not otherwise anything special. *Araucaria araucana*, the Monkey Puzzle, seldom does itself justice as a mature specimen in our climate and loses its lowest branches untimely. *Arbutus unedo*, the Strawberry Tree, is certainly valuable as one of the few more or less hardy evergreen trees that are not conifers, but its leaves are only so-so.

I must give official mention to *Castanea sativa* 'Albo-marginata' because I dote on it. This is a sport from the Spanish Chestnut and has pure white leaf margins. Sometimes this whiteness distorts and puckers the leaf but not to its disadvantage. How big it will grow and whether to tree size, I don't yet know, having never seen a mature specimen, but I have placed it at the back of my 15 ft. border and can always prune it if it grows larger than a large shrub. However, it would make a good lawn specimen on its own.

Catalpas have spitefully dull foliage except for the golden form, which is more useful as a shrub than as a tree, which brings us to the cedars. Undoubtedly the most striking as to its foliage is the popular blue-leaved *Cedrus atlantica glauca* but the colouring varies greatly from tree to tree, so it is wise to choose your plant by eye. Most of the best nursery stock has been grafted on the Continent and imported. This cedar should be accorded as much lateral space as will allow its branches to sweep the ground. Golden cedars are a dirty yellow.

And so to the far more important though less magnificent coniferous genus *Chamaecyparis*, of which Lawson's Cypress, *C. lawsoniana* is the linchpin, having given rise to an extraordinary number and variety of mutations. We shall doubtless have to come back for some of these when considering the shrubs but many grow into trees of conical habit and 60 or more feet high.

A visit to the National Pinetum at Bedgebury in Kent (only 10 or 12 miles from my home) has refreshed my memory in between the last paragraph and this.

A point that should be noted about the foliage of all cypresses and junipers is that there are two types. The juvenile leaf sticks out obliquely from its twig and is sharp-pointed – usually described as awl-shaped but perhaps the reader is as unfamiliar with the awl (? a cross between the owl and the awk) and its shape as I am. The mature leaf is scale-like and lies flat against the twig on which it grows. Every seedling starts by having the juvenile type of leaf but whereas some continue in this way for the rest of their lives, as does our wild juniper, *Juniperus communis*, others gradually change over to the adult scaly leaf while yet others continue, in maturity, to combine both leaf types on different branchlets. The juvenile leaf-type gives a much more feathery texture to a bush or tree than does the adult. Whipcord hebes have scaled-leaves similar to an adult cypress's.

Among the largest Lawson cultivars is 'Triomphe de Boskoop'. It is a dark glaucous green in winter (which it is as I write) and a rather gloomy feature, but makes a 60 ft. cone very rapidly, has an open, informal texture and is a beautiful shade of pale blue on the young shoots in spring. It is a good background tree for the yellow conifers. Allumii is another glaucous cultivar and a popular hedging variety. It is excessively dismal in winter and has no redeeming features as a tree. Its branch system becomes coarse and threadbare with age. In 50 years it grows as many feet. I am also disappointed in Green Hedger as a tree. It is not objectionable but is practically featureless and a very ordinary green. As a hedge it is another matter, having an upright habit and being slow growing enough to require no trimming in many situations, in which case it cones freely.

Elegantissima dates back a century and is well named. It grows about a foot a year (growing in turf, that is) and is pale green with a hint of silver in it. The leaf-bearing branch tips are dense and overlapping with a pretty spraying habit. Filiformis grows to 35 ft. or so in 50 years and is then 12 ft. across at the base. The scale leaves are minute and this gives a thread-fine outline to the branchlets; they ramify like seaweed. It strikes me as more interesting in detail and hence for cutting than in the mass. It is a dimmish green in winter. Intertexta, 60 ft. by 8 after 45 years, has a spire-like habit but a very open branch system, the terminal branchlets being widely spaced and graceful. Having written that from my direct observation and notes, I now see that Bean writes 'It is the stoutness and remoteness of the ultimate ramifications that give this variety its unique appearance', which tells the same story only better.

Now we come to one of my favourites, though Bean seems to have disliked it. 'A curious rather than beautiful form', he remarks of Wisselii, and 'too thinly furnished to be pleasing'. Perhaps he had a Victorian preference for clutter. Wisselii grows slowly to 60 or 70 ft. by about 8 ft. across. The branch work being sparse, you can, although they come down to the ground, see a pleasantly rugged trunk through them. The branch habit gives an impression of great strength, being horizontal or slightly downward pointing near the trunk but turning upwards and becoming vertical at the leafy tips. It has the beckoning lines of a Chinese pagoda. The foliage branches are very dark and dense, in chunky blobs: rather glaucous. The scale leaves are tiny. This is an ideal tree to act as background to the autumn display of highly coloured deciduous shrubs or trees.

Albo-maculata, which is probably very like if not the same as Argenteo-variegata (from Hillier) is a gay creature, by contrast (we are still among the Lawsons). At 30 years it is 30 ft. by 10 – a broad cone. Its shoot tips are some of them green, some cream and some a mixture of green with cream splashes. They are effectively displayed both close to and at a distance.

There are a number of yellow-leaved forms of Lawson of which I consider the brightest in winter to be Aurea Smithii, obtainable from Four Winds Nursery at Holt Pound, Wrecclesham, Surrey. But Lutea, Lanei and Stewartii are all good and make telling cones to 60 ft. C. *obtusa* 'Crippsii', however, is slighter and dumpier, 30 ft. by 15 and is brighter as to its young leaf shoots than any of the foregoing. It almost froths. I love it at every age and it has the habit, in accentuated form, of all yellow cypresses, of the second year leaves changing to green and thus making the tree's own background for the bright young shoots.

Returning to the Lawsons I must next attempt to put the reader off a popular group of spire-like habit. The lure is that they look very attractive in youth, but as they will reach a height of 30 or 40 ft. in time, it behoves us to look ahead. There are several snags. First, an almost vertical branch habit. This mode of growth invites lasting damage by snow. There is a new method for getting round this by wrapping the whole tree in a sleeve of soft netting. At Bedgebury they use a 6 in.-square mesh of black

Netlon that is practically invisible after the tree has been growing through it for a year. The panels are 6 ft. wide and are joined length-ways round the tree. At Wakehurst Place they are using a much smaller-mesh net in that virulent and unnatural shade of green which the manufacturers apparently dote on, thinking, perhaps, that it is gay and colourful.

Second drawback: the trees tend to get broader as they get taller, and an inverted spire looks top-heavy. And third, these conifers go bare at the base, revealing legs that are no more elegant in middle age than our own. So, don't equip yourself with Pottenii, Erecta Viridis, Erecta Aurea or Erecta Anything-else. Erecta Aurea additionally burns or scorches very badly. Fraseri is better built, with strong horizontal branches that become vertical where they become leafy, making rich glaucous-green, upright fans. In 20 years it grows 20 ft. by 5 across.

A real charmer, though it can be damaged by snow, is Fletcheri. Its foliage is juvenile and its growth soft and feathery, coloured greyish blue but by no means sombre. It is often planted on rock gardens but you must be prepared for it to grow 30 ft. tall in 40 years and it becomes quite broad-based, some 12 ft. across. Its rather free habit being part of its charm, this would not be a suitable subject for a net jacket.

As the luck of the alphabet has it, a clutch of coniferous trees comes all together. *Cryptomeria japonica* is a harsh, unfriendly looking tree, but that is in its adult form. The juvenile leaf is unrecognisably different, like a juniper's only more wide spreading, fluffier and softer. *C.j.* 'Elegans' is composed entirely of juvenile leaves. Green in summer, they change to purple in the cold weather. The tree grows into a 20 ft. narrow-based cone, but is unstable and is often seen in a Pisa-tower condition or even recumbent. If you have the space to let it lie on its side, it gets along quite happily that way. However, seeing that your plant is becoming unstable, you can cut it back as hard as you like and it will grow again from old wood. Alternatively, *C.j.* 'Elegans Compacta' (syn. 'Elegans Nana') is root-firm, though it hardly qualifies as a tree.

You are pretty certain to have the Leyland Cypress, *Cupresso-cyparis leylandii*, in your garden. Everyone (including myself) is planting this fashionable cypress which grows so quickly and is invaluable for shelter, but is a coarse and uninteresting foliage subject.

The true cypresses in the genus *Cupressus* have a reputation for tenderness that is not altogether justified. Often it is simply a question of planting a hardy geographical form. The fastigiate cypress that one so greatly admires in Mediterranean gardens is *C. sempervirens stricta*. I collected seed from a cemetery outside Urbino, quite high in the Apennines where the winters are severe. That was in September 1956. The seeds germinated almost immediately; the resulting plants all (about ten of them) survived the 1962–63 winter and the tallest is now, in 15 years, 30 ft. Luckily it is as fastigiate as I could wish. Seedlings are very variable in this respect; ideally one should take cuttings from a good narrow clone.

These cypresses tend not to be root firm in youth and it is important to plant them out as young as possible, before their roots get curled up in circles in a pot. On the other hand they are at their most vulnerable to cold when young, so you should plant in spring and protect them in their first winter, as I did not (but it was a singularly mild winter).

The leaves are small and a warm, friendly green; the branch system is elegant and cuts well for the house.

C. macrocarpa, from the Pacific seaboard of the States, makes a valuable windbreak near the sea but is a cumbersome tree whose better characters are not sufficient to encourage risks on behalf of a not so very hardy constitution. However, there are several yellow-leaved cultivars of tremendous appeal. As soon as you begin to want a plant, you point out that it is not nearly as tender as a jumpy, neurotic public likes to make out and is well worth a slight risk. Donard Gold is one of the finest cultivars. It grows at a great rate, and should have an open, sunny position for the brightest colouring. Lutea is almost as fresh and appetising. Neither, I should add, is either yellow or gold, but a fresh yellow-green.

C. arizonica is not the species usually grown as such in British gardens, which should be referred to *C. glabra*. Still, if you see a plant listed as *C. arizonica conica* or *C.a. pyramidalis*, get it, for you are on to a good thing. It grows quickly into a tall cone and is a marvellous glaucous colour. Furthermore, the scale leaves are arranged on their branchlets like samphire (the sort that grows by the sea and you eat like asparagus) and have a wonderful texture. Cones are freely borne at an early age. This is dependably hardy.

Elaeagnus is a valuable genus for foliage; mostly shrubby, however, but *E. angustifolia* and *E. orientalis* do make small spreading deciduous trees. The latter is sometimes treated as a variety of the former. Anyway, it is the better plant. Their leaves are silvery underneath and rather willowy. In spring they are covered with tiny, insignificant buff flowers which draw attention to themselves with a delicious scent.

There was never an ugly Eucalyptus. At their most relaxed, many of them grow to enormous dimensions but their characteristic foliage, lanceolate and hanging vertically, is always pleasing while the ghostly pallor of their peeling trunks is a marvel for colour and texture.

Eucalypts belong to that scarce and precious band, the non-coniferous, hardy evergreen tree – when they *are* hardy, that is, for there's the crux. Many are tender, or they will be hardy in one part of Britain and not in another. You cannot even pin your faith on a particular recommended species. All eucalyptus are propagated from seed and much of this seed is sent us from their Australasian homeland (though it is worth adding that if you can get a supply of seed from trees that have grown in a reasonably testing part of the British Isles, your chances of success are rosy). In their homeland, the geographical range of any one species may vary by as much as 5,000 ft. altitude. Seed from the higher level will certainly give rise to the hardiest plants but few of us will be in a position to know where the seed we procure was collected. Another catch: it is often wrongly named, either through accident or carelessness or simply because gum-trees hybridise naturally and you may have seed of mixed parentage.

But it is always worth experimenting on however small a scale, and you have little to lose. Eucalyptus grow so fast that losses are soon replaced and the larger the tree has grown the greater its chances of continued survival. Young plants are the tenderest but they are also the most expendable.

Most gum-trees have (in common with all conifers) two kinds of foliage: juvenile and adult. Based on this fact, there are two main ways of growing them: as natural trees with adult foliage or as regularly pollarded shrubs, which will continue to bear juvenile foliage. The juvenile leaves vary much more in appearance from one species to another than do the adult, and they have a great attraction for flower arrangers. In the room next to where I'm writing I have a large foliage arrangement, made three weeks ago and likely to last for as long again or longer if I want it to. Half the material is of juvenile branches of *E. gunnii* and the even more glaucous *E. pulverulenta*, from shrubs that I regularly cut for this purpose. I try to time this cutting to be before the first hard frost – just before Christmas in this instance.* Vigorous, pruned eucalypts go on growing right into the winter until the cold stops them. Their youngest shoot tips are as frost-tender, alas, as they are pretty.

If you prune your plants back to within a foot or two of the ground each year, they will (if they survive) grow during the following season into shrubs between 6 and 15 ft. tall, according to soil and variety, and you can use them tellingly in mixed plantings. *E. perriniana* is one of the most arresting for this purpose, though not one of the hardiest. Its juvenile leaves form a series of almost circular discs, entirely surrounding and clasping the stems. There is something toy-like about them reminding me of an articulated wooden snake I had as a child.

Supposing it is a small natural tree you want, *E. niphophila*, the Snow Gum, should be your choice. It grows only 20 ft. tall and as well as glaucous adult foliage its peeling trunk in grey and white becomes a focal point at an early age. If you can take a large tree, then one might suggest *E. gunnii, E. coccifera* or *E. urnigera*, but there are many other possibilities.

When a eucalyptus becomes pot-bound before it is planted out, it is difficult to get it wind-firm and independent of its stake – though a stake will always be needed in the early years. Plant out young, when the roots begin to show through the bottom of its pot, and aim to plant in spring when late frosts are no longer a danger. Thus it will have the whole summer in which to become

* A year later; I have killed my *E. pulverulenta* by cutting it too hard!

27

established before encountering its first cold weather. There is no need to be greedy or impatient with eucalypts. A foot-tall specimen provides the best planting out material, and will double its height in a few weeks. If you plant in a slight, saucer-like depression, this facilitates watering in the first season and you can fill in the saucer so as to cover the young tree's stem along its lowest inch or two. Far from causing collar rot, as this would with many trees, it acts as a safeguard. Should the tree's aerial portions be killed in the winter (and a polythene guard is advisable the first winter or two), new growth will often develop from the earthed-up section of stem.

One of the most delightful foliage variants in the common beech is *Fagus sylvatica heterophylla*. This is a finely cut-leaved beech. The tree grows full-sized and looks feathery all over. Occasional branches revert to the ordinary leaf and must be removed. There is also a slower growing, purple-leaved form called Rohanii.

So-called copper beeches are the most commonly planted. I write 'so-called' because the purple beeches *purpurea* and Riversii normally do duty for the copper epithet. Any purple beech's seedlings tend to come more or less purple and may be grown on as trees, so a good deal of variation in what one sees is to be expected.

Are these heavy purple trees an asset, by and large? They are ravishing in spring, admittedly, but soon settle down to ponderous middle age. Singly and with airy associates like robinias or deciduous cypresses, they are acceptable, but never in battalions. As a spring association I recently enjoyed seeing a purple beech against the pale lime green of *Quercus rubra*, the Red Oak, and it struck me then that we too often think in terms of dark backgrounds. A light background for a dark feature can be just as effective.

Hedges of purple beech have the great advantage that they go on producing young shoots and leaves, the latter almost pink, right up to the time, in late July, when the hedge is clipped.

The Common Ash, *Fraxinus excelsior*, is a study in contrasts: the naked tree with branches thick to their very tips, looks stern, and yet its pinnate foliage gives it a lightness which remains even in late summer, when most deciduous trees are at their most sullen.

3. *Mahonia lomariifolia*, gaunt but stately, the supreme member of its genus.

4. ABOVE, Koster's blue spruce, *Picea pungens*, in a procumbent form. BELOW, the shore juniper, *Juniperus conferta*, is a relaxed ground coverer with fresh green foliage.

For the garden, I should prefer *F. angustifolia*, whose branches are slenderer and whose leaflets are narrower. It is a very graceful tree and has a weeping form, Pendula. For leaf colour I can recommend *F. pennsylvanica* 'Aucubifolia'. The tree is not very large at maturity, perhaps 40 ft. The leaflets are large and mottled in gold and green, this colouring being retained throughout the growing season.

The extraordinary *Ginkgo biloba* is a conifer. To look at, you would never think it. Indeed it looks like no other tree and when one learns that it dates back to the era when coal was laid down and is known in fossil form, one is not surprised. It is called the Maidenhair Tree and its leaves do resemble a maidenhair fern's on a large scale. They are fan-shaped with radiating veins and arrive at two shallow lobes at the apex, with a cleft between them. They turn yellow in autumn.

This is a beautiful hardy tree and not just weird. Eventually, and when suited, it grows enormous, 80 or more feet high and perhaps 40 across. And yet young plants are fastigiate for many years and often they make little or no progress, in which case they look peaky and give scant pleasure. Ginkgos should be grown in the best possible soil and will then do you and themselves proud, requiring plenty of room for development.

I don't think the Honey Locust, *Gleditsia triacanthos*, is worth growing in its typical form except in a collection, although the pinnate leaf is inevitably attractive and turns a good yellow in autumn. But there are at least two outstanding cultivars. The one called Sunburst is suddenly on everyone's tongue: there is a real vogue. It is a fast growing tree but probably best treated as a shrub, cutting it pretty hard back each winter so as to encourage young shoots and leaves over as long a growing season as possible. The young leaves are bright yellow changing to rich green as they mature. Yellow against green again. Trap: the branches are brittle, so this is not for a wind-swept garden.

G.t. 'Elegantissima', by contrast, is slow growing and in no danger of blowing to bits. It makes an upright, semi-fastigiate feature, suitable as a lawn specimen or for emphasis at the corner or on the promontory of a border. Eventually growing to 25 ft. or so, my 20-year-old plant is now about 12 ft. tall. It has no obvious charms like Sunburst and yet, to its devotees, gives immense satisfaction at every time of year, whether clothed in its fresh green, pinnate leaves or whether showing its shining brown, naked stems.

Gymnocladus dioicus (syn. *G. canadensis*) is also a legume but with a leaf to beat its other hardy brethren hollow. There is a specimen in Holland Park that makes your mouth water. The tree is small and very slow; some 30 feet high and nearly as spreading, with low branches. Each leaf is 2 ft. long but doubly pinnate, and thus subdivided in geometrical fashion into a very great number of leaflets. This is certainly the acme of elegance.

The tree has to be propagated from seed and the seed coat is so hard, in common with many other legumes, that it responds to no ordinary method (such as soaking, chipping, or abrading in a mincing machine) normally employed to facilitate the imbibing of water and hence the germination of the embryo. It is interesting to learn that resistance can be broken down without damage to the embryo by soaking the seeds for 4½ hours in concentrated sulphuric acid (popularly known as oil of vitriol). This is a dangerous chemical and needs handling with respect, but it is what the pros use. The seed is then thoroughly rinsed in running water and thereafter stratified in sand, being left out in the cold through the winter (again with the object of breaking dormancy). When brought into the warm it germinates within three days.

The Sea Buckthorn, *Hippophaë rhamnoides*, is a tree in shrub's clothing. It has the soul of a tree. Single specimens may be a mere 12 or 15 ft. high, but they become attractively gnarled with age. Their leaves are silvery and lanceolate.

Females bear translucent orange berries and it pays to plant a group: 1 male to 4 or 5 wives. You can buy sexed plants from Treseder's of Truro, Cornwall.

Not only are there some 300 different species of holly, but there are scores of cultivars, mostly variants of the common wild holly, *Ilex aquifolium*. Some are compact bushes; others make trees, in time, but 'in time' is the operative phrase, especially where the gold- and silver-variegated cultivars are in question. The only one I grow is Golden King. It was given to me as a small, rooted cutting and is now a 9 ft. bush, after 18 years. The margins of its leaves are almost smooth and prickle-free, and they are gold in a more or less narrow band, the central area being dark green. I love this in winter (against a yew hedge background) as much as *Elaeagnus pungens* 'Maculata'. Golden King is a female and I read recently that it is shy-berrying. This is not true; it berries freely in its good years but I prefer it without fruit, which the birds soon see to on my behalf.

A holly I should like to find room for is *I. altaclarensis* 'Camelliifolia' (for practical living purposes you can forget the *altaclarensis* business and just concentrate on Camelliifolia). It is vigorous and forms a 20 ft. tree furnished down to the ground with enormous, lustrous dark green leaves: perfectly smooth along their edges and on their glossy surfaces; up to 6 in. long and 2½ in. across. It is a berrying female, ripening its fruit in late autumn. Such of the silver-variegated hollies as I have met have been prickly. Best known is Silver Queen, whose young foliage is tinted pink and then cream, forming a gorgeous mosaic on a clipped bush.

My favourite juniper of those attaining tree status is *Juniperus chinensis* and I should prefer the yellow-tinted Aurea to the type-plant. Its young foliage is particularly beautiful. This makes a shapely pillar, only 3 or 4 ft. across when 20 ft. tall.

Although its leaves account for scarcely half its total merit, I shall bring in *Koelreuteria paniculata* because it is a medium-sized tree deserving wider recognition (that phrase has admittedly been grossly overworked by horticultural journalists and nurserymen striving to gain the public's jaded ear). It makes the prettiest and shapeliest of trees, 30 or 40 ft. high and spreading, with pinnate leaves varying in size but often over a foot long. Charming yellow flowers are borne in terminal panicles in July or early August. At least they should be charming and they will be borne in the warmer parts of Britain, for the tree benefits from baking. In many strains, and also in the variety *apiculata*, the flowers are minute and make no impression, but in a good strain they are about the size of a shilling.

These are followed by a handsome crop of bladder-like seed pods, flushed red in youth. The leaves colour yellow in autumn. The tree is all too easily raised from seed, which may not give you the best flowering forms, but it also roots easily from stem cuttings. I was allowed to take a shoot sprouting from the trunk of the magnificent old specimen in the Chelsea Physic Garden in August, three years ago, and it rooted in a cold frame.

In the golden-leaved form of the common laburnum, *Laburnum anagyroides* 'Aureum', the colouring comes and goes and you can never be certain of it. At flowering time one doesn't particularly want yellow leaves as well, but afterwards they can look effective, especially, as I have seen this, against a purple-leaved prunus. A cultivar called Quercifolium has markedly indented and scalloped leaflets. It flowers well and is a pretty thing.

The well-known Incense Cedar, *Libocedrus decurrens*, is now being pretty generally referred to as *Calocedrus decurrens*, which is a nuisance. It makes a pencil specimen 60 ft. tall by 6 ft. across (in 40 years) and looks marvellous if you can make room for a group of well spaced pencils. The green is always fresh and the fan-like leaf branches are arranged in loose rosettes which makes for a texture of great originality. The tree apparently grows more bushily in Ireland and the west country than here in the south-east.

Liquidambars belong to the *Hamamelis* family but the palmate foliage of the popular *Liquidambar styraciflua* is strongly reminiscent of a maple's. This is a good leaf form, regardless of anything else it may do for us. Liquidambars are, in fact, expected to change to dramatic purple and red shades in autumn. They almost as often do nothing of the kind. Soil and climate can be responsible for these disappointments but a likelier cause in this instance is the fact that most liquidambar trees have been grown from seed. Seedlings are of variable performance and no clones have been developed that are known to be reliable colourers. Nurserymen are aware of this and something may be done about it in the future. *L. styraciflua* makes a large tree and is of easy cultivation except on dry or chalky soils.

5. This young scarlet oak, *Quercus coccinea*, has not yet attained its full colouring, but is even more interesting in the intermediate stage. Its large, boldly lobed leaves look well at all times but those of the red oak, *Q. rubra*, seem to me to make a prouder impression.

Tulip trees here and in America

The Tulip Tree, *Liriodendron tulipifera*, is even larger and should definitely not be planted fecklessly in a small garden. But in any plot of an acre upwards, yes indeed. The leaves are wonderfully cut, the freshest green and as smooth as smooth. They nearly always change to a clear yellow in autumn. The interesting though modest flowers may be borne on trees aged 15 years upwards.

Although *Maackia amurensis* has a pinnate leaf, and flowers, obligingly and prettily, in August, I shall pass it over and pause fleetingly with *Magnolia*, known as tulip trees in America and actually related to *Liriodendron*. These are mainly flowering trees and shrubs but its foliage is the most notable feature in the dark evergreen *M. delavayi*. Except in mild districts, it is usually grown as a wall shrub but is quite capable of standing free in London, at any rate. The leaves are about a foot long and eight inches wide and of great distinction. The cream-white flowers are not as large and important as you might expect but are deliciously fragrant.

M. acuminata, known as the Cucumber Tree on account of the shape of its fruits, will be grown for its large deciduous leaves or not at all – usually the latter.

The only apple that I should want to grow for its leaf is *Malus trilobata*, which is indented and uncommonly like a hawthorn. It colours well in autumn and is an interesting small tree, listed by Hillier.

So much has been written about the Dawn Redwood, *Metasequoia glyptostroboides*, known only in fossil form until its discovery in China in 1945; now widely planted and of the easiest cultivation, that there seems little to add. It is a deciduous conifer after the style of *Taxodium distichum* but much faster growing and

6. ABOVE, *Helichrysum splendidum* is a remarkably hardy grey shrub that always looks its smartest in autumn. Its rounded habit contrasts with the vertical lines of the individual shoots. Its flowers don't hurt and there is nearly always a sprinkling of them. BELOW, the cardoon, *Cynara cardunculus*, at its most luxuriant in early May. Too closely planted neighbours are easily enveloped and killed by it. Later, the artichoke-like inflorescences rise majestically to 8 ft. As they need support of the stoutest calibre, some gardeners prefer to remove them altogether.

not nearly as pretty. Still, only the comparison renders it odious. The leaves are a fresh green in spring and change to rufous shades in autumn. The trunk becomes furrowed and buttressed with age. I personally like to see the tree forming a narrow cone with branches right down to the ground.

Nothofagus, the southern hemisphere beeches (not beeches or remotely related) some of them make evergreen trees, which is not in itself quite sufficiently momentous to detain us, while *Nyssa sylvatica* is little or nothing apart from its capricious autumn colouring, though the tree is a pleasant shape, withal.

Once established, *Pittosporum tenuifolium* is remarkably hardy, though I should advise against siting it in the most gale-stricken or draught-ridden spot in your garden. Its foliage is beloved of florists and, for that matter, all flower arrangers. The leaf is not quite 2 in. long, shiny on top and wavy-edged. It is evergreen and displayed to advantage among stems that are very dark, almost black. The leaf's own colour is olive green but with a hint of silver on its undersurface.

My bush was planted out in 1959 and is 15 ft. tall by 10 ft. across, after 12 years. It is just becoming a tree. In May, it is covered with blossom; tiny, bell-shaped chocolate-coloured flowers. The first time I noticed them was by their scent. There is none by day but I happened to be weeding close to the shrub at 7 p.m. one evening (Ah! if there were only more dedicated gardeners like Lloyd). Their scent is powerful and has something of the quality of vanilla but is unpleasantly rank at close range. Bean, however, describes its 'exquisite honey-like fragrance'.

This, the hardiest pittosporum, is also a good wall shrub where space can be allowed for it to form a buttress. You can cut branches for your arrangements to your heart's content, without doing any damage and this is also a good hedging plant in milder districts.

It has several cultivars including the variegated Silver Queen and the very nice Purpureum, with leaves that become purple as they mature, having started green. I recently planted this next to a golden catalpa, but the latter disobligingly died. *P. tobira* is coveted for its 4 in.-long leaves, which are highly polished, and for its orange-scented, creamy blossom. This is not at all too hardy but a good risk against a warm wall. A friend with a London garden gave me a seed pod from her specimen and I now have three babies, still in pots in a cold frame.

Several poplars deserve our attention, but always with the reservation that their roots are destructive and should be planted well away from drains or foundations of any kind. As the roots often come right to the surface, they can make lawn mowing awkward.

The one I was brought up to call the Silver Poplar is really the grey *Populus canescens*, making a large tree with horizontal speckles on its trunk and larger branches. The leaves are not deeply indented; deckle-edged, rather, and are grey underneath – pretty in the wind. The White Poplar, *P. alba*, is much whiter as to the underside of its leaves and they are often deeply lobed. This species makes a smaller tree (particularly valuable near the sea) and has a useful fastigiate cultivar in Pyramidalis.

My own preference is for a poplar with golden foliage – to be accurate, it is lime green – namely *P.* 'Serotina Aurea'. It leafs out late and is coppery at first but retains its bright yellow-green adult colouring right into autumn and is most effective against other darker-leaved trees. Although it roots easily from hardwood cuttings, I have had difficult in establishing young plants in their permanent quarters when this was rough grass. They probably don't like competition when young.

P. lasiocarpa makes a fairly small tree but has huge leaves, some 8 in. long by 6 in. wide, bright green in youth with red stalks and veins. It goes into an early autumn decline and looks utterly disreputable then.

P. candicans 'Aurora' has a largish smooth leaf, variegated in green, pink and cream. It can be treated as a shrub, pollarding it hard each winter, in which case the variegation is brightest early in the season, the whole shrub turning green later on. If allowed to make an unpruned tree, however, it's the other way about: green in spring, variegated later on. You have to make a choice.

Prunus cerasifera 'Pissardii' (we seem now to have returned to this old name after dallying with Atropurpurea for some years) and the even darker *P.c.* 'Nigra' are both good background trees whose purple leaves will set off some paler feature. Perhaps they are grown mainly for their early blossom, but as they age, blossoming unaccountably ceases.

Pterocaryas do make very beautiful and large trees. By far the best known species is *Pterocarya fraxinifolia*, whose pinnate leaves may, on a strongly growing specimen, be up to 2 ft. long. The trunk is fissured in diamond-shaped relief. On moist soils this is a tree of gratifyingly rapid growth but it does seem to need the warmer, drier climate of the south and east to ripen its wood and thus withstand winter damage. *P. stenoptera* is good too, with leaves of a fresh green right into autumn. It is perfectly hardy in Mr Maurice Mason's Norfolk garden.

The Weeping Pear, *Pyrus salicifolia* 'Pendula' is enjoying a considerable vogue, and deservedly. It makes a small tree, 25 ft. or so tall, and it is a good plan to help a leader to make height, in its early years, by tying it to a central stake. The leaves are lanceolate and willowy, silver on both sides when young; becoming green on top but still silver underneath, later on. The flowers are white, as in all pears, and pretty enough though seldom borne in sufficient numbers to make any impact.

But this is a delightful tree either as a solo specimen in a lawn, or forming an item in a large association of shrubs.

Of the oaks, Hillier's list several score. They specialise in the genus, which is as varied as are the hollies. A form of our native *Quercus petraea* called Mespilifolia, has an elegant leaf, long and narrow that I use as a book-marker in my Bean. It is 9 in. by 1¼ and has a gently undulating margin. The tree grows large and beautiful. It would be a change if this sort of oak or another that was unfamiliar were planted on commemorative occasions when it is usually a common oak that has been grown from an acorn in someone's small front garden, that is honoured. The seedling grew too large for its position (and too large to be easily moved), but along came a convenient coronation or royal marriage or perhaps a visit by a T.V. star, and it was moved (at the wrong season, of course) to the village green or town recreation ground. There it died forthwith and was surreptitiously replaced in the autumn.

Another eminently suitable species, except that it is not British (I don't think it can even claim to be Commonwealth) would be the Pin Oak, *Quercus palustris*. Again a large tree whose strong lines are tempered by the graceful down-drooping habit of its young branches. The leaves are carried on exceptionally long stalks and are themselves deeply scalloped. Strongly recommended.

Q. coccinea, the Scarlet Oak, is well known and much grown for its autumn colouring, but for foliage through the season I prefer to it the Red Oak, sometimes listed as *Q. rubra*, sometimes as *Q. borealis*. Its large, interestingly shaped leaves are a wonderfully tender lime green in spring and change to several shades of rich brown in autumn. It regenerates in this country and I have a self sown seedling from a neighbour's large specimen.

Some of the oaks with 'coloured' foliage throughout the season are noteworthy. The golden oak, *Quercus robur* 'Concordia', so strategically sited at one end of the Palladian bridge at Wilton House, near Salisbury, is justly famed. It is so slow growing that there is no danger that it will attempt to outshine or dwarf the bridge itself. Visitors to Inverewe, in north-west Scotland, will remember the beautiful little cream-and-green-variegated oak on the edge of the front lawn, there. This is *Q. cerris* 'Variegata', a sport from the Turkey Oak. It is continually sporting back to the plain green type-plant, and these reverted branches have to be pruned out annually, so it is just as well the tree is no larger.

Quercus pontica is no more than a large shrub or small scrub tree but has very big leaves: up to 8 in. long. Still, I cannot say I'm enthusiastic about this one.

Of the evergreen oaks, *Q. ilex*, the Holm Oak, often known simply as ilex, is the best known and makes a vast round-headed tree in the southern counties. It stands up to salt spray well but is not too hardy in cold, inland districts. I reckon that one ilex makes a quorum. Several in a group become unduly heavy. This is an excellent subject for a tall evergreen clipped hedge too – say you wanted one 12 ft. high. The plants could go in 6 ft. apart. One thing the ilex won't tolerate is being cut back into old wood: it doesn't break. Also it moves badly and must be planted small and young.

The Cork Oak, *Q. suber* is another evergreen and hardy enough in the south and in East Anglia, but the cork bark is its main distinctive feature. Hybridised with the Turkey Oak it gave rise to the Lucombe Oak, *Q.* × *hispanica* 'Lucombeana', which is semi-evergreen. You meet it a lot in the south-west. Evergreen oaks are particularly unpopular with professional gardeners, who take their habit of shedding leaves over a long period, and especially in late spring, as a personal insult.

The False Acacia, *Robinia pseudoacacia*, gives me a small thrill whenever I see one. First, and to our purpose, its leaves are pinnate, light and freshly coloured all through the summer; smooth and cleanly outlined. Its fragrant white racemes of pea flowers are not borne freely every year, but when they are (in June) they look radiant. In old age, the trunk becomes deeply fissured and picturesque like an Arthur Rackham tree.

Robinias are deep-rooted and won't starve out their neighbours but they do throw suckers now and again. Furthermore, their branches are lined with rather nasty spines. They go in couples and need respect. One last defect: the tree is fast-growing and like most such the branches are brittle. So it should not have too exposed a position. It is admirable for street and town square planting: much more used on the Continent than here, however. In north France you usually see it parasitised by mistletoe.

There are a number of good cultivars. Pendula doesn't flower but its weeping leaves are up to a foot long; narrow for their length and with widely spaced leaflets. The leaves in Tortuosa are curled up and hang in ringlets as though they were green flowers. This is delightful. Frisia is a post-war introduction and very like the type-plant except that its leaves are bright yellow, the colour being retained throughout the summer and autumn. They make a sunny day seem twice as bright. This will doubtless make a good-sized tree, in time, and there is no reason why it shouldn't flower.

I shall deal with the willows later, confining myself to the shrubby ones or those that I should treat as shrubs. *Sophora japonica*, the Chinese Pagoda Tree, belongs to the same family of legumes as *Robinia* and is not unlike it, with airy pinnate foliage but darker and the young stems are dark green too. There are no spines, no suckers and no particular inclination to snap its branches. It is a fine tree, easily raised from seed and growing up to 60 ft. tall. I planted a seedling in 1950 and it is now about 25 ft. tall. When mature, these sophoras can cover themselves with tiny white blossoms, in September, especially if the summer has been hot. The flowers fall to the ground, strewing it like grains of rice. Bean says flowering does not commence till trees are 30 or 40 years old, but a litter brother to mine flowered at Wye College in Kent in 1969, so I am full of hope.

Most of the rowans have pinnate leaves but they are not essentially foliage trees. Some of the whitebeams, with a silvery underside to their large oval leaves, do qualify. Our native *Sorbus aria* of the chalk and limestone, is at its most scintillating in spring, when the unfolding leaf buds look like white magnolia blossom. This stage is soon past, however. For the garden there are improved forms like Lutescens, which is woolly on both leaf surfaces and Pendula, a pretty weeper.

The Swamp Cypress or Deciduous Cypress, *Taxodium distichum*, is certainly the prettiest deciduous conifer: arguably as pretty as any tree you could choose as a lawn or waterside specimen. Its pinnate leaves are arranged like a double comb, as in the yew, but are much more petite. They maintain a wonderfully fresh green colouring all through the summer doldrums when elm, beech and sycamore are at their darkest and glummest. In autumn, they change to brilliant russet. The tree itself acquires a fine shape by the time it is 50 years old. The variety called Pendens, with drooping branch tips, is said to be even more exquisite.

The Swamp Cypress has the invaluable attribute of growing happily in boggy ground (wherein it makes its famous knee-roots), but it is equally happy on any well-drained loam that does not become dry in summer. As boggy places tend to be low-lying, and low-lying areas tend to be frost hollows, this tree often suffers, in youth, from late frosts on its young shoots. Its development is thereby checked. Once its leader has grown above the frost line, all is well, but it may take some years to make up its mind whether it has a leader. Taxodiums are much slower growing that the comparable metasequoia (though they attain 80 ft. in the end) and there is all the predictable difference between the one and the other, of quality and restraint versus quantity and coarseness.

The finest lime for foliage effect is *Tilia petiolaris*. The leaves hang on long stalks and you can thus see their grey under-surfaces almost as easily as the green top-side – especially if there is any wind to twist them. This is a park tree and requires plenty of space in every direction. Its branches hang almost vertically and will sweep the ground. It is a tree you will find yourself constantly turning to and looking at again.

Except on dry soils, the Western Hemlock, *Tsuga heterophylla*, is an excellent and fast-growing coniferous tree. Its leaves are arranged like a yew's but are much shorter and less coarse, and are more or less glaucous underneath. The leafy branches hang obliquely, giving the tree, which is broadly conical in outline, a relaxed appearance. Speed in growth and grace in form are rarely so well combined. Whatever you do, avoid the clumsy Canadian Hemlock, *T. canadensis*, which never makes one trunk and always looks a shapeless lump.

The shape of an elm leaf is basically unpretentious if not boring. Our main interest is therefore in its colouring. You expect the plant bearing a variegated leaf to be considerably less vigorous than its green prototype, but at Petworth House in west Sussex there is an 80 ft. specimen (from memory) of the green-and-white *Ulmus procera* ('Argenteo-variegata'). Seen against a blue sky and with a lowish sun shining across it, you get a wonderful view looking through its branches from underneath. Why one should not see this cultivar more frequently I cannot imagine.

There are quite a lot of different kinds of Golden Elm. The creamy-yellow-leaved Wych Elm, *U. glabra* 'Lutescens' is said to be more satisfactory than *U. procera* 'Louis van Houtte', which is a golden form of the common elm. I have no personal experience of these but I suspect that the latter reverts to green pretty readily.

By far my favourite – and it seems to have no inclination to revert – is Dickson's Golden Elm, *U. sarniensis* 'Dicksonii', also known, among its several pseudonyms, as *U. carpinifolia* 'Aurea'. It has an upright habit, and the leaves are arranged in two ranks along the young branches. They overlap like feathers. This will make a 40 ft. tree but you can restrict it by pruning the young shoots back in winter and retaining a slim fastigiate habit.

Sunshine from a bush elm

Another worth-while elm is U. *viminalis* 'Aurea' (or U. *plottii* 'Jackie'). The leaves are deeply toothed and they are obovate (broadest near the tip) and twisted. When young they are gold, becoming green with age. As growth continues through the summer, you see gold against green. This is slow-growing; a bush rather than a tree, for many years, gradually reaching to 20 ft. by as much across (if you let it spread). There is a specimen in Maurice Mason's Norfolk garden and it is something we never leave out of a tour but always stand and admire for quite a long time. However dull the day, it creates its own pool of sunshine.

CHAPTER 4

Planning a Border

*

FOLLOWING my individual treatment of trees for foliage, I should, logically, deal next with shrubs in the same way, and then with hardy plants and then with annuals and tender perennials. However, a break chapter will be welcome to the author, and perhaps to the reader too.

Trees generally have to be considered singly or in pairs or in quite small groups. But the other, smaller units can be combined in larger numbers and in all sorts of permutations. Of them, we can make our borders. Now, I am taking this word 'border' in the broadest sense, as an area of (initially) cultivated ground to be planted up with ornamentals – in our case with foliage plants. The area may be quite tiny (more readily described as a bed than a border) or it may be the fringe of a piece of woodland, and very large. What I want to steer clear of is the concept of the shrubbery; the herbaceous border; the bed for annuals. This is a bad, lazy old habit and stultifying. Always mix your ingredients as much as it suits you to do so. Don't worry about whether they are shrubs, herbs, roses, succulents or whatever.

The first thing to consider about a border is where to have it and in what size and shape. I shall not say much about this as I am not writing a book on garden design. But I shall make a few personal observations.

Aim at simplicity and broad effects (even in a small garden) rather than a mass of busy detail. If you have the alternative choice between making two small borders or one large, make it a large. If you have the choice between a narrow border and a wide, make it wide. This gives you more scope in the range of plants you can use and in the boldness of the effects you can create.

There is a fashion, nowadays, for borders of informal outline. In an informal setting, these will generally be appropriate. But fidgety outlines, sudden kinks and wiggles and meaningless bulges are distracting. You keep looking at the border's shape rather than at its contents. Try to make your lines easy and flowing and appropriate to the slope of the ground or to the position of a key feature, such as a tree.

It should not be necessary, in the majority of cases, to make a garden of formal outline look as though it were informal. Far better, usually, to accept a rectangular frame and to plant informally within it. Let the plants supply the informality. Most of them will be only too happy to do so.

When you have made your border, you must decide what to put in it, and this is very confusing, but there are many ways in which the field can be narrowed. And anyway you should always remember that it is a great deal more fun to have made your own bed and to have to lie in it than to have to give the credit to an outsider for making it for you. Because you are inexperienced, your mistakes will be numerous, but experienced gardeners do and indeed should make many mistakes also. They should always be living on the frontiers of their experience; always be experimenting and trying out something new. It's only those who are afraid of having to admit to mistakes who are frightened of making them.

Still, you can forestall many of your troubles. Make a list of factors to be taken into consideration when choosing your plants, as it might be:

1 Soil
2 Drainage
3 Sun or Shade
4 Exposure to wind
5 Temperatures
6 Rainfall and Humidity
7 Maximum Plant Height Acceptable
8 Season of interest
9 Viewpoints
10 Backgrounds
11 Slope
12 Acceptability of ingredients
13 Special Factors

Let us consider these headings in turn.

Soil. First, is it acid, alkaline or more or less neutral? You can buy yourself a soil testing kit from a chemist or garden sundries shop and find out for yourself. Ericaceous plants like heathers and rhododendrons as well as quite a number of others, like camellias, will not grow in alkaline (chalky, limy) soils. On the other hand the calcicoles (lime lovers) *will* grow on acid soils.

I have never in my life done a test of the soil in my garden, having learned all I need to know about it from the behaviour of the plants that were there when I was born. But to go the proper way about it is obviously more economical, especially if you are starting a garden from scratch and have no examples of established shrubs before you to supply clues.

Is the soil light and free-draining, warming up quickly in the spring but drying out in the summer? Or is it heavy and water-retentive? Many plants are better adapted to the one condition or to the other.

If you are the first occupant of a new house, you may find that the builders have overlaid your natural top-soil with subsoil from the building's foundations. It is pretty well hopeless to try and garden on sub-soil: even a lawn won't take. So you will have to put things to rights and you may have to buy in some top soil. Gardeners in industrial towns also find it profits them to replace their worn out, polluted (I had to work that word in somehow) top soil from time to time, with good earth from the country.

Drainage. Very few plants can live happily with wet feet. A border in which the water hangs about during wet spells will certainly need to be drained before anything else. Tap-rooted plants particularly need good drainage.

Sun or Shade. Sun loving plants and shade loving plants are equally numerous and desirable in their different ways, but you want to know which to include. A shade-loving fern like *Blechnum tabulare* will survive and increase in sun but will make fronds of only half the length and lushness that would come naturally to it in damp shade. I know, because I planted a group in the shade of a large old tree peony, *Paeonia delavayi*. The peony became a martyr to botrytis and had to be extracted and this has left my blechnums high and dry and looking, incidentally, rather silly.

On the other hand a sun-loving plant like *Senecio cineraria*, if grown in shade, will not have nice white-felted leaves but will turn a sort of nondescript grey-green and develop into a spindly shrub. All grey-foliaged plants are sun worshippers.

Plants with large, soft leaves are often shade-fanciers, but there are exceptions.

Moist shade is a boon in the garden. Dry shade is a bane. Few plants tolerate, let alone enjoy, the dry shade you get underneath a beech tree, for instance. The beech's surface-feeding roots mop up all the moisture and all the soil nutrients. Don't lose sleep over this situation. Bare ground underneath a tree is not necessarily an eyesore. It is a perfectly natural condition and may look a great deal more dignified than futile attempts at gardening.

Exposure to Wind. It is a common human failing to buy or build a house on a ridge or high slope, for the sake of the magnificent view (regardless of how your house affects the view back to where you've sited yourself) and then to grumble endlessly about how impossible the wind makes it for gardening. Either you must plant your view out, making shelter to grow a wide variety of subjects in your garden; or you must garden with your blessed view, confining your choice to ground huggers that can take what's coming to them. So much for your plants. That leaves you. Not much basking on the patio, I fear. You'll have to take refuge behind your splendid plate glass picture window. Bad cess to you.

Temperatures. If you're not the kind that builds on a ridge then you're probably a seeker after an old priory or water mill, or converted boat house or 13th-century *columbarium* mouldering away in a valley bottom with a stream tinkling past your boundary, willows growing aslaunt it and Ophelia or the Lady of Shalott floating down on gala occasions. Aside from the fact that the stream will become a raging torrent and flood your garden and ground floor once a year, your main discovery will be that you live in a frost hollow. This is bad enough in winter, when most plants are dormant, but much more serious in spring and autumn, and leaves you with a bare three frost-free months. By day, of course, the frost hollow becomes an oven.

Soil temperature makes a vast difference to plant growth.

There are many bedding plants which will perform successfully or not according to whether or not the summer is a good one. A difference of a degree or two (Fahrenheit) in mean soil temperature will make the difference between success and failure with cannas, *Melianthus major* and similar plants. Not only the summer but what part of the country you live in, affects what you can grow, the south-east experiencing the highest summer temperatures.

Then, the slope your border is on. If tilted to the south, the sun's rays will hit it at right angles and the cannas will relax and flourish. If facing north, the sun hits your slope obliquely and much less effectively. You must take advantage of the fact by growing plants that enjoy cooler conditions.

Rainfall and Humidity. As far as British gardening is concerned we are lucky indeed to have the climate we have and not the Mediterranean sort we think, from a human point of view, we should prefer. Rainfall is spread over the year; the atmosphere is generally moisture-laden. Some of the foliage plants that we most enjoy have large leaves and large-leaved plants mostly appreciate a humid climate with plenty of soil moisture. Inasmuch as your western seaboards enjoy a moist Atlantic climate and in the east we are drier and Continental, the moisture-loving, furry-leaved rhododendrons do best under the former conditions. If we grow them in the east (and we do when we can) we shall need to irrigate in times of drought.

The benefits of hotter drier conditions in the south-east are less applicable to foliage than to flowering plants.

Plant Height and Border Size. Turning now from factors edaphic and climatic to more particular questions of what suits our purpose: very tall plants in a narrow border look silly. We can rule them out. As a rough guide to height suitability, it may be said that a border viewed from one side only (it will probably be backed by a wall, fence or hedge) should have plants in it no higher than the width of the border from front to back. But an island border, viewed from all sides, should have plants in it no higher than half its width, and they, of course, will be near the centre.

Season of Interest. A foliage border will automatically give us a

far longer season of interest than one in which flowers are pre-
dominant. But even foliage has its seasons. If we insist on the
border looking uniformly agreeable the year through, we shall
have to confine ourselves to hardy evergreens whose foliage does
not get spoilt by wintry blasts. This kind of safe planting is more
appropriate to an institutional garden – a hospital, say, or a
school for nit-wits – than to the private gardener and plantsman
who enjoys variety.

How much do we use or gaze upon our gardens in winter?
Not such a great deal, surely. I think we should be content, in
winter, with a few strong features while concentrating our creative
efforts on the spring to autumn season. This will allow the liberal
use of deciduous plants.

We may, of course, be planning a border or borders in a holiday
home that we visit, to any extent, only in July and August. In that
case our attack can be even more concentrated.

Viewpoints. These affect not so much what you include in
your border as where you site the plants.

If you have a large rectangular border with a service path along
one side separating it from a narrow border against a wall or solid
fence, it obviously doesn't matter what the border looks like
from the service path. It does matter what it looks like from the
other side when approached from either end. It may matter even
more how it looks viewed head-on across a lawn from the kitchen
window, let's say. A border viewed head-on is more exposed, as
to its weaknesses, than a border seen end-on. The end-on view
conceals those nasty gaps or drab patches. But a head-on or,
better still perhaps, an oblique view from some way away is the
most satisfying if the border is full and well integrated.

Backgrounds. Dark backgrounds are a great help to flower
borders but are less necessary to foliage. Foliage can develop its
own backgrounds but it does, ideally, require plenty of elbow-
space in which to do so. Otherwise your entire border can easily
be eaten up by background foliage, leaving no room at the front.
In island beds it is the same story. For the finest effects you need
to be able to devote a large central area to shrubs (mainly) that
will set off the marginal features.

Slope. If the border is set on a slope, it won't show on your two-dimensional plan but you can easily remember to make allowance for it. If the slope faces your viewpoint, then your plants can be more nearly of the same height from the border's front to the back, because the slope is varying their heights for you. If the slope runs away from your viewpoint, you're in some difficulty, because differences in plant heights will need to be much more sharply defined if the farthest away from you are going to be seen at all.

Acceptability of Ingredients. Personal likes and dislikes come in here. Also the question of how much work you want the plants to do for you; how much you are prepared to do for them. If the border has to be labour-saving it will, again, be of the institutional kind: steady ground-covering evergreens that need little attention. But if you like to exercise your faculties then you may be prepared to go through the annual fiddle-faddle of lifting and storing cannas, keeping their rhizomes plump through the dormant season, starting them off under warm, humid conditions in spring and planting them out when danger of frost is past. It all sounds a great fag when you've never done it. Once you have, you realise that the routine is simple and much less troublesome than feeding your dog daily.

Special Factors. Sea spume may blow through your garden. You may be bombarded with sulphur dioxide fumes in an industrial area. You're a hard-driven business man who normally has leisure to enjoy his garden only in the evenings, and so you'll site your border on the garden's east side to catch the evening sunlight. These are special factors and they are legion.

7. ABOVE, a half-wild tangle of bindweed and all sorts in which the vivid September colouring of the true Virginia creeper, *Parthenocissus quinquefolia* predominates. Divided into five fingers, the foliage of this self-clinging climber is far more elegant than the more commonly planted *P. tricuspidata*. BELOW, the rich purple, light-reflecting foliage of *Perilla atropurpurea* 'Laciniata' as planted at Wisley in effective association with African marigolds. The perilla is almost always seen in public gardens, scarcely ever in private ones, which is certainly a wasted opportunity as it can be treated like any other half-hardy annual.

THE LIST

Now you must make a list of possible ingredients. You will include plants you have admired in parks and other gardens; others that sound nice from what I have written about them or (more likely) that look nice in their photographs. You will include plants that you bought on impulse or that were given you and are still kicking their heels in a spare plot. You will, since I have told you to on this occasion, concentrate on foliage plants but you will also include some flowerers because you fancy them in a setting of foliage or because you are desperate for a home for them. On the other hand you will exclude all those that fail to conform with the requirements we have just been studying.

I think it is time we took a concrete example.

8. ABOVE LEFT, when the holly, *Ilex aquifolium* 'Silver Queen', is treated as a clipped specimen, you get the strongest impression of the pink colouring in its young foliage, wherein the margins later change to cream. RIGHT, a newcomer to my garden, the variegated strawberry, that has quickly settled down and makes handsome ground cover in sun or in shade, throughout most of the year. MIDDLE LEFT, young shoots (late in May) of the variegated figwort, *Scrophularia aquatica* 'Variegata', before inroads have been made on its complexion by the several pests that feed on it. *Helleborus foetidus* behind and *Fatsia japonica* (looking a bit tired at this season) to left. RIGHT, variegated balm, *Melissa officinalis* 'Aurea', in a late spring association with the perennial cornflower, *Centaurea montana*, whose warm honeyed fragrance is also in contrast to the balm's pungent spiciness. Both plants are best cut to the ground in late June, to make them start over again. BELOW LEFT, the amphibious *Glyceria maxima* 'Variegata' here seen in our horse pond with a background of waterlilies (Rose Arey in foreground). This grass colony was later destroyed by water voles. It makes an excellent herbaceous or bedding plant in an ordinary border, provided its invasiveness is understood and checked. RIGHT, a bold and vigorous variegated ivy, *Hedera colchica* 'Dentato-variegata', here flowering, in November. This self-clinging climber will make a sombre north wall cheerful at every season.

OUR GARDENER AND THE GARDEN

The garden is in a self-conscious Surrey commuting area. The soil is light, sandy and acid. Water is available for irrigation. The border in question is a new one; an island site in a lawn and receiving all the sun that's going. There is a laburnum near by but it is on the border's north side and anyway laburnums are no great problem as to their roots.

I intended the husband to plan this bed because he's a safe sort of fellow and I want a safe example to start off with. However, it soon became obvious that he wasn't the slightest bit interested in foliage: it was his wife who was pushing the theme (with cutting material for the house at the back of her mind) and he quickly turned the whole project over to her, saying that he would concentrate on the dahlias.

The wife is a nervous gardener. If anyone brings up the subject of frost, she points out that their garden gets more than anyone's in the neighbourhood. It's the same with wind and drought. Nobody can imagine what they have to battle with. So she starts off with a determination not to take any risks in her choice of material. Everything must be hardy and everything must be reliably perennial. There must be a good proportion of staunch evergreens but she doesn't object to deciduous shrubs and herbaceous material mixed in.

She made her list of possible ingredients from plants she had seen and made notes about at the time (sensible woman). Here is the list she started with:

> *Acaena* 'Blue Haze'
> *Acanthus longifolius*
> *Acer palmatum* 'Dissectum Atropurpureum'
> *Alchemilla mollis*
> *Anaphalis triplinervis*
> *Artemisia palmeri*
> *Artemisia pontica*
> *Ballota pseudodictamnus*
> *Berberis thunbergii* 'Atropurpurea'
> *Berberis thumbergii* 'Atropurpurea Nana'

Bergenia cordifolia
Bergenia purpurascens
Catalpa bignonioides 'Aurea'
Cotinus coggygria 'Notcutt's Variety'
Crambe maritima
Euphorbia wulfenii
Helichrysum splendidum
Helictotrichon sempervirens
Hydrangea quercifolia
Iris pallida 'Variegata'
Juniperus communis 'Hornibrookii'
Kniphofia caulescens
Leucothoë catesbaei
Lonicera nitida 'Baggesen's Golden'
Mahonia 'Undulata'
Miscanthus sinensis 'Zebrinus'
Origanum vulgare 'Aureum'
Phlomis chrysophylla
Rubus thibetanus
Rubus tricolor
Ruta graveolens 'Jackman's Blue'
Salvia officinalis 'Grandiflora'
Santolina neapolitana
Sedum maximum 'Atropurpureum'
Sedum telephium 'Variegatum'
Senecio cineraria 'White Diamond'
Senecio laxifolius
Thuja occidentalis 'Rheingold'
Viburnum davidii
Weigela florida 'Variegata'

The items that eventually featured in the plan are numbered from 1 to 38 in the order that they were set down. We will follow the making of it from start to finish exactly as it happened. On her left, she had her list, over which she constantly ran her eye for the next inspiration; on her right, a sheet of graph paper on which the outline of the border was marked using a scale of one inch to three feet. She marked everything in with a B pencil, and a soft rubber was handy for alterations to group outlines.

Where a group consisted of only one, two, three or four plants, she marked in their positions at once, because the numbers she wanted to use could influence the shape of the group. Where it was a case of a lot of plants filling in a given area, she marked in the area first and then worked out how many plants she would need, giving them the spacing indicated by various books of reference, or what she felt they would need from what she had seen of them.

She started her plan with a feature she knew she wanted, and that she knew should go on a promontory: the Japanese Maple, *Acer palmatum* 'Dissectum Atropurpureum' with the prostrate blue-leaved *Juniperus communis* 'Hornibrookii'. The maple's cut-leaved purple foliage would form a low knoll but would trail into the juniper at its margins. Something bright yellow would cheer up the purple and blue, so the golden marjoram, *Origanum vulgare* 'Aureum', went in next. It grows barely a foot tall. The grey, narrow-leaved sage she had admired at Hidcote would look nice behind that. It grows up to 3 ft. but that wouldn't matter and anyway you can cut the shrubby sages hard back in spring, if they are straggling. At Hidcote and in Robert Poland's list (of Brook House Nursery, Ardingly, Haywards Heath, Sussex) they call it *Salvia hispanica* but the recent supplement to the R.H.S. Dictionary gives that species as an annual. The more probable name given it at Kew is *S. officinalis* 'Grandiflora'.

Continuing along the border's margin, something with a rather boldly formed but plain green leaf now seemed to be called for; it should be the oak-leaved *Hydrangea quercifolia*, which also carries handsome cones of white flowers in late summer.

She wanted to use the middle of the widest part of her bed for the tallest shrubs in her list, and *Mahonia* 'Undulata' would fill the bill. Its evergreen pinnate foliage is hard and very shiny and there is a seductive twist to the leaflet margins. The colour is green in summer but bronzy purple in winter and tight terminal clusters of bright yellow flowers are carried for ten days or so in April. The bush can become pretty bulky but, again, responds extremely well to cutting back, which is best done immediately after flowering.

As a complete contrast to this, the golden catalpa, pollarded

annually in winter and kept as a low bush. Low for a catalpa,
anyway. The great heart-leaves are a beautiful euphorbia yellow
and they retain their colouring throughout the summer. As the
catalpa would be continually advancing and retreating, she wanted
something pretty adaptable and tolerant on its other side and the
palest silvery grey. The 4 ft. *Artemesia palmeri* seemed to fill the
bill. It is a little bit of a thug but she was prepared to see that it
didn't swamp the maple. Anyway, their colouring would look
well together. And she decided to have another purple and silver
combination between them and the border's eastern margin. She
had seen it in a garden near Eastbourne called Folkington Place
and had determined to copy it. *Sedum maximum* 'Atropurpureum',
a 2½ ft. herbaceous plant with thick fleshy purple leaves crowned,
eventually, with a head of small flesh coloured flowers, is a
favourite with all flower arrangers but its gawky habit and sulky
colouring are awkward to place in the garden. As she had seen
it, it had been set off and enlivened by one of the whitest of all
hardy grey-leaved plants: *Senecio cineraria* 'White Diamond'. Its
leaves are felted and not very deeply cut, carried in rosettes. To
keep the shrub neat and to prevent it from flowering (its flowers
being highly undesirable little yellow daisies) you cut it hard
back, so that not a leaf remains, in April each year. It is not 100%
hardy, but much the hardiest of its tribe and she was prepared to
take a risk with it because she wanted it badly. The sedum grows
slightly the taller. She was going to mix the two together (as at
Folkington Place) but with rather more of the taller partner
behind, rather more of the silver in front.

Next, but again under the catalpa's skirts, *Acanthus longifolius*;
quite a power in its own right and well able to look after itself.
It has deeply indented, double-comb-shaped leaves and is very
free flowering – hooded spikes in purple and off-white. Coming
between this and the border margin must be something that
wouldn't get squashed right out. She thought of *Rubus tricolor*
here: a trailing, prickle-free evergreen with handsome, heart-
shaped rich green but beautifully lustrous foliage, purple at the
margins. But it might go all over the lawn and her husband would
be ruthless with the mower. But she'd seen another rubus that
looked much the same only on a miniature scale, without the

octopus tentacles: *Rubus calycinoides*. She decided to have that instead.

Euphorbia wulfenii, now sometimes known as *E. characias* subspecies *wulfenii*, would look wonderful on the north-east side of the catalpa and mahonia, with its statuesque columns of deep glaucous green, lanceolate leaves. She was determined not to have *E. characias* itself with clear green inflorescences and two chocolate coloured spots in the centre of each flower. Though good of its kind it is not as dramatic as the larger columns of *E. wulfenii*, which are lime green throughout. She would have to question the nurseryman closely about this.

Now what could go between that and the edge? She fancied something grassy and a golden colouring would show up well against the euphorbia as one walked around the border on its north-east side, but there was nothing appropriate in her list. Then she remembered a dwarf bamboo she had seen in Christopher Lloyd's garden at Great Dixter, only 2½ ft. tall and striped in green and gold: *Arundinaria auricoma*. Next to that would be a good place for the small-growing prick-eared *Bergenia purpurascens* (often listed as *B. delavayi*). Its neat oval leaves turn purple in winter and it flowers well in spring – a cleaner magenta than *B. cordifolia*.

Another grass, but a real one and tall at that, could stand against the mahonia's north flank: *Miscanthus sinensis* 'Zebrinus', the Zebra Grass. Its basically green leaves (see Gertrude Jekyll's description, p. 16) are cross-banded in a most unusual style with yellow. It can flower prettily, in October, but one doesn't depend on that.

Something to round off the mahonia's neighbours on its west side. It could be a 4 ft. shrub. She wanted to work in another purple and 'blue' association she had admired in a garden on the chalk downs: *Berberis thunbergii*, in its purple-leaved form Atropurpurea, with Jackman's Blue Rue, a steely blue clone of *Ruta graveolens*. Actually it was the dwarf form, Atropurpurea Nana, of this berberis that she had seen with the rue. She could use that too, but build up behind it with a plant of the taller kind. She hoped they would blend and that the rue wouldn't grow taller than the dwarf berberis where the latter turned in behind the former. But anyway, she intended to cut the rue hard back each spring (that sort of pruning takes no time at all) so as to keep it shapely and to get the bluest foliage colouring from it.

Now she would bring in her favourite and indispensable, grey-leaved *Senecio laxifolius*. This was the narrowest part of the border but she would be pruning it back into old wood every 2 or 3 years, and if it made a height of nearly 4 ft. from time to time, no great harm would be done. In the years when it hadn't been pruned, the senecio would cover itself with yellow daisies, but she liked them and they would stand out well among all the surrounding foliage.

She had been dealing in rather bitty foliage lately, so, next to the dwarf berberis she would site *Kniphofia caulescens*, with its grey-blue, leek-like strap-leaves. It is a woody stemmed red-hot-poker, flowering in September, and reputedly not too hardy, but she had seen it outside at Wisley, not many miles away, and her soil was light and the position sunny.

She had been glancing uneasily at the other end of the border, on the plan, for some time past. Promontories are important, and she decided to get this fixed next. Standing back from the edge she would have a specimen conifer, *Thuja occidentalis* 'Rhein-gold', which would grow into a broad-based, conical bush, yellow in summer but taking on burnished coppery tints in winter.

This should be flanked by two low evergreens with dark green leaves. *Viburnum davidii* has them oval but they are saved from dullness by their deep parallel veining. This is a chunky, solid shrub which she hoped to keep down to 2½ ft. It can carry clusters of berries in a most intriguing and unlooked-for rich blue shade, but you need female bushes to carry the berries and a male to ensure that the fruits are fertilised and develop at all. Many of her nursery catalogues were unhelpfully vague about this, commenting that the females would produce bright turquoise blue berries when planted with a male, but not telling you what or which you would be buying from them. Exceptionally, Treseder's of Truro, Cornwall, unequivocally offered their plants singly or in pairs. So did Bodnant Garden Nursery attached to the famous gardens at Tal-y-Cafn, Colwyn Bay, Denbighshire. She decided to sandwich one male between two females and then, coming round the elbow, to have a group of the tough-leaved elephant-eared *Bergenia cordifolia*, which is indispensable to all flower arrangers. Old leaves die off in vivid scarlet, carmine and orange shades while the healthy ones turn an attractive liverish purple in winter (attractive if you are fond of liver, anyway, and fortunately she was). The heads of flowers, in April, are a raucous bluish magenta shade, carried on red, rhubarb-like stalks. One cannot help admiring and being repelled by them simultaneously.

Now she wanted to link up with the rest of her plan and decided on the grey, shrubby *Helichrysum splendidum* (also listed, she had discovered, as *H. alveolatum* and as *H. triliniatum*), to go behind the kniphofias. The greyness of the one would emphasise the blue element in the other. The helichrysum has small, ribbed leaves but they are arranged around vertical spikelets which give the whole shrub considerable individuality when viewed at a distance.

Joining up the kniphofia with the bergenia, a variegated iris. There are more than half a dozen different irises in cultivation with variegated forms, but *Iris pallida* 'Variegata' struck her as looking particularly fresh, with its strong upright fans of glaucous green-and-white-striped leaves. She had bought one plant from Treasures of Tenbury, Worcestershire at 50p, a couple of years ago and found that it increased very readily by cutting the rhizomes up each spring and making sure that there was just one 'eye' on each piece.

What could look better behind this than the strongly contrasted, broad crinkly foliage of Seakale, *Crambe maritima*? This is a palish glaucous shade, rather similar to the kniphofia's. Its great pouffes of honey-scented white flowers, at the 2 ft. level, in May, would be a welcome bon-bouche.

She decided to tuck in a group of *Leucothoë catesbaei* (correctly *L. fontanesiana* and once *Andromeda*) behind the thuja. Its arching stems are lined with glossy, sveltly pointed green leaves turning purple in winter, and are invaluable to flower arrangers. They look just right with spray chrysanthemums in yellow and burnt orange shades. This leucothoë need never grow much more than 3 ft. high: her cutting would see to that. The feathery grey foliage and waxy grey stems of *Rubus thibetanus* would make an appropriate neighbour. The friend who had given her suckers of this shrub had warned her that it was apt to travel a bit, but an annual chop round with a sharp spade would look after that. This rubus is pretty at all seasons. When the leaves fall in autumn, the naked, white-washed stems are fully revealed. They arch outwards and are seldom more than 4 ft. tall. Only in spring does the whole plant need cutting right down to ground level, so that it can start all over again with fresh young shoots.

There was surprisingly little variegation in her border and she was next going to fit in a specimen of the good-natured *Weigela florida* 'Variegata', which will grow 6 ft. tall in time. It does carry a mass of pale pink, tubular blossoms, in May, and they are very sweetly scented. At this time the leaves are pale green and silver, but the silver later changes to gold and the green deepens. Only in early December does the shrub finally shed its foliage.

On the outside of the border on another bend, she eventually decided on *Hosta plantaginea* 'Grandiflora'. True, hostas like moisture and her soil was light, but she could water it quite easily, there. Its leaves remain such a fresh and spring-like yellow-green all through the summer and up to its flowering time in September. The flowers themselves are surprisingly large, pure white trumpets and swooningly scented in the evenings. By its side a shrubby willow she had admired in several Scottish gardens: *Salix lanata*. Indeed, it is a rare native of Scotland. Its leaves are rounded and grey on a compact, slow-growing shrub and the male pussies make a charming display in spring. This, again, might want extra moisture, which was one reason for siting it next to the hosta.

Neither the hosta nor the willow featured in her original list, but then that had been drawn up with drought-tolerant plants in mind, and she was prepared to make a concession. Indeed, the list was beginning to run a bit short of the sort of plants she was now looking for. For instance, something rather heavily green to link *Senecio laxifolius* and *Rubus thibetanus*. Casting around, closing her eyes and then staring into vacancy by turns, she eventually pitched on a laurel, of all things, but a neat, slender-leaved, glossy Cherry Laurel, *Prunus laurocerasus* 'Zabelliana', with a pleasingly horizontal habit. Not that it altogether fails to make any height, but its branches tend to grow in layers and the white blossom is borne in spikes on their top sides – mainly in spring but quite freely in autumn, too.

Then, as a pair, Notcutt's deep purple form of the Venetian Sumach, *Cotinus coggygria* (or *Rhus cotinus*) with its paddle-shaped leaves, behind our old friend *Alchemilla mollis*, with umbrella-shaped, glaucous leaves and a haze of tiny lime-green flowers in June and July.

Knowing that the laurel would eventually spread to the border's margin, she didn't want anything important in front of it. Again departing from her list she decided to move a few bits of *Euphorbia robbiae* from another part of the garden. It is certainly invasive but by no means uncontrollable in this sort of situation and its foliage makes neat, dark evergreen rosettes against which the pale green inflorescences show up well in spring.

How was she to fill in the rest of the north side of her border? There would, for instance, be quite a lot of shade under the tall zebra grass, which her list didn't cater for. None of the greys would be happy there. After a bit of pencil chawing, she pitched on a mixed association – ten of each, evenly interplanted, of two saxifrages, *Saxifraga fortunei* and *S. cuscutiformis*. *S. fortunei* makes clumps of more or less circular leaves, ruffled at the edges. They die away in winter, but in October there comes a haze of delightful white flowers, prettily irregular, with long petals on the flower's lower side, short on the upper. Wada's form has more distinctive leaves, inasmuch as they are purple on their undersides, but the plants are not so bonny and she didn't feel like risking a miff. *S. cuscutiformis* is like the better known *S. stolonifera* (alias *S. sarmentosa*) which one sees under greenhouse benches, but its orbicular, evergreen leaves are handsome, being marked with rich purple, radiating stripes along the veins. This could be relied upon to fill in the gaps between the *S. fortunei* clumps, having a way of spreading by over-ground runners, rather like a strawberry, but with just the one plantlet terminating each runner.

Three plants of the shrubby *Lonicera nitida* 'Baggesen's Golden' would fit in between *Senecio laxifolius* and the zebra grass. This shrub's foliage only develops a good colouring if it receives a fair amount of sun, but if she allowed it to grow 4 ft. tall, she reckoned it would get sun enough.

She was now faced with a 10 ft. long, 2–3 ft. deep, marginal stretch that she was inclined not to chop up, fussily, but to treat as one unit with something reasonably shade-tolerant that would make a carpet. Again, her original list didn't help. At last she had it: the hardy, herbaceous plumbago, *Ceratostigma plumbaginoides*. True, its leaves are not specially interesting in the summer, but they take on glorious fiery tints in autumn, and in early autumn the heads of dark blue flowers open successively. The plant can be relied upon to flower well in our southern and eastern counties but is more inclined to vegetate in the cooler, damper north and west. Had she been more of a purist, she might have chosen that tough, evergreen ground-coverer, *Pachysandra terminalis*. It is a fresh shade of green; or, as a change, there is its green-and-white-variegated-leaved form.

Actually, reviewing the border as a whole, it will be found that at least half the plants included have worth-while flowers. About half of them are evergreens that will look presentable in winter. Only two – *Leucothoë* and the maple – are lime-hating. Curiously enough, our gardener's planning methods happen to coincide almost exactly with my own, which I find encouraging, because no other planners of my acquaintance have ever told me how they set about it.

THE FINAL LIST

in the order that its contents were selected:

1 *Juniperus communis* 'Hornibrookii'
2 *Acer palmatum* 'Dissectum Atropurpureum'
3 *Origanum vulgare* 'Aureum'
4 *Salvia officinalis* 'Grandiflora'
5 *Hydrangea quercifolia*
6 *Mahonia* 'Undulata'
7 *Catalpa bignonioides* 'Aurea'
8 *Artemisia palmeri*
9 *Sedum maximum* 'Atropurpureum' and *Senecio cineraria* 'White Diamond'
10 *Acanthus longifolius*
11 *Rubus calycinoides*
12 *Euphorbia wulfenii*
13 *Arundinaria auricoma*
14 *Bergenia purpurascens*

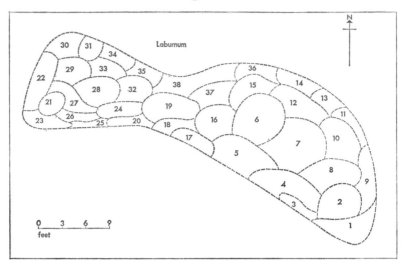

15 *Miscanthus sinensis* 'Zebrinus'
16 *Berberis thunbergii* 'Atropurpurea'
17 *Ruta graveolens* 'Jackman's
  Blue'
18 *Berberis thunbergii* 'Atropurpurea Nana'
19 *Senecio laxifolius*
20 *Kniphofia caulescens*
21 *Thuja occidentalis* 'Rheingold'
22 *Viburnum davidii*
23 *Bergenia cordifolia*
24 *Helichrysum splendidum*
25 *Iris pallida* 'Variegata'
26 *Crambe maritima*

27 *Leucothoë catesbaei*
28 *Rubus thibetanus*
29 *Weigela florida* 'Variegata'
30 *Hosta plantaginea* 'Grandiflora'
31 *Salix lanata*
32 *Prunus laurocerasus* 'Zabelliana'
33 *Cotinus coggygria* 'Notcutt's
  Variety'
34 *Alchemilla mollis*
35 *Euphorbia robbiae*
36 *Saxifraga fortunei* and *Saxifraga cuscutiformis*
37 *Lonicera nitida* 'Baggesen's
  Golden'
38 *Ceratostigma plumbaginoides*

CHAPTER 5

The Principal Shrub Ingredients for Mixed Plantings

*

HAVING suggested what I believe to be a good way of using one's material, I must go on to describe the material itself in a fairly orderly (alphabetical) manner, starting with the shrubs.

Where a procumbent or recumbent blue **conifer** of bold design was required, the obvious choice would be a form of the Blue Spruce, *Picea pungens* (see p. 89). But my own preference would be for *Abies concolor* 'Glauca Compacta'. It makes a wonderful slow growing specimen, with leaves arranged more or less in two ranks, of clean outline and beautiful glaucous colouring. When crushed, they smell of tangerines.

The **Japanese maples** comprise two species, *Acer japonicum* and *A. palmatum*, both having a large number of attractive cultivars. I always enjoy seeing happy specimens in other people's gardens but, since I grow only one of them in my own, and that for its bark, I cannot write with quite that note of personal lyricism that I should wish to sound.

Autumn colour is one of their fortes but does not necessarily go with a leaf that is specially interesting at other times. One of the best of all golden-leaved shrubs, retaining its colour throughout the summer, is *A. japonicum* 'Aureum'. As is the case with so many yellow-leaved plants, you need, in siting them, to strike the right balance between allowing them too much shade or too little. Too much, and the colouring tends to be greenish rather than yellow; too little, and the yellow becomes hectic with necrotic brown spots, although this will largely be prevented if ere is plentiful soil moisture.

A. j. 'Aureum' is so slow growing that it may be treated as a shrub, although it will reach 20 ft. in course of time. *A.j.* 'Aconitifolium' has a nicely dissected leaf with deep cuts between lobes that are themselves lacy.

I described the best known cultivar of *A. palmatum* in the last chapter, namely Dissectum Atropurpureum. Basically the leaves are quite large, but so cut up as to be all lace-work. The green-leaved Dissectum colours with particular brilliance in autumn. Osakazuki is famed for autumn colouring but is not too interesting at other seasons. The clone that used to be called Septemlobum, now Heptalobum Elegans Purpureum, is a rich purple throughout the summer and grows into a wide-spreading large bush or small tree.

Although not out and out calcifuge, none of these maples are mad about alkaline soils in general. They can be ruined in spring by cold and cutting winds on their young foliage and they hate being dry at the root in their growing season. But they are thoroughly winter hardy. When they do well they do very well; often, however, they cause their chagrined owners to wring their hands and gnash their teeth in baffled despair.

It is pleasant to achieve a simulation of flaunting exoticism in an English garden with little effort and less risk. This can sometimes be worked by treating a tree as though it were a shrub. **Ailanthus altissima**, the Tree of Heaven, is much planted in London, as it puts up with adverse, smoky conditions. It grows 60 ft. high and has pleasant pinnate foliage with a good number of divisions, but you might not look at it twice. Grown as a shrub, however, you cut it down almost to ground level every early spring, and then allow just one stem to develop. It will grow perhaps 8 ft. in one season, and the leaves clothing it will be up to 4 ft. long, with ever so many divisions. This is exciting. The tree is easily raised from seed. Repeated pruning is weakening, so you should feed well and expect to have to replace exhausted plants from time to time. See also *Paulownia, Rhus, Catalpa* and *Corylus* for the same treatment.

Two of the most splendid of all variegated (albeit deciduous) shrubs are cultivars of **Aralia elata**, the Japanese Angelica Tree. There is the yellow-and-green Aureo-variegata and the silver-and-green Variegata, alias Albo-marginata. The leaves, without any funny business by pruning, are some 4 ft. long by 2½ ft. wide and they are twice pinnate. You can estimate that the shrub will grow about 6 or 8 ft tall, and it benefits, visually, from a dark background. It is very expensive – let's say, allowing for inflation between writing this and you reading it, £10. All plants have to be grafted; they are raised in Holland and imported. Even so, there may be several pounds' difference in retailing prices from one nursery to another. Don't dig round your plants if you can help it. By damaging their roots, you will induce them to sucker, and the suckers will be of the stock.

What shall we say of **Aucuba japonica**, infamous denizen of soot-bedizened Victorian shrubberies? It has the misfortune of being able to exist in dry shade, where not much else will. But existing and living are two different things. Give the aucuba its chance – in shade, if you like, but nice damp shade and not too dark – prune it for shape, choose your cultivar carefully and you will be rewarded.

There are a great many aucuba cultivars (Hillier lists fifteen) and confusion is worse confounded when we bring in sex and mention that females can bear red or yellow berries. It is not my business in this book to play the role of accoucheur. If you are content with any old spotted laurel, you will have no difficulty in finding one and you won't be bothered whether it's a him or a her. If you want something rather special, I do recommend (though I've only seen, not grown it) Goldenheart, from Treseder's of Truro, Cornwall. The whole of the centre of the leaf is golden whilst the green margin has gold speckling.

Ballota pseudodictamnus is one of those plants that shrub specialists deny is a shrub while herbaceous plant specialists are equally clear that it is not herbaceous but shrubby. I have just been out to look at my group in their mid-January aspect. No doubt about it: they are shrubby. You need several plants together to make an impression and some of mine are looking remarkably comely, considering they were weighed down for a fortnight by snow. The others haven't recovered quite so well from their annual trim, which I do in August. This is an ever-green with felted, grey, heart-shaped leaves. They look greener than grey just now but the plant is at its best in May, June and July. Its basic height is 1½ ft. The flowering spikes add to this but they tend to flop sideways under their own weight. They are pretty at first – a string of greenish grey bobbles – but go to pieces when the flowers (which are quite insignificant) actually open. All flowering spikes should then be cut back into old wood. There are different, but undifferentiated, clones of this plant in circulation, so you want to make sure you're buying a good one.

Bamboos. The work to consult on this subject is *Bamboos* by A. H. Lawson, published by Faber in 1968. Dr C. E. Hubbard's notes in the 1969 Supplement to the R.H.S. Dictionary of Gardening, are also helpful.

Bamboos belong to the grass family: they are shrubby grasses, evergreen but often a sorry sight in winter. They are (unlike many other grasses) entirely foliage plants. The one thing they are required not to do is to flower. Flowering, indeed, occurs in most cases at only long intervals. A flowering bamboo at best looks scruffy (in this country, anyway), at worst is killed outright. If the whole plant flowers, it dies; if flowering is only partial, the plant can recover and eventually return to normal, but after several years.

However, the best thing is to forget about flowering and its attendant ills, until it happens to you.

Bamboos are very beautiful plants (with certain exceptions). They have a shimmering elegance in their foliage as well as stateliness and poise in their habit. There are many ways of using them but there are two things you want to know before making your selection. First, how hardy any particular species is. Second, what to expect of its habit of growth.

Bamboos spread by suckering. Many of the best, from the small-gardener's point of view, throw up their new canes so close to the parent clump that they can hardly be said to be suckering at all. In warmer countries they might have a greater suckering propensity, but here they behave. These make admirable lawn specimens. They can also be used where there are planting spaces or built in, raised beds on terraces and in courtyards. Reasonably upright types should be used here, where space is restricted; otherwise, with the arching kinds, you'll receive a shower bath every time you swish past a plant, following rain. Bamboos in

9. ABOVE, *Salvia officinalis* 'Tricolor', most gaily coloured of the many varieties of common sage.   BELOW, the trifoliate *Helleborus corsicus* associated with *Lamium galeobdolon* 'Variegatum', which needs strictly controlling.

10. *Hebe andersonii* 'Variegata', one of the least hardy of the shrubby veronicas, but deliciously fresh in green and cream.

courtyards cast beautiful shadows, especially noticeable in moon-light.

The well-behaved bamboo is also suitable for inclusion in mixed plantings. It should be placed so that it is much the tallest feature among its neighbours. Then you will be able to appreciate its habit. It is not difficult to chop round the thinner-caned species once a year with a spade, to make sure they don't increase their perimeter.

Mr Lawson is so fond of his bamboos that he is like an indulgent parent towards them and their spreading proclivities. 'Only wanders at the edges', he will write, equably, of a species one had always thought of as rather redoubtable. But even he admits that some are a rampant menace. Of *Sasa* (*Arundinaria*) *palmata* he tells us that an ideal way to confine it is on an island! Shades of Napoleon on Elba? But even the rampers have their uses as an alternative to docks and nettles in some awkward corner.

Quite a large number of the most desirable bamboos are hardy, but they do dislike cutting winds, so should receive reasonable shelter. Those with thin-textured leaves are best in shade – in my part of the country, anyway, but not in west Scotland. Most dislike drought. The time to plant is in warm, late spring weather, when growth is just starting and they can establish quickly. Nurseries supplying bamboos include Reuthe's at Keston in Kent, Hillier's at Winchester and Treseder's in Cornwall. If you buy from Treseder's, say, it is quite likely the offsets or clumps they supply will be ready to send before your own weather and ground are congenial for establishing them. The wisest thing is to pot or box up the material on arrival and keep it in a greenhouse or even in a reasonably warm shed, until growing weather comes along.

The worst thing about bamboos is the confusion in their naming. Each one has several synonyms and the botanists will not agree on how they should be classified. I will give some alternative names in brackets.

There are three principal genera, if you're not a splitter, like the Japanese botanists. These are *Arundinaria*, *Phyllostachys* and *Sasa*. The last is sometimes included with *Arundinaria*. I like *Sasa* as a name; it's got something. But as a genus it is the least attractive; dwarf, with large leaves that often become blasted at the edges. At a distance, you think what a pretty variegation, but on coming closer you realise that the pale areas are dead, and not at all attractive. Also sasas are runners, often difficult to control. Two dwarf arundinarias are similarly barbarous. Of *A. pumila* Mr Lawson says 'very free moving', which is a nice way of putting it. Of *A. vagans* (vagans means roving) Dr Hubbard tells us that it is 'very vigorous, rapidly spreading, and a nuisance anywhere if not thoroughly isolated or rigorously kept in bounds'. Mr Reuthe, who sells it, says 'excellent ground cover, even under trees. Will stifle all weeds'. Set a weed to catch a weed.

Turning to the desirable arundinarias, there are two charming dwarf kinds that could be grown in any not too dry garden. *Arundinaria auricoma* (*A. viridistriata, Pleioblastus viridistriatus*) grows only about 2½ ft. tall with me and increases all too slowly. You can divide it in spring, but it won't forgive you for at least a year. The leaves are striped in green and gold, the gold being the brighter for siting the plant in a sunny position. *A. variegata* (*A. fortunei, Pleioblastus variegatus*) is handsomely striped in green and white. Most bamboos look horribly battered in winter, but this one in my garden, in January, is looking really smart with its cleanly striped, green and white foliage. I have had it now for four years and it has just about settled down, though still only 2 ft. tall. In Holland Park, Kensington, it must be quite 4 ft. It makes a thicket with its slender canes and becomes something of a traveller, once established in moist soil.

The biggest of the hardy arundinarias is *A. fastuosa* (*Sinarundinaria fastuosa*), a stately, upright bamboo 15 ft. tall and making a fine specimen on its own in a large lawn, for instance. *A. aponica* (*Pseudosasa japonica*) is the hardiest and commonest of the larger bamboos, a dull and scruffy object, as usually seen, with over-large, coarse leaves. Far more appealing for the same purpose, that is as a boundary boskage or a filler under trees – anywhere, in fact, where its running proclivities will not be a nuisance – is *A. anceps*. It grows 10 to 15 ft. and has small leaves, carried in billowing swags. Curiously, I can find no synonyms for this one.

Two similar species have great elegance and polite garden

manners. They make good specimens and increase their circum-
ference only slowly. These are *A. nitida* (*Sinarundinaria nitida*) with
purple stems and *A. murielae* (*S. murielae*) with green stems. They
are happy in full sun in Scotland but in the hotter south-east of
England are better in shade; otherwise their leaves tend to curl
up. Their foliage is airy and neat, carried in masses. Height:
8–10 ft.

A species with a particularly small and fragile leaf and a fragile
constitution to go with it is *A. falconeri*. In Ireland and the mild
west it grows to 25 ft., but it is not reliably hardy in most parts of
Britain. However, I read that it was an excellent tub plant, so I
transferred the seedling that a friend had given me from a pot in
the greenhouse to a 2 ft. cube tub in the garden. It grew at a
tremendous rate and I have been delighted with it for two seasons
now. The young canes are almost leafless except at their tips.
They are very slender and bend over after rain with a string of
silver raindrops suspended from their undersides. With the first
autumn frost (in November, here), we move it into a cellar where
it receives only a little dim light from a dirty window, and is
watered on Saturday mornings. It has lost most of its foliage by
the spring, but soon picks up.

Most *Phyllostachys* are clump-formers having only the slightest
colonial tendencies. Their canes are a great feature and are usually
displayed to advantage. The only one I know is usually called
P. boryana but should probably be *P. nigra* 'Bory'. Its foliage is
gold-green with olive green stems and a pleasingly sparse habit.
P. nigra itself has canes that are jet black at maturity in the best
clones so make sure you get hold of the best clone but don't ask
me how. There are a number of other phyllostachys available and
they all sound worth owning.

I have left a lone wolf to the last: *Chusquea couleou* (*C. andina*),
from Chile, looks like no other bamboo. It makes a splendid
specimen. If worked in among other shrubs, let it tower head and
shoulders above them. It usually seems to grow 10 to 18 ft. tall
in this country. The canes are very thick – if you want one as an
offset from an old clump, a saw is necessary. The leafy branches
are thickly clustered in a semi-circular arc, on opposite sides of the
stem alternately. The leaves themselves are small and slender. In

the aggregate they look like a great feather brush. I long to re-place a rather scruffy old ball-and-saucer clipped yew, in our front lawn, with one of these. Reuthe of Keston, Kent, lists it but says 'fabulously rare', so you know what to expect.

One final word about bamboos. Many owners seem to think that, once established, they can be left to get on with it for ever-more. So they can, but they will look far handsomer if you will take the trouble to cut out all spent canes, once a year, and give them a feed.

The **barberries** are grown mainly for their flowers or for their fruit. Some of the deciduous types colour brilliantly before leaf-fall and some of the evergreens have rich, glossy foliage. The only ones I want to mention by name as out-and-out foliage plants, however, are a few of the deciduous barberries with coloured leaves. Most are derived from *Berberis thunbergii*, and the best known are *B.t.* 'Atropurpurea', 4–6 ft. tall, and *B.t.* 'Atropur-purea Nana', 1½–2 ft. tall. Both are very useful purple-leaved shrubs. The former is often raised from seed – much less trouble-some a method than cuttings – and there is consequently a good deal of variation in the intensity of the seedlings' purple colouring. The same goes for *B. vulgaris* 'Atropurpurea': you want to be sure of selecting a good seedling. This is an even larger shrub, to 8 ft., and its leaves being larger also are that much more telling. There is a new cultivar of *B. thunbergii* called Rose Glow, whose basically purple leaves have patches of pink and white in them. The colour-ing is pleasant but the pale patches have the effect of distorting the leaf shape and young shrubs look peaky. Still, this is good.

Of the **heaths** with coloured foliage, most work has been done on ling: cultivars of *Calluna vulgaris*, which is the typical Scots heather. They have proliferated with horrid abandon and abound in good selling names like Blazeaway, Multicolor (but why not Joseph's Coat?), Gold Haze and Golden Feather (which is really rather good). Sometimes the colouring is remarkable, but what is the use of colour without form? True, they are efficient ground cover but in any but the largest garden with room for an extensive heather feature and an admixture of more interesting shrubs, they look utterly inappropriate. Their adoring public will heartily disagree and are welcome to do so but it's no good looking to me for kind words that would stick in my gullet. Heather is for grouse.

The Golden **Catalpa**, *Catalpa bignonioides* 'Aurea', is a most excellent foliage plant when used as a shrub as already described (see pp. 52-3). The green leaf of the unadorned species is dull, but there is a wonderful luminous quality in the golden form. You can buy it grafted as a standard, but more than half the point is to be able to associate it with leaves of different shapes and colouring from its own, and this is most easily achieved at shrub level.

Taking another quick look at the vast genus of the false cypresses, **Chamaccyparis**, the one that has flooded the market of recent years is *C. pisifera* 'Boulevard'. No doubt the o-la-la (yet pronounceable) Frenchness of its name has been a contributory factor. This makes a conical bush of soft, juvenile foliage, blue in colouring but drooping at the shoot tips so as to reveal the pale grey resin ducts on the leaves' under-surfaces. In winter the general colouring becomes overlaid with a slight purple flush. It is a pretty shrub growing large in time but most gardeners will be happy to cross that bridge when they come to it.

Boulevard was a sport from the scarcely less popular though cacophonously named *C.p.* 'Squarrosa', which is very similar and eventually grows into a small tree.

The purple colouring that so many evergreens assume in winter can make for fascinating contrasts, as in *C. thyoides* 'Andleyensis', where the overall colouring is dark green, this forming a background to the purple of the shoot tips. Andleyensis consists largely of adult foliage, with minute scale leaves. In *C.t.* 'Ericoides' the foliage is all of the pointed, juvenile type and stands out at right angles to the stems, again turning purple in winter. This does really remain a small bush and is therefore more suitable in the long term for small spaces than those so far mentioned. It will, however, look very small for many early years.

Slower still are *C. obtusa* 'Nana' which is dark green and *C.o.* 'Nana Aurea', the golden version. In these, the leafy shoots are arranged in distinctive fans. They are especially suitable for culture as miniature trees or bonsai, and there are examples in this country (but originating in China) some 250 years old but still only 18 in. tall by 3 ft. across.

A form of *C. obtusa* that I find most attractive, especially when young (it does grow rather inconveniently large and woody in its later years) is *C.o.* 'Tetragona Aurea', in which the gold-green young shoots are encrusted like a lichen. When I bought my plant some years ago, it arrived with more top than roots, and no soil on the roots. Fearing that it might not 'take', I made three cuttings from its leafy shoots, forthwith. This is often a wise insurance against accidents. In fact, the plant grew perfectly well. The cuttings all rooted, so I now have 3 extra plants which would be nice, supposing I wanted them.

The **dogwoods** are an extraordinarily mixed lot (taxonomists are eager to tear them apart into four or five genera), but one feature they all have in common is a dull and dreary oval leaf. And yet they have managed to transcend this defect to a point where we are obliged to spend quite a time with them and enjoyably at that. Most dogwoods are capable of good autumn colouring, but that would not be a sufficient recommendation by itself. No, it is through their variegated cultivars that they win fame and acclamation.

To take the commonest first: *Cornus alba*, the dogwood that we grow for the carmine colouring of its young stems in winter. This has three variegated forms. Best known is *C. alba* 'Spaethii', whose leaf is green in the centre with a broad yellow margin. It is a vigorous shrub and can cope with a setting of rough grass in any boggy place. Likewise *C.a.* 'Variegata', with green-and-white variegation. These both earn their keep in winter, too, with coloured stems but are not nearly as brilliant in this respect as *C.a.* 'Sibirica', which also has a white-variegated cultivar, sometimes called Sibirica Variegata, sometimes Elegantissima. But you need to know that this is not nearly as vigorous as the others, which may or may not be a convenience, according to whether you are using it for wild gardening or for tame.

C. mas, the Cornelian Cherry (it has red, cherry-like fruits) is valued for its clusters of small, greenish-yellow flowers carried on the bare wood of a large shrub or small, spreading tree in late winter. So far, so good, but like many other winter flowering shrubs, its summer dress is undistinguished or worse. However, this is redeemed by *C.m.* 'Variegata', whose leaves have a broad margin of white. It flowers as freely as the type-plant but is less vigorous. Another cultivar, Elegantissima, has leaves variegated yellow and pink. I have not seen it.

Now we come to the two stars of the genus. *C. alternifolia* 'Argentea' is one of the loveliest of all variegated shrubs. It grows to 8 or 10 ft. in time and builds up in tiers from a dense foundation to an airy, transparent tiara, blue sky making the best of backgrounds. The leaves are quite slenderly elliptical and thin-textured, green in the middle with a broad white band. Sometimes there are additional pink tints. *C. controversa* 'Variegata' is built even more markedly in layers. Its leaves are larger, giving the shrub a stronger appearance and the marginal shading is pale yellow. It is a more decided and imposing shrub and may even be preferred to *C. alternifolia* 'Argentea' (not by me).

The number of good purple-leaved shrubs not being so very great, I feel I must include **Corylus maxima** 'Purpurea' among the greater shrub luminaries, although it is coarse growing and apt to take up a good deal of space. However, this does not really matter, as you can prune it severely to the ground, every other year at least. This is a hazel (or filbert), with large rounded leaves. The catkins, as well as the leaves, are purple.

Perhaps the most sought after of purple shrubs are the darkest forms of the **Venetian Sumach,** long known as *Rhus cotinus.* This group, with their simple, paddle-shaped leaves, look so different from the pinnate sumachs, that one is hardly surprised they should have been separated into a genus on their own. The only pity is the clumsiness of the specific epithet. How is one to say coggygria? I have never learned to mouth the word with either confidence or comfort. Anyway *Rhus cotinus* is now *Cotinus coggygria* and the darkest purple-leaved cultivars are Notcutt's Variety and Royal Purple. Watch out what you buy. Foliis Purpureis sounds like the goods but, when correctly named, it is a clone whose leaves start purple, when young, but change to an indeterminate greenish purple shade later in the season.

If you can site your purple sumach so that it can be seen with the sun shining through its foliage at the beginning or end of the day, that'll be ideal. Each leaf will appear to be glowing with its own inner source of light and warmth.

Danaë racemosa looks something like a dwarf bamboo though not, in fact, related. It is an excellent evergreen shrub for a shady place under trees, for instance, but needs a reasonable amount of moisture to do itself justice. It is perfectly happy on chalk. You need several plants in a group, for the best effect. It is one of those botanical trap plants, in that what appear to be leaves are really cladodes – leaf-like stems. One has to mention this as a kind of insurance against pedantic criticism (not that anything really protects you against the pedant rampant). The slenderly tapering lanceolate 'leaves', then, are bright green and glossy and of firm texture, coming through the worst of winters without scars. They are borne in sprays on branching stems. On a well established and flourishing plant, the stems may be as much as 4 ft. tall. I only wish mine were, but they have only achieved 2½ ft. to date. However, I keep splitting my plants up (rather than buy more, which is expensive) and they take a long time to get into their stride, so I live in hopes. A fresh crop of shoots is thrown up from ground level each spring. When these have fully developed, in the summer, don't forget to cut away the previous year's shoots; they are no longer needed and become progressively tattier, spoiling the plants' general appearance, if allowed to remain.

Now I include a shrub that many readers will never have met but which is remarkably hardy and most handsomely attired. **Daphniphyllum macropodum** belongs to the *Euphorbiaceae*, but has leaves like the common man's idea of a rhododendron. (It pleases the childish type of mind that derives a sense of superiority from deceiving friends and acquaintances in this question of identity). Now, for a plant to look like a rhododendron is no more cheering than for a person to look po-faced, but this daphniphyllum brings it off, first by the smoothness of its leaves' texture, second, by the glaucous colouring of their lower surface and last by the bright red shading of the leaf stalks. It will make a big shrub, after many years, and is good in shade, enjoying some shelter as is to be expected of any large-leaved plant.

The best known **Elaeagnus** are evergreen. Of the deciduous species, I have already mentioned *E. angustifolia*, under trees. Remains *E. commutata*, once so much more descriptively known as

E. argentea. Its leaves are broadly ovate but with wavy margins. They are covered with brown, glandular speckles underneath, but are shining silver on top and have a very special look about them. This is a suckering shrub and can make a thicket, 3 or 4 ft. tall. It is never a nuisance except that in many gardens, including my own, it is afflicted by a die-back disease, and scarcely makes any headway at all. Still, it's worth trying. Its inconspicuous yellowish bell-flowers, in spring, are deliciously scented.

Far and away the most famous of the evergreens is *E. pungens* 'Maculata' (till recently, *E.p.* 'Aureo-Variegata'). It is a singularly enlivening shrub to contemplate in winter's sunshine or in winter even without sunshine for it is a source of warmth in itself.

The ovate leaves have puckered margins. Their upper surface shines and is occupied by green and yellow patches and streaks. The proportion and distribution of each, varies greatly. On the whole, the yellow tends to occupy the centre of the leaf. As Bean tells us somewhere, this is generally an unstable condition; plants having it, tend to revert to plain green. *E.p.* 'Maculata' certainly does, and you must always watch out for the trouble and remove reverted branches as soon as they reveal themselves. Young shoots and leaves are brownish. This is nothing to worry about but they do give the shrub a nebulous and indeterminate cast in its growing season.

I have just been comparing this shrub's leaves and branches with those of the holly, *Ilex* 'Golden King', which I like just as much (see pp. 30-1). The elaeagnus has the more lustrous upper surface to its leaf and hence sparkles more, but it has an awkward and angular habit of branching. The holly is more graceful. The yellow in their leaves is almost identical but the holly's have suffered to some extent in recent frosts while the elaeagnus has not.

E.p. 'Maculata' is a shrub that seems desperately slow-growing to start with, but you must allow it plenty of space in the long term, because it eventually grows 8 ft. tall by as much across and makes rapid progress when fully established.

There are other variegated cultivars of *E. pungens* of which Dicksonii, with marginal variegation and scarcely any reverting tendencies, is well known. I never thought a lot of it, but a gardener whose opinion I respect has recently championed it so enthusiastically that I must look again.

Flower arrangers go on about *E. ebbingei* – a vigorous plain-leaved hybrid, grey on the underside, but I find it a dull thing. Sybil Emberton much prefers its parent, *E. macrophylla*. It has the R.H.S. Award of Garden Merit. Even so, I don't know it.

The majority of deciduous **Euonymus** colour pink or carmine in autumn but are poor looking objects otherwise (their fruit apart). *Euonymus europaeus* is our native spindle. The evergreen fraternity look quite different. And yet, if you should see an unclipped specimen of the hedging species, *E. japonicus*, you may be surprised to find it carrying red fruits just like the spindle's, only smaller. This is a fine shrub, however common and despised, but all the better for being allowed to grow freely, in which case it will attain 10 or 12 ft. each way. The oval leaves are a strong shade of bay green and they are highly polished. This species has a great number of cultivars, many of them with yellow or white variegation. All are pleasant and worth growing. Some are apt to revert but still look nice with patches of yellow and others of green. For use where space is restricted, as in a courtyard, one or other form of the dwarf, small-leaved *E.j.* 'Microphyllus' is especially well suited. I would recommend the golden variegated Microphyllus Pulchellus.

More popular with the sophisticated (i.e. self-conscious) gardener are the cultivars of *E. fortunei* (formerly *E. radicans*), especially Silver Queen. This makes a low (2 ft.) but spreading bush that is as gay as any flower. The central leaf area is blotched in two shades of green while the margin is cream-white with additional pink stains in cold weather. Actually, there are a number of variegated clones of *E. fortunei* and they differ markedly in their will to grow and thrive or, on the contrary, to sit and mope and just look scruffy. I suggest a sunny position, although they are shade tolerant (tolerance and enjoyment are not synonymous). Some, like *E.f.* 'Variegatus', have the ability to transform themselves into self-clinging climbers up to the second storey, when they have their backs to a wall.

The leaves of *E.f.* 'Coloratus' are green but change, like so many evergreens, to purple in winter.

Several shrubby **spurges** have a claim on us. Our native wood spurge, *Euphorbia amygdaloides*, has a purple-leaved form, Purpurea, that is especially eye-catching in winter. It comes more or less true from seed, but you can select better or worse coloured seedlings. There is also a cream-edged form, *E.a.* 'Variegata' – not easily come by.

E. robbiae, a rampant species, useful as ground cover in shade – even dry shade – has dark green leaves arranged in a terminal rosette.

The shrub we used to know as *E. wulfenii* is yawing helplessly from one name to another. At present we seem to have a choice between *E. characias* subspecies *wulfenii* and *E. veneta*. I have already described this (p. 54). For finest foliage effect, plant it in sun. Then it will make a compact, not a sprawling, bush. Even so, you want to cut flowering stems right out, immediately they have flowered, and leave room for the young stems growing up from the bottom of the bush.

Fatsia japonica, once known as *Aralia sieboldii*, is the largest-leaved evergreen shrub that is hardy through most of the British Isles. And what a leaf! Shaped like a nine-fingered hand, it measures up to 15 in. across by 10 in. long and is carried on a long, strong stalk of 18 in. or so. The leaf texture is solid – wind never tears or bruises it – the surface is beautifully glossy, rich green with boldly delineated pale veins. There is also a good variegated form, *F.j.* 'Variegata', with white splashes near the tips of the leaflets.

This shrub is commonly, but erroneously, known as the castor-oil plant. We shall come to the real castor-oil when dealing with tender foliage plants (p. 168-9). *Fatsia japonica* does very well in shade – as a pot plant it is quite often stood in a dim fireplace in the sort of position where you might expect to meet an aspidistra. In the garden, however, it should be allowed a good deal of space, for it will grow 8 ft. tall by as much across. Old leaves tend to get hung up in the fabric and want pulling out, from time to time, to keep your plant looking smart. The one pest that often disfigures it is the capsid bug, which feeds on the sap of very young leaves so that, when they grow up, they are found to be riddled with holes.

Fatsias do flower, quite pleasingly in their subdued way, in October and November, with umbels of small white blossoms on a branching inflorescence. These look like ivy blossom and point the close relationship, as do the black berries that follow in spring, and from which they are easily propagated.

A number of **fuchsias** are used by parks and public gardens for the colour of their foliage in bedding out schemes. Golden Treasure is one of their favourites, and mine too, when really well grown: that is to say on well manured and, above all, on regularly and thoroughly watered soil. It then grows with a will and looks like a more exotic, fleshier-leaved version of golden privet, not flowering at all. If allowed to go dry, it scorches badly. Sunray has an exciting leaf; 'a delicious confection of strawberry and cream and fresh green' is how H. E. Bates (who introduced me to it) describes it. But the leaf form and texture are on the coarse side. The elegance of its leaf is one of the main assets of Genii, which is a hardy fuchsia that has successfully passed its trials as such in the Northern Horticultural Society's gardens at Harlow Car in Yorkshire. The leaf is narrow and pointed, pale lime green, the stems red. There are flowers, late in the season, too; red and purple, the sepal tips curled back. I know nothing about the hardiness of Autumnale, but its leaves are elegant and interesting, being basically lime green but with a darker flush and salmon-copper veins. Scarcely any flowers to distract you.

F. gracilis 'Variegata' is a weakish grower, but with bright cream and green variegation with a dash of pink thrown in. It is not sufficiently robust in the garden. Of more general use, because so much tougher, is *F.g.* 'Versicolor', also known as Tricolor. Its colour is always changing. Sometimes, at midsummer, the bush is nearly all a sort of ashen green. At others it is liberally sprinkled with vivid carmine pink shoots with flecks of cream here and there. The fact of the matter is that the young shoots are this pink colour. That is what you first see when the plant returns to life in May. Later on, the capsid bugs get busy on it, eating out all the young shoots so that the bush consists mainly of mature, ashen leaves. But, come the autumn, the capsids disappear and, if you are lucky and don't get a frost till November, the fuchsia is at its most radiant in the preceding 6 or 8 weeks, covering itself all over with a flush of young shoots.

On heavy, moisture-retentive soil, which is what all fuchsias relish (they are marvellous in those dismal summers when it rains and blows every day and all your other flowers go mouldy), Versicolor grows from nought to 3½ ft. with a graceful, arching habit. Always cut your plants down to ground level, in early spring. Even if the old shoots survived, much the strongest growth is produced from the base. When this is about a foot high, you will notice that a number of shoots have reverted to plain green. Grasp each of them low down and give a tug. They will break cleanly away at their point of origin and you will have no more trouble from them for another year. But if you omit this small task, the bush will steadily become greener and lose nine-tenths of its charm.

The leaf of **Griselinia littoralis** is oval but very far from dull. It is evergreen and unusually solid, almost fleshy, of oily smooth texture, 2 or 3 in. long. And the colouring of both leaf and stem is bright yellow-green, this spring-like shade being retained throughout the year. It is particularly cheering in winter. Everything hinges on the shrub's hardiness. It is absolutely in its element in coastal regions anywhere from Land's End to John O'Groats and makes a first-rate shelter belt against the full blast of salt-laden winds. Inland, it is often hardy, too, especially on well-drained soil. It cannot abide wet feet. You must just try it out, planting in spring. It makes a handsome clipped hedge (but clip it in spring for safety); an even handsomer free-growing bush to 10 or 12 ft., generally.

Griselinia is usually propagated from cuttings, but if you have a male and a female (the shrub being dioecious), the latter will self-sow freely. *G.l.* 'Variegata' is a beautiful variegated form with streaks in its foliage of different shades of green as well as cream. But, as is always the way, it is less hardy than the type plant and has succumbed with me in Sussex, though there is a large specimen in the gardens at Inverewe in North-West Scotland. All very tantalising.

The genus **Hebe**, from New Zealand and thereabouts, comprises the shrubby veronicas. They can vary in appearance to an extraordinary degree. Some have tiny overlapping scale-leaves that make them look like miniature cypresses. These are the whipcords and I will take them first. They are attractive small bushes and they are hardy – a point that always has to be mentioned in respect of hebes, many of which, especially the glamorous flowering types, are anything but.

Hebe armstrongii is a honey. Its young shoots are, indeed, a deep honey colour and of such an unusual and accommodating shade that it associates with and flatteringly offsets practically anything you can think of planting near it. At Hidcote, the National Trust property near Chipping Camden in Gloucestershire, they have this burnt yellow hebe with the grey of *Salix lanata*, the green of a dwarf shrubby pine, *Pinus densiflora* 'Umbraculifera', and, as upright features, the glaucous Irish Juniper, *Juniperus communis hibernica* and a young *Chamaecyperis lawsoniana* 'Erecta', with bright green, vertical fans. The only flowering feature (in September) was a pale yellow shrubby potentilla. More was not needed; everything you could wish for was there in leaf and shrub colour, form and texture. The hebe carries its branchlets in sprays, which give it extra individuality. Like all its brethren, it needs full sun to look its best. Having said all this, I have to admit that I may have been writing all the time about another species, namely *H. ochracea*, which has commonly been grown as *H. armstrongii* in gardens, according to Messrs Hillier's latest catalogue. The branches of the true *H. armstrongii* are coloured olive-green.

H. hectorii has the same neat leaf and branch construction and is a warm green. *H.* 'Edinensis' has slightly larger scale-leaves that overlap but stand out a little from the stem. This is bright green and a good front line plant, forming a fairly loose mat about a foot tall. One of my favourites, because I have had it for more than 30 years and it has given me such valuable service, never requiring the slightest attention, is *H. propinqua* (often grown as *H. salicornioides* 'Aurea'). As it is raining and blowing outside and my dachshund puppy, asleep in front of the fire, is giving me a moment's peace, I shall describe this one without holding a sprig in my left hand (the safest practice). It is another whipcord, with a loosely (but not too loosely) branching habit making a $1\frac{1}{2}$ ft. mound but gradually spreading laterally to a width of 3 or 4 ft.

– more, if it can layer itself as it goes, but mine is on a ledge, over which it cascades on one side and there is a lawn on the other. The scale leaves are small and overlapping and they are a very bright yellow-green, always looking sunny, even on the dullest day.

H. cupressoides continues to carry its conifer mimicry act to a smell of cedar pencils. This is airborne and I have even been able, on occasion, to detect it in the unpromising circumstance of bleak February weather with wet snow falling. The tiny leaves are dusty green, as though the shrub grew near a dirt track. Also, with age and notwithstanding full exposure, it does become quite tall, to 4 or 5 ft., and a thought leggy. But I don't resent this, as it has character. Some people's bushes did succumb in the 1963 winter, including the parent of mine in Margery Fish's Somerset garden, but it is pretty dependable.

Enough of the whipcords. A number of hebes have glaucous foliage, notably *H. pinguifolia* 'Pagei', which is a low, sprawling shrub, giving a generally grey impression, and *H. pimelioides* 'Glauco-caerulea' which is much bluer and has lavender-coloured flowers. *H. albicans*, at least in the form I have, is very compact, making a small, rounded bush with larger greyish leaves than the others, and they are pointed. It has spikelets of white flowers briefly at midsummer but in great profusion, and its chocolate-coloured anthers show up prettily.

Two hardy hebes with narrow, purplish foliage, particularly dark when young but becoming greener with age are the 2 to 3 ft. Mrs Winder and the 2 ft. Waikiki. Both are quietly pleasing the year round and a good contrast to most other foliage.

I have two variegated hebes and used to have a third but got fed up with it. This was *H. franciscana* (often classified as *H. elliptica*) 'Variegata'. It is a 2 ft. shrub with obovate leaves having a broad cream-coloured margin. You see this a lot in London window boxes planted under contract, which perhaps accounts for its world-weary, institutional expression. In the country it is generally tender (except by the sea, where all hebes are in their element). However, I don't feel like putting up any sort of a fight for it; the leaves are too closely arranged for their size and the whole plant looks smug. *H. andersonii* 'Variegata' is every bit as tender – probably more so – (though I have just picked a perfectly fresh leaf from the garden in mid-winter) but I would never give it up. Its leaves are 3 in. long by 1¼ in. wide and are loosely arranged (though in opposite pairs, as always). The central leaf area is in two shades of green, the paler only thinly overlying the cream colour which comes to the surface in an uneven band at the margin. At its best, the plant has remarkable freshness. Put it in a sheltered place near your south-facing garden door. It may survive quite a few winters but you should always take the precaution of making a cutting or two in the autumn. They root with the utmost ease and grow quickly thereafter. Flowers are borne in large, deep-lavender spikes.

Third, *H. glaucophylla* 'Variegata' (also found as *H. darwiniana* 'Variegata'), which was given me as a cutting and I don't really know much about it yet except that it's very pretty with quite tiny, close-set lanceolate leaves in green and cream on surprisingly long strands. I should think it will grow 2½ ft. tall, and it appears to be hardy. Another variegated hebe that I am determined to acquire is Tricolor. In habit, leaf size and general tenderness it resembles *H. andersonii* 'Variegata', but the leaf colouring is pale green in the centre becoming cream farther out but purple along the margins and on the undersides. The flowers are reddish purple. This is exciting without seeming over-busy.

Insofar as they concern us in this book, the **helichrysums** are grey-leaved shrubs. The tender ones will be dealt with later. From South Europe are several very similar species; *Helichrysum angustifolium*, *H. fontanesii*, *H. italicum*, *H. plicatum* and *H. siculum*. I hope Mrs Underwood has sorted them out for us. This much I can say, speaking for myself. *H. angustifolium* (which Hillier is now calling *H. serotinum*) wafts the strongest smell of curry. Whether that is an asset or not depends on your craving for curry. I think this a pretty miserable plant with squinny little leaves and looking weedier than ever when it comes into flower. All this lot have linear foliage, almost needle thin. I had *H. siculum* for many years but it might have been *H. plicatum*. At its best, which is in early summer before it flowers, it looked good. Then came the unwelcome mustard yellow flower heads on long stems, then the moment when you have to cut everything hard

11. ABOVE, *Viburnum davidii*, a low evergreen shrub of firm texture, with deeply grooved leaves. BELOW, an old and famous specimen of *Euphorbia wulfenii* at East Lambrook Manor, the late Margery Fish's Somerset garden.

12. Grey foliage plants of moderate hardiness and excellent for bedding. ABOVE LEFT, *Senecio cineraria* 'White Diamond', is the palest clone. ABOVE RIGHT, *S. cineraria* 'Ramparts' has more deeply cut foliage while, BELOW, *Centaurea gymnocarpa* is laciest of all.

back to restore some semblance of order (for flowering sends this
2 ft. shrub sprawling all over the place), then follows a long period
of recuperation followed by winter, which kills half your plants.
On my clay soil, that is. On chalk or sand you'll do much better.
H. fontanesii looks to me the best of the bunch, but I have never
grown it. The leaves have a little more substance than the others,
and I believe it has a less compulsive desire to flower. One that
is commonly grown in public gardens as *H. rupestre* should, it
seems, be known as *H. italicum*. It is very like (if not the same as)
H. fontanesii and there is a reasonably hardy strain of it in commerce.

We now come to a South African species which, to everyone's
amazement, even in the heart of Perthshire, appears to be perfectly
hardy. This, for the moment, has the official blessing of *H.
splendidum*, by way of a name, but you are equally likely to find it
listed as *H. alveolatum* and *H. trilineatum*. It is a solid shrub (but
best grouped, I think, in a unit of three together), growing 4 ft.
tall but becoming scraggy by then. However, it responds beautifully to the cutting-back technique – hard back into old wood in
April, and this operation needs to be repeated only once in 4 or
5 years. The narrow, blunt-tipped grey leaves are densely arranged on stiff, upright shoots which give the whole shrub a
vertical lift, although, in fact, its outline is rounded and bulging.
It looks its best in late summer and autumn and is then, I reckon,
one of the most satisfying features in any garden. I love it.

Every shoot is terminated by a cluster of tiny yellow button
flower heads. They are borne the year round, but are of no
account, neither enhancing nor detracting from the shrub's
appearance. Its really bad season is spring, when a large proportion of the older leaves have died on the bush. But it grows out
of this state in May and June. I think it could be used as a
low edging hedge, like santolina (cutting it back annually), but
hardier. Unaccountably few people appear to be growing the
shrub.

Every self-respecting garden will be represented by one or both
of two shrubby **hellebores**. They are evergreen and shade tolerant,
ideal for growing under trees or tall shrubs. *Helleborus lividus* spp.
corsicus seems, at the moment, to be the taxonomists' preference

for the plant we have meekly known on earlier occasions, according to the latest directive, as *H. corsicus* and *H. argutifolius*. Its faintly glaucous-green leaves are ternate with mock prickles on their margins. The central leaflet is regular in outline but the outer leaflets are enlarged on the lower- or outer-side with a bulge like a pelican's pouch. *H. foetidus* is our native stinking hellebore (it doesn't stink at all), usually found wild in woodland on calcareous soils. Its leaves are a sombre green but beautifully fashioned. They are palmate with nine leaflets. The central one is a direct continuation of the leaf stalk, but the fans on either side of it arise from a double arc. The whole leaf takes in three-quarters of a circle with each leaflet receiving its fair share of light. Both these hellebores have just started blooming as I write (24th January) and will continue opening their multiple inflorescences into April. *H. corsicus* has light green saucers; *H. foetidus* has green bells staining maroon around the mouth as they mature.

These (and other) hellebores are subject to a wretched fungal disease, against which the plants carry on a running fight. Leaves and stems are attacked, the latter often rotting at the base. Whole plants may die in this way. On the other hand these species regenerate by self-sown seedlings all the time. You can help them by spraying with a protective copper fungicide, especially in the spring months. Also by removing infected material. The leaves develop dead areas, which are rippled with concentric rings. They are easily recognised.

I have already brought in **Hydrangea quercifolia** (p. 52). Its jagged leaf toothing makes for a strong outline. Why this North American species should still be shunned as tender, in England, beats me. It is a good deal hardier than most of the *H. macrophylla* cultivars – the general run, that is, of hortensias and lacecaps. The leaves sometimes colour brilliantly in autumn. *H. sargentiana* (now, it seems, considered a subspecies of *H. aspera*) is mainly interesting for its foliage. The leaves are broadly ovate, usually a foot long and very furry. It is hardy but must have moisture, shade and wind protection if its leaves are not to suffer. It is worth hunting for the right spot for this noble shrub, which can grow very large indeed, say 8 ft. by 10, when suited. It gradually increases its range by suckering. The pale bluish mauve lacecap inflorescences are quite charming.

There are a great many worth-while **junipers**, and I shall scarcely do more than scratch the surface of the possibilities here. Conifer enthusiasts will turn to a specialist work on the subject. Actually, the junipers seldom go wrong: few, even of the man-made varieties, are repulsive.

The Irish Juniper, *Juniperus communis* 'Hibernica', makes a tight-knit glaucous pencil specimen, for many years, and it can look self-conscious and smug as often seen with heather or on either side of a house doorway. With age it loses its slimness and symmetry, and grows 12 or 15 ft. tall. At just this stage, when it has ceased to be what its owner intended, I begin to find it attractive.

J. squamata 'Meyeri' makes a handsome glaucous bush with juvenile leaves all pointing forwards. It grows slowly and if you allow it 6 ft. each way, you will not be dismayed for a good many years. At Knightshayes Court in Devon there is a specimen which I reckoned to be 20 ft. tall by 25 ft. across, but plants do grow, down there.

J. media 'Pfitzeriana' makes a bold feature in landscape planting. It reaches a height of 6 ft. but is mainly spreading. Aurea is a variant with yellow young foliage. If you were making a large shrubbery or mixed planting, this juniper would associate well with shrub roses, rosemary, regal lilies and with colchicums at the margins.

Coming down the scale, *J. sabina tamariscifolia* grows no more than 3 ft. high but pushes out horizontally in a peculiarly satisfying manner. Its growth is densely ground-covering and its shoots pile up in overlapping layers. It is a good bright green with a hint of blue included. This makes a fine lawn feature and can be allowed, gradually, to take over and engulf as much grass as you care to relinquish.

The really prostrate junipers can also be used in this way. There are a lot of them. *J. horizontalis* 'Douglasii' is glaucous in summer, taking on purple tints in the cold weather. I find this a shade dismal, but *J. conferta*, with a mossy habit, is such a pale green as to be almost frivolous. Its foliage is of the juvenile type with ½ in.-long leaves. It grows wild on sandy shores in Japan and is not as hardy as the rest.

J. communis 'Hornibrookii' is a fine blue prostrate juniper, excellent ground cover, piling up on itself to 2 ft. Its leaves are juvenile.

Sufficient mention has been made of **Leucothoë catesbaei** (p. 56) so let us pass on to **Ligustrum**, the privets. True, their leaf shape is not generally very stimulating, though the larger types, like the glossy *L. lucidum*, are pretty well as handsome as the average camellia's. Golden Privet, *L. ovalifolium* 'Aureum' is so bright that a little goes a long way. One specimen bush, allowed to grow reasonably informal, will give far more pleasure than a clipped hedge of it.

L. lucidum 'Tricolor' is unfortunately not hardy but *L. sinense* 'Variegatum' is, and has much the same colouring in a lanceolate leaf. This is in two shades of pale green, with a white or pink-tinged margin. I have just bought a plant and am intrigued to see that it has been grafted. You would think that any privet would strike from cuttings with laughable ease, but this is not the case. Some just make a large knob of callous and refuse to root.

The form of **Lonicera nitida** called Baggesen's Golden see-saws between sparkling gaiety and wan dejection. In January, it is looking anaemic but new buds are already expanding and by March it will have pulled round. The young shoots are a pretty gold green and, as this lonicera has a long growing season there are young shoots for a large part of the year. I recommend trimming a bush with secateurs annually, in February. It is usually 4 ft. tall but can be allowed to grow taller if you wish.

You must grow this in a sunny place. In shade, the leaves are merely pale green. But if the sun gets very hot and the soil dry,

13. The border in which those plants feature is devoted entirely to foliage and is located at Crathes Castle in north-east Scotland. The main feature is *Hosta undulata* in a form having most of the variegation in the centre of the leaf; golden marjoram, *Origanum vulgare* 'Aureum', in front; the maple-like leaves of *Kirengeshoma palmata* behind. There are a mahonia and a bergenia in part-shadow in the distance.

there will be some leaf scorch. Of *L. pileata,* sometimes recommended as ground cover, sometimes as an alternative hedging material to *L. nitida,* than whose leaves *L. pileata*'s are bigger, the best I can say is that it is inoffensive.

Mahonias are closely related to berberis, but are distinguished by their pinnate leaves. This, indeed, is what gives them their distinction and qualifies them as foliage shrubs. They are all evergreen but most, alas, are too tender for the majority of gardens, unless they are given special consideration.

The most popular species is *M. japonica.* Flower arrangers love to use its bold leaves, either singly or in large terminal whorls, as they are naturally borne. Each leaf is some 20 inches long with about 14 pairs of sharply toothed leaflets. Mere size is no particular recommendation, as I see it. There is a certain flatness and regularity about these leaves that I find tiresome. They are fairly glossy but only fairly and the quality of green is worthy without firing the imagination. The longer I live with this shrub the less I like it – apart from its flowers. They make all the difference: strings of pale yellow bells opening from October to April and scented like lilies-of-the-valley. Obviously one cannot be without such a valuable winter-flowerer. It is best in shade and given some shelter for its foliage from fierce winds.

M. lomariifolia, by contrast, has me weak and babbling with admiration. If only it were hardier. Still, it seems to be perfectly happy in London gardens and if you can find a sheltered position for it, should do well enough in most parts of the south and south-

14. ABOVE, part of my Long Border in late October. Phloxes and Japanese anemones have faded but the border is still held together by its foliage: *Gleditsia triacanthos* 'Elegantissima' left; *Hedera canariensis* 'Variegata' climbing a pole, centre; *Eryngium pandanifolium* in subdued flower, right; the Jerusalem sage, *Phlomis fruticosa* at front has recovered from its annual, post-flowering trim. There are two plants of Jackman's blue rue with seed heads of the white, late-flowering *Allium tuberosum* between. BELOW, an effective yet unusual summer bedding-out scheme at Kew Gardens. The dark purple foliage of Coleus 'Roi des Noirs' (propagated from cuttings) is offset by the pale grey of *Artemisia arborescens* and the variegated form of *Pelargonium crispum.*

east. It is a tall (8 ft.) and leggy shrub, but this is a part of its charm. Any mahonia, incidentally, can be pruned quite brutally back into old wood, if the urge is on you, doing the job in spring. The leaves of *M. lomariifolia* have the delicacy of a fern frond although they are actually hard and spiny. Each leaflet curves forwards and down at the margins. As a bonus, short upright spikes of the usual yellow mahonia flowers are borne in clusters in November. They have no scent.

This species has been crossed with *M. japonica* and the resultant clone called Charity has been widely acclaimed. It will have no beginning in my home. Charity combines the worst features of both its parents. It has the leaf of *M. japonica* (with very little of the elegance of *M. lomariifolia*) but it flowers in autumn and has little or no scent.

M. aquifolium is the hardiest and easiest member of the genus, and has been extensively planted in woodland as cover for pheasants. It is extremely shade tolerant and spreads by suckering. Usually you find it no more than 3 ft. high, a bit scrubby but less so in an open situation where its leaves become pleasantly bronzed in winter. The clusters of yellow flowers in April have a warm scent, *not* of lilies. Better than this, as a specimen in the garden is *M.* 'Undulata'. The leaves consist of only seven leaflets but they are very glossy and beautifully undulate. In winter, they become purplish but glowing red along the veins. See p. 52 (first plan).

With its fresh evergreen leaves, its hardiness and its capacity for covering the ground in difficult shady places, even dry shade, **Pachysandra terminalis** (albeit mildly calcifuge) is a plant to be reckoned with. Far superior, for instance, to the dismal *Gaultheria shallon*, which has similar mechanical properties. I haven't the sort of garden that produces tracts of bare ground needing cover. The only pachysandra I grow is the much less vigorous *P.t.* 'Variegata'. It has a twisted, constipated expression and I am not sure that I like it but it's not getting in my way or doing any harm under a vast *Buddleia alternifolia*.

As a foliage plant for exotic luxuriance, **Paulownia tomentosa**, which is by nature a medium-sized tree, should be raised from seed and then treated as a shrub in the same way as *Ailanthus* (p. 62). Its hairy, heart-shaped leaves can be as much as 3 ft.

across. Such an expanse of sail demands a sheltered position; otherwise it becomes sadly battered.

Philadelphus, the Mock Orange, is a genus of coarse, fast-growing shrubs, makeshift in habit and with uninspired foliage. Some of the small-leaved kinds get away with it on account of their smallness but the only one that makes a positive contribution with its leaves is *P. coronarius* 'Aureus', with golden or lime-green colouring. And this is very good indeed, standing out as a feature among more ordinary neighbours, from right across a fair-sized garden. In too much shade, the shrub is too green but if fiercely exposed to sun its leaves turn a hectic, unhealthy yellow with necrotic patches developing. You must strike a balance. *P. coronarius* is the common old 'syringa' (that grew in my grandmother's garden) with the dullest, smallish off-white flowers; Aureus flowers in the same way but the scent is likewise more powerful than in any of the more glamorous species and cultivars. It grows about 6 ft. tall.

There is more than one strain in cultivation of the well known Jerusalem sage, **Phlomis fruticosa**. The best has a markedly undulate leaf. The colouring is always a slightly dirty grey (with a hint of yellow in it). However, this evergreen shrub looks presentable throughout any reasonable winter but is undoubtedly at its most beautiful when the young shoots are expanding and before it flowers, in June. The flowers themselves are hooded, dusky yellow, borne in whorls, one or two to a spike. I like them but some don't. I have heard them described as looking old-fashioned and this is apt. It can be taken as a compliment or not, as you please.

After flowering, a bush should be cut over with secateurs fairly drastically, removing the terminal leafy shoot among a group of flowered spikes as well as the spikes themselves. Unless unduly exposed, the shrub will grow large and sprawling in an attractive manner; perhaps 4 or 5 ft. tall by 10 ft. across and becoming a little thin in the middle so that you can grow violets underneath it and perhaps a not too vigorous clematis like the indigo blue, non climbing Durandii, or the climbing *Aconitum volubile*. The branches of *Phlomis fruticosa* are brittle and break easily under snow. It is not all that hardy and should be given shelter in cold midland or northern gardens. Like all the greys, it needs sun.

Even better than this is the much less well known *P. chryso-phylla*. It is a paler, more effective and silvery grey; the leaf is smoothly outlined and narrower. It makes a less sprawling shrub and flowers very little, which can be an advantage, because the bush doesn't have to go through a drab and threadbare post-flowering period.

Phormium is known as New Zealand Flax. The two species, *P. tenax* and the smaller growing *P. colensoi* do indeed come from New Zealand and the former is used there, like flax, to make rope and twine, from its tough, strap-shaped evergreen leaves. But there is no relationship with flax; rather with yuccas and agaves, but the leaves in *Phormium* are produced all in one plane, in fans.

There are at least 50 cultivars of *P. tenax,* which is easily raised from seed as well as by division, in spring. It makes a large, imposing, sub-tropical-looking clump with, typically, dim green leaves some 8 or 10 ft. tall. Mature clumps quite readily produce their multiple inflorescences of dusky red flowers. These are interesting and grotesque; only marginally beautiful. The plants' principal attraction is in their leaf form and colouring. The purple-leaved Purpureum is more interesting than the green, but the green-and-cream-variegated phormiums make far and away the liveliest features and are much to be coveted, in a good strain and *if* they are hardy with you. They are certainly kittle-cattle in this respect. *P. colensoi* also has variegated forms, e.g. Tricolor, with green-and-white-striped leaves, margined in red. Variegated plants produce variegated seedlings, but in some the variegation is very weak, so you want to know what you're getting before it arrives.

The only phormium I grow is the very dwarf, purple-leaved *P. tenax alpinum* 'Purpureum', which is only 18 in. tall and never flowers. It seems to be pretty hardy but may not be easy to locate. This looks well in a group at the edge of a border near something pale grey or glaucous, like rue. That its outline and characteristic sit may not be blurred by taller features, there is a strong case for making of it an isolated feature in gravel or paving.

I am not sure why I left **Picea pungens** out of the tree chapter, but it will fit in very well here, as it has a ravishing prostrate form and also because the tree itself is more striking while still a shrub and before it reaches maturity. *P. pungens* is the Colorado Spruce and it has a number of blue-leaved cultivars of which Kosteriana is the best known. In youth it looks like a Christmas tree of duck's-egg-blue colouring. The needles, moreover, are longer and the shoots hence plumper than in any Christmas tree. A young specimen with branches down to the ground is a quite extraordinary feature and pretty well impossible, in my opinion, to fit into the context of a garden but I am in the minority, for this is one of the most popular of all conifers, selling on sight.

That is the trouble. The Blue Spruce has to be propagated by grafting and the nurseryman, finding himself short of propagating material, uses some that is quite unsuitable, resulting in a lop-sided bush. So you should choose your specimen by eye (not trusting to a mail order) taking into account first the brilliance of its colouring and second the symmetry of the bush. It should have a vertical leader surrounded by a whorl of evenly spaced laterals.

The Blue Spruce has some prostrate mutants which are much easier to fit into a garden setting, especially in a rock garden or overhanging a pool. Names to look out for (and you will have to look out for them for stock is scarce) are Procumbens or Glauca Procumbens or Koster's Prostrate. A plant under the last name is the pride of the Northern Horticultural Society's gardens at Harlow Car, by Harrogate, and deservedly so, but it is competing with a mat of heathers that appear to be suffering from a bilious attack.

Another, quite different dwarf spruce that is readily available, is *P. glauca albertiana* 'Conica'. It makes a perfect dwarf cone of dense consistency and dim green colouring and will do duty as a vegetable gnome. It is much easier and more rewarding to be unfair about plants you don't like than to say nice things about the ones you do. Speaking for myself, anyway, the snide aside and caustic cut come the more naturally. Reining myself in, I will therefore add that, gnome or not, *P. albertiana conica* (as it is generally known) looks delightful as you see it in Maurice Mason's Norfolk garden, where it appears to grow out of a cube of rock;

like a tame woolly bear, towards which you smile and bow indulgently, in passing.

Pieris formosa, in one of its better forms like the well known *P.f. forrestii*, looks ravishing in spring when the terminal tufts of young leaves are unfolding. They are lance-shaped and laurel-like but a brilliant shrimp red. If subjected at this stage to hot sunshine, especially following rain, they are burnt to a frazzle, so the shrub should be given overhead shade, as from nearby trees. Being ericaceous it also needs acid soil. When mature, it carries panicles of small, waxy white flowers at the same time as the young foliage is unfolding. Quite lovely.

Good in a different way is the variegated form of *Pieris japonica*, with a white margin to leaves that are arranged in rosettes. It is slow growing but will attain 6 ft. in time. Here, of course, you have your display the year round. *P.f. forrestii* is uninteresting for 11 months out of 12.

Prunus cistena is a hybrid plum of shrubby habit that is grown principally for its glossy purple foliage, and this is undoubtedly excellent. It also carries tiny white flowers in early spring. It is frequently recommended for use as a low, informal hedge, say for a rose garden, and the recommended treatment is to prune quite hard (perhaps 'clip' gives a better idea of what's needed), immediately after flowering. The young shoots produced during the summer will provide the next spring's blossom.

Unfortunately *P. cistena* is often a flop. It seems to make no headway. It is propagated from cuttings, as a rule, and I am told that it is often unthrifty on its own roots. However, there is a beautiful planting of this grouped with shrubby yellow potentillas at Harlow Car. *P. cistena* is effective as a single, grafted specimen among other shrubs and plants, and not pruned at all. It then grows quite 8 ft. tall by as much across and is a fine purple feature.

Then there are the other kinds of prunus, the Cherry Laurel, *P. laurocerasus*, and the Portugal Laurel, *P. lusitanica*. The former takes up much space but is handsome when unclipped. And I have described a smaller, horizontally branching narrow-leaved cultivar, Zabelliana (p 57-8). Otto Luyken is another good dwarfish one of more upright habit. Sybil Emberton describes a beautiful variegated form, but I have never seen this. However, I do know and own *P. lusitanica* 'Variegata'. Its oval leaves are margined in cream and it also has deep red petioles and young stems. At its best, on rich soil (for it is otherwise very slow-growing) and in sun, this is a first-rate foliage shrub.

As a hardy evergreen shrub with neat, silver-margined foliage, it would be hard to improve on **Rhamnus alaterna** 'Argenteo-variegata'. This is a buckthorn. The leaves are only $1\frac{1}{4}$ in. long, quite narrow and polished on both sides. The shrub will grow large in time and I have sited it at the back of my 15-ft.-wide border. It transplants badly and should find its final position while young.

And so to the revered genus **Rhododendron**. Many of the most popular hybrids gain admittance to our gardens purely on account of their overpowering floral display. This lasts a fort-night or less. For the next 50 weeks, we have to endure, as best we may, a lump of the gloomiest foliage imaginable. If flower power is our yardstick of excellence, these are the rhododendrons we shall, perforce, continue to grow. But once we start consider-ing flowers as only one aspect of a shrub's various potentialities, we shall stop worrying about whether they are carried in the shrub's youth or even regularly after that. The foliage gardener has already reached this state in his education – not that he will have eyes for foliage alone. But, having developed eyes for that, he will also be receptive to the rhododendron's habit, the colour-ing and texture of its trunk or stems, the scent of its flowers and their season. His selections within this versatile genus will be varied and he will enjoy its manifold subtleties. All of which may sound a little smug, but the rhododendron enthusiast has something of smugness in him too and I have probably caught a share of it.

I do not grow many, but I keep finding room for another two or three each year. The exciting large-leaved kinds, however, quite apart from their deficiencies in hardiness (which have been con-siderably exaggerated) are unsuited to a small setting. They need to be grown among trees and informally. Few of us can accom-modate more than one or two of them and many of us will be wise to eschew them altogether.

Rhododendron sinogrande is at the top of this particular ladder of desirability, its leaves up to 2 ft. long, with a beautiful grey-white felting underneath. This felting is called the indumentum, and is a major asset in the rhododendrons possessing it. The trouble with a large leaf, from a cultural point of view, is the damage to it that can be done by wind. In this case the wind waggles the leaf to and fro and round and round on its stalk till it breaks off. Finis.

Given the necessary wind shelter and also overhead shade from hot sunshine, this rhododendron is not too difficult at all. If grown in the drier, colder east (rather than the mild, moist west, which it prefers) it will often flourish but will adapt itself to circumstances by having much smaller leaves, probably no more than a foot long. This is a practical adaptation and very welcome. But there are close relations that are easier to grow and are much more suitable for eastern gardeners. R. *macabeanum*, for instance, presents no problems. Its leaves are up to a foot long, deeply veined on top, greyish white beneath. The flowers are bell-shaped, cream white or, in the best forms, pale yellow. Mine is a seedling and about to flower for the first time (after only five years in my service) so I am all agog. Its parent was the First Class Certificate form, but anything may turn up.*

Then there is R. *falconeri*, with a deeper rust indumentum and growing into a magnificent specimen shrub. Again it is quite an easy species. I have a cross between this and R. *sinogrande*, which

* Anything did turn up. I was (accidentally) sold the wrong plant, and it turns out to be R. *eximium* with dirty pinkish white flower trusses.

15. ABOVE, summer bedding in my own garden where the purple of heliotrope Marine and the red of *Verbena* 'Huntsman' are linked and knit together by the invaluable pale grey *Senecio leucostachys*, which comes equal first in my esteem as an interweaving foliage plant for bedding and other purposes with BELOW, *Helichrysum petiolatum*, here seen flowering out from an ornamental pot. Four of these stand as sentinels above our sunken garden and the zonal pelargonium Maxim Kovaleski provides highlights with its orange flower heads. The walls are colonised by the little Mexican daisy, *Erigeron mucronatus*, which flowers non-stop for six months.

was given me four years ago as a layer from a shrub that I have admired in a friend's garden for many years. It is a real beauty, especially when the pale young leaves are expanding in spring. But it didn't flower at all for the first 40 years and then only 2 or 3 trusses at a time at most. I really don't care; the leaves are quite enough and I have perched it half-way up a steep bank so that from the bottom I can see their undersides in comfort. And I have placed R. *hodgsonii* in the same way. The upper surface of the leaves, when young or fairly young, has a glistening, silvery speckling that has been likened to mica but reminds me of the trails left by slugs. You know how they catch the light. Slugs, of course, are unattractive, but their trails, divorced from the creature, are rather beautiful. The undersides of the leaves are woolly and fawn-coloured. On mature specimens the trunks peel and expose a smooth grey surface. I have not seen the flowers; I believe they are usually a poor magenta.

A much smaller-leaved rhododendron with the brightest indumentum of all – a warm chestnut brown – is R. *mallotum*. Its flowers are dark red. It can grow well in my part of the world but is distinctly temperamental. The first thing my plant did, although I fetched it from the nursery and interred it with horticultural

16. ABOVE, a planting for foliage effect in the Victoria Embankment Gardens next to Charing Cross Underground. The foreground is dominated by the broad heart-shaped leaves of *Coleus blumei* hybrids. Other ingredients include grey dots by *Chrysanthemum ptarmiciflorum* (front) and *Senecio cineraria* (middle distance); the non-flowering *Pelargonium* Mme. Salleron at front, backed by one of the lemon-scented pelargoniums (probably a variegated form of *P. asperum*); also iresines and cannas (both purple) and the bipinnate green foliage of *Grevillea robusta* seedlings. BELOW, a restful planting of shrubs at Hidcote Manor, a National Trust garden near Chipping Camden in Gloucestershire. Conifers include the Irish juniper (left) the bright green *Pinus densiflora* 'Umbraculifera' (centre back) and *Chamaecyparis lawsoniana* 'Erecta Viridis' (right) which is pretty as a baby but should be scrapped when past its first youth. The grey willow *Salix lanata* is in the foreground and the *Hebe* generally known as *H. armstrongii*, with dusty gold foliage, plumb in the centre of the picture. Only a shrubby potentilla is contributing flowers.

reverence, was to shed all its leaves. Five years later it appears to be slowly readjusting itself to a new life, but is still very small. Worth a shot, though, and it is not too tender. And I can recommend R. *bureavii*, where space is limited: it grows only 4 or 5 ft. tall and wears leaves only 4 in. or so long that taper to elegant points, are glossy green above and thickly felted in rust brown beneath. This is an easy species.

Some forms of R. *arboreum* have bright rust undersides to their leaves: Campbelliae, for instance, though its flowers are a particularly revolting bluish pink. Far preferable is Sir Charles Lemon, which is white, if it flowers at all, but wholly adequate as a foliage plant. In a moist climate it will grow 20 ft. tall and more. The young foliage is for a long time held pointing obliquely upwards as though expressly intending that we should admire and enjoy its best feature. It is not entirely hardy but a good deal more so than is commonly accepted.

R. *campanulatum* is a really hardy 8 to 10 ft. shrub of which Knap Hill is the best cultivar, with clusters of large bells coming as near to blue as you could wish, of a rhododendron. This, again, is red-brown on the leaf undersurface. R.*c. aeruginosum* can be vividly pale glaucous on the upper side of its young leaves and like white kid below. I say 'can be', because like so many species that are commonly raised from seed, it varies a lot and I rather fear that the plant I have bought is going to prove a non-starter in this most important respect.

The glaucous colouring in many of the rhododendron leaves we most fancy, is associated with a smooth and waxy texture quite different from the types so far considered. The wax, indeed, is there as a bloom on the young leaf and unfortunately wears off a good deal with age. Still, the leaves are often, additionally, of a pleasing shape, rounded or cordate. Such is R. *orbiculare*, even broader than long and glaucous underneath. The open bell-flowers are borne in loose trusses, with charming informality; the only pity is the blue in their pink colouring. R. *thomsonii* has a similar leaf, though longer. Its flowers are a sumptuous red. There are good and not-so-good strains of this.

I think R. *concatenans* is my favourite of the glaucous fraternity – a wonderful colour all through the summer. It has apricot-

A variegated rhodie

coloured flowers. R. *cinnabarinum*, its orange flowers in longer funnels, is closely related and has a good leaf, often deliciously aromatic on the air, when young. The last four will all grow into large bushes, 6 or 8 ft. high and as much or more across, in time, but can be fitted into the larger plantings in medium-sized gardens. A baby of 2 ft., by contrast, is R. *lepidostylum*, with brilliantly verdigris young leaves. No one could fail to fall for this. I've no idea what its flowers are like. Pale to mid yellow, Mr Reuthe's catalogue says; the R.H.S. Dictionary doesn't include the species. It is semi-deciduous and looks nothing in winter.

R. *decorum* has a generally well-oiled and glaucous appearance. In a good strain, the dormant flower buds are the same blue colouring. The shrub grows large in time and always looks pleasant. Its white flowers, in April and May, are fragrant.

R. *oreotrephes* is another species I have bought on the strength of the blue colouring on the undersides of its young leaves, which are prick-eared at first. I fell for it at Inverewe, one July (so the colouring lasts well), where it is tellingly combined with a purple-leaved *Cotinus coggygria* and the deep blue berry trusses on *Berberis darwinii*. They were all about / ft. tall.

Very different from any so far mentioned is Moser's Maroon. In shape, its leaves are large and dull like the common gardener's idea of how a rhododendron should be, but they are an extraordinary shade of deep red in youth and the flower trusses are deeper still. As a young plant on a nursery, it is irresistible, but it has a horribly lanky habit of growth. A mature specimen looks a wreck. Regular pruning (sacrificing the flowers) might be a good idea.

And then, wait for it, a variegated rhododendron! Of course, there had to be, but why only one? Haskin and Hillier stock it and it is a form of our old friend (or enemy) R. *ponticum*, that sows itself incontinently all over the commons of Surrey, the hills of Scotland, anywhere it can get a foothold. Its variegated change-ling is a real sweetie, with neat, slender leaves, their margins cream-white, stained just now, at midwinter, with currant-juice-purple.

I'm sure there are many more I should mention but I am not a rhododendron specialist; there are many other plants I want to

95

grow and most of the rhododendrons I like best make huge shrubs or trees, even. Inevitably, my contacts with them are limited though my rhododendron friends are kindness itself in sharing the pleasures of their gardens with me. You should see them in some unlikely month like November. It's surprising how much these shrubs have to show us even then, and this is thanks to their foliage, to their trunks and to their noble bearing.

The Smooth Sumach, *Rhus glabra*, and the Stag's horn Sumach, R. *typhina*, are among the commonest large shrubs or small trees seen in small gardens. They can seldom have been bought, I imagine; suckers are freely (over-freely) produced and are passed around between friends and neighbours. Their pinnate leaves are much more interesting in the laciniate forms, where the leaflets themselves have lacy margins. R. *typhina* 'Laciniata' is the one to go for.

These make gaunt shrubs of a peculiarly depressing winter aspect. They flare up in autumn – rather incongruously, as a rule, popped in by themselves with a red or yellow brick house for background. The happiest treatment is surely as a foliage component in a mixed border. Given hard-pruning treatment (see *Ailanthus*, p. 62), their leaves can grow up to 3 ft. long. Being already much dissected, they put up with wind a great deal better than *Paulownia tomentosa* in the same role. For *Rhus cotinus*, see p. 71.

Healthy **rose** foliage can be a joy to behold (perhaps for its rarity value), and it may have considerable character of its own, as in the glaucous tones of *Rosa alba* cultivars. It is seldom the main reason for growing any rose. Exceptionally, we have R. *rubrifolia*. It grows 8 ft. tall by about 6 ft. across and has dusky purple leaves. They make a valuable contribution to mixed plantings. The flowers are dog-rose type, a bit darker – of no great account, but the clusters of hips that follow can make a great display.

Another foliage species is R. *virginiana*. The leaves are exceptionally glossy and begin to change to an extraordinary range of fiery tints quite early in autumn. The display lasts a long time and is augmented by the red colouring of the young stems and the crimson of the small globular hips. This shrub is rather of a

17. Two cultivars of common ivy, *Hedera helix*. ABOVE, Buttercup develops its yellow colouring most brightly on those leaves that get most sun. BELOW, Goldheart, also most boldly patterned and coloured in a light aspect.

18. ABOVE LEFT, the variegated comfrey *Symphytum asperum* 'Aureo-variegatum', is smartest before and again after flowering. ABOVE RIGHT, a figwort, *Scrophularia aquatica* 'Variegata', that should be discouraged from flowering, as here. BELOW, the rose plantain, *Plantago major* 'Rosularis'.

spreading than an upright habit, making a suckering thicket 4 or 5 ft. high. R. *nitida* might be likened to a lower growing version of the last, only 2 ft. tall. Both come from the eastern States of North America.

Among the general run of popular modern cultivars, Rosemary Rose is conspicuous for the plum purple colouring of its young foliage, this being especially noticeable on pruned bushes in May and June before flowering commences. I recently saw this asset turned to good account in a friend's mixed border, where she has grouped some *Tellima grandiflora*, with its scalloped evergreen heart-leaves and loose racemes of green flowers in late spring (more on this anon), in front of two or three bushes of Rosemary Rose. Perhaps I can work this one into a plan, later on.

Rubus is the genus of the blackberry and raspberry, and I have already discussed the three that interest me for foliage (pp. 53-4 and pp. 56-7), these being R. *tricolor*, R. *calycinoides* (syn. R. *fockeanus*) and R. *thibetanus*. R. *tricolor* makes a delightful ground cover, best appreciated in sun, and can hoist itself up 2 or 3 ft. into nearly shrubs. I have it weaving among the much larger foliage of *Bergenia cordifolia*. The two together are more than twice as interesting as each separately but any interweaving of this sort does require a vigilant eye and an occasional restraining hand to ensure that neither party (the bramble, in this case) gets the upper hand.

I have said enough on R. *thibetanus* except to remark that its grey pinnate leaves have great elegance, the leaflets tapering to fine points.

Ruta graveolens was also included in Chapter 4 (pp. 54-5), using Jackman's Blue Rue, which has the steeliest colouring. No doubt I shall use it again: the plant is unique, not so much for its colouring as for its compound pinnate leaves, each leaflet being round-tipped. This adds up to a quite different sort of featheriness from the usual pinnate form. The cleanest and brightest foliage effect is obtained by cutting your bushes back every spring, and in this way they grow no more than 2 ft. tall. They should also have full sun, theirs being a colour that is lost in shade and is not so intensely developed without sun, anyway.

There is a pretty variegated rue in cream and green, R.*g.*

'Variegata'. Seedlings from variegated plants will often, if not always, be as variegated themselves and yet this is an unpredictable cuss. A plant will sometimes turn plain green, only to change back to what it should be, subsequently. Young plants raised from cuttings have a special propensity to greenness, but do not despair, they usually pull round.

Rue is not quite as hardy as one would wish, especially on heavy, wet soils. Free drainage usually ensures longevity.

There are many different kinds of **willow** in cultivation, from the largest trees to tiny prostrate rock plants, and they are grown for a variety of attributes, among which foliage is one.

Some don't look like willows at all. A notorious trap species is *Salix magnifica*, with broad leaves closely resembling a Magnolia such as *M. sieboldii*. It grows into a very large shrub or shrub-like tree, and becomes progressively more threadbare. Unless you must have your little joke, this is a poor investment. By contrast, *S. fargesii*, although equally un-willow-like, is a beautiful shrub if you can grow it well. Like several others in this tribe, it is seen at its best in Scotland but can be a bit of a struggle in the south. My specimen is growing far too slowly and loses its leaves prematurely in late summer. Still, this is partly my fault because it can be healthy even down in the South-East.

Its young branches are sturdy and polished, coloured red-brown. The young buds are an even brighter red and so are the leaf stalk and main vein. The leaves themselves are a good 6 in. long and 2½ or 3 in. wide, and stamped with a conspicuous pattern of veins. This species makes a strong and thickset shrub, perhaps 8 ft. tall by 10 or 12 ft. across as I have seen it in North-East Scotland, but usually only 5 ft. high down my way. It has great distinction and is worth pleasing.

S. lanata is also at its best in Scotland, which is its native stamping ground. I have described it in Chapter 4 (p. 57). Considering that so many shrubs with grey foliage are on the borderlines of hardiness, one is particularly grateful to the grey-leaved willows for being out-and-out tough. They do, however, have the disadvantage (if you consider it as such) of being deciduous. *S. lanata* will grow 3 ft. each way in the warm, dry parts of England, but up to twice that size in the cool damp north.

S. repens argentea is another native worth cultivating: about 4 ft. high but not short jointed and densely twiggy like the last. This one has wand-like young shoots (lined with catkins the next spring, so be sure to get a male), and neat little heart-shaped grey leaves. You can prune it to encourage the production of young shoots, as much or as little as you like.

There is a grey-leaved willow, *Salix exigua*, which I greatly admired in Maurice Mason's garden and which he had from the Edinburgh Botanic, but is not in commerce as far as I know.* Despite its name it grows 12 ft. tall and has a most elegant habit with drooping branchlets and narrow 5 in.-long leaves, grey on both surfaces. It increases its range by suckering, if allowed to. I have not met this habit in a willow before.

I find *S. alba* 'Sericea' a useful shrub and it has the A.G.M., so it must be – again with typical willow-shaped leaves and silver. It would grow into a small tree, if allowed to, but I group it near the back of my border and keep it pruned to 3 ft. in winter, which means that it reaches about 8 ft. in summer. It looks pretty with the broad yellow foliage of Dickson's Golden Elm (see p. 40) both having the dark green of yew for a background.

S. friesiana is grey rather than silver, its leaves so narrow as to be linear. It makes a beautiful specimen on its own near a stream: only a shrub, but a very large one. You can always cut it back if you want to restrict it, however. This has a terrible lot of synonyms and I really don't know which is correct: *S. elaeagnos, S. incana, S. rosmarinifolia.*

I must mention *S. cinerea* 'Tricolor' although I don't like it. A bush of 6 ft. or so, its leaves are pink, yellow and white, but twisted and diseased looking.

Cooking **sage**, *Salvia officinalis,* is a 2 ft. evergreen shrub and a dull thing but it has some interesting cultivars. Purpurascens has purple young shoots, ageing greyish. Icterina is grey and yellow while the jazzy Tricolor is cream, pink, red and purple against a grey foundation. They should be lightly clipped over in spring to keep them neat. None are out-and-out hardy, so sun and light, well drained soil is the right recipe.

I have already brought *Salvia officinalis* 'Grandiflora' into the

* It is now listed by Hillier's in their fabulous 1971 catalogue.

plan in Chapter 4 (p. 52). Its leaf has more elegance, the plant more dignity than any of the others.

Our wild **elder**, *Sambucus nigra*, is one of the commonest shrub weeds. Birds gobble its berries avidly, and so you find it coming up everywhere, particularly in waste places like old rubbish tips, but also in gardens. You might think it has little horticultural scope, but you would be wrong, because it has sported into a large number of different forms, both interesting and beautiful.

Best known is the Golden elder, *S.n.* 'Aurea' – a large shrub to 12 ft. in which the leaflets (the leaves of all elders being pinnate) are themselves broad and substantial. Elders are very tolerant of shade, but this one must be given sun to bring out its colouring. There is, even then, always a mixture of shades from gold to green in any one bush, which suits it well. I don't know if it seeds and comes true from seed; I should have thought not, but in Scotland it is so common a feature of the countryside as to be seeming wild. It is an under-valued shrub, looking particularly fine with sun on it, against a stormy sky. If you cannot be sure of organising your sky, put it against a dark tree or shrub, as it might be *Acer platanoides* 'Goldsworth Purple' (see pp. 19-20).

Then there is a beautifully cut-leaved elder that is a marvellous sight when in full flower. The lightness of its foliage added to the froth of blossom makes the whole shrub look as though ready to become airborne. This is Laciniata. In Heterophylla the leaf area is so much reduced that it consists mainly of thread-like stalks. It is a pretty green bush, about 6 ft. tall, and does not flower. Pulverulenta is well named: green and white are so inextricably mixed that the entire shrub appears to have been powdered. At a distance, this is effective; close to, you get an uncomfortable feeling because of the agonised distortion in the leaflets.

The finest jewel in the elder's crown belongs not to this species at all. It is *S. racemosa* 'Plumosa Aurea'. *S. racemosa* is naturalised, especially in Scotland; it has a paniculate, not a flat-topped, corymbose inflorescence, and its berries are red; not purple. Plumosa Aurea is golden and the individual leaflets are heavily fringed. In youth they are coppery, soon changing to a pleasing yellow. This one, however, should be grown in shade: the leaves become scorched in hot sunlight. Indeed, the shrub is altogether more robust in the cool, moist north, but it does very well with me and gives the best results, I find, if pruned fairly hard each winter to a framework built gradually to a height of 4 or 5 ft. It then makes 3 or 4 ft. long branches during the summer. This prevents it from flowering (which is a good thing) and encourages well-developed leaves.

There are three valuable foliage species of **Santolina**. *S. chamaecyparissus* (syn. *S. incana*) and *S. neapolitana* are grey. *S. virens* is green. They are not altogether hardy, but most gardeners can accept them as such. Their leaves are subdivided into stumpy leaflets, arranged longitudinally in four rows. Lavender Cotton, *S. chamaecyparissus*, was introduced at the end of the 16th century and has long been used as a low, clipped hedge surrounding parterres or outlining knots. Its leaves are barely an inch long. I much prefer *S. neapolitana*, whose 1½-in.-long leaves contribute, with a looser habit, to a more graceful plant. The leaf segments are larger too and more distinct. The shrub should annually, in April, be cut back to about 9 in. This keeps it from falling apart. It will make a perfect hummock, during the summer, of very pale foliage to a height of 2 ft. and can be used for edging and hedging just like *S. chamaecyparissus*. Both species have a pleasant scent.

Not so *S. virens*, but never mind. The 18-in.-tall bush is bright green and a mossy texture. Its button flowers are pale yellow and, being an asset, one tidies the bush up *after* flowering, removing all the flowered trusses, together with a central leafy shoot, back to the base of the bush.

Sun and good drainage for these.

There are some 1,300 species of **Senecio**, the largest genus of composites – perhaps of any family. They range from annuals like groundsel, through tender perennials like the florist's cineraria, succulents like the popular candle cactus, bouncing hardy perennials like *S. tanguticus*, to shrubs and even small trees, as found in the alpine flora of Central Africa.

The South European *S. cineraria* (also known as *Cineraria maritima*) is among the most valued of low grey shrubs. It can easily be raised from seed and the progeny are always worth looking at but are very variable, both as to leaf form and hardiness. It is better to acquire a cultivar, propagated from cuttings and of a known standard of performance. The leaf outline is basically ovate but deeply or less deeply cut. Ramparts is very lacy; Alice, even more so, and short-jointed, making a compact bush especially useful in bedding schemes. White Diamond has a less cut leaf, but is the whitest of all the greys. (This must not be confused, incidentally, with a seed strain put out as Diamond, and having no particular merit.) The leaves of White Diamond, are pinnatifid: that is to say the re-entrants stop short of the main vein. The spurs are themselves lobed. It is a particularly hardy cultivar, but should nevertheless be planted in spring and given as good drainage and open a position as possible. Plants grow up to 2 ft. tall, in the summer, but must be cut back to the bone in April. This keeps your bushes neat (they fall apart otherwise) and stops them from producing their wretched little yellow daisies.

A point to note about all greys and very noticeable in this one, is that the young shoots produced after the annual pruning will be green at first, gradually changing to grey and then to near-white. When the leaves are wet, they again turn greenish and spotted, at any age, so you should never judge a grey plant's foliage when it is damp.

I suppose I ought to deal with *S. leucostachys* in the tender-plants chapter, but it'll be tidier to bring it in here and anyway I'm too fond of it to wait that long. Surprisingly this one comes from Patagonia – the windswept southern area of the Argentine. It is much more cut-leaved than *S. cineraria*; in fact it is pinnatisect – divided pinnately into leaflets which are themselves deeply lobed, not quite back to their central veins. All the segments are quite narrow and filigree.

The plant's great merit is in its rambling habit. It will interweave with all its neighbours and is thus invaluable for inter-planting as a background to more sombre foliage; or in front of something taller than itself that you would like it to climb into. Plants may survive the winter, but more often succumb. You should take cuttings in the autumn and overwinter them under well ventilated glass. Put out in spring, they grow very rapidly and seldom need planting nearer than 2 ft. apart.

This senecio demonstrates another feature common to the

greys. Their foliage is at its whitest and hence most attractive under starvation conditions. We can't all provide poor soil in our gardens. On the contrary, we are for the most part striving to keep it in good heart, as the saying goes. To get the best of both worlds, some gardeners will plunge *Senecio leucostachys* in their border, pot and all. I recommend the measure where you are cramped for space. In any fair-sized border, though, I like to give the plant its head. Even if its leaves become a little on the green side of grey on their upper surfaces, they will remain grey enough.

And now we must scamper across the Pacific to New Zealand, where the senecios are solid shrubs and grow very much like their kinsmen the olearias, also natives of that region.

S. greyi and *S. laxifolius* are so much alike that I really cannot say which of them it is we are most of us growing in our gardens. Of *S. greyi*, the R.H.S. Dictionary says: 'Rare in gardens, *S. laxifolius* being often grown under the name. . . .' Hillier's catalogue, compiled by Roy Lancaster who is hot on taxonomy, says of *S. laxifolius*: 'Closely related and similar to *S. greyi*, but a rarer plant, differing in its rather larger, less undulating leaves.' So you pay your money and you take your choice. Some are now splitting the difference by claiming that a hybrid between the two species is what we're growing.

Let's call it *S. laxifolius*; I brought it into the plan in Chapter 4 (p. 55). It is indispensable, but apt to straggle (a) if grown in shade and (b) if not cut fairly severely back every 2 or 3 years. You can cut it back every year, in spring, if you don't want its flowers. If you do, tidy the bush up in July, after flowering. The oval leaves are green on top but grey underneath and the stems are grey. They are evergreen, of course; of fair substance and excellent by the sea but also hardy in most inland gardens.

S. reinoldii is better known to us as *S. rotundifolius*. It comes from the very exposed coastal region of the south-west of New Zealand's South Island. It is really only hardy, in Britain, within smell of the sea, but I knew one gardener who succeeded with it in London and although I'm 10 miles inland from the coast, I have a 4 ft. specimen in my border. But I take a lot of trouble over it, considering it well worth the effort. In early December the entire shrub is enveloped in a double layer of polythene sheeting, forming a tube (kept rigid with stakes) to 4 ft. The top is left open in mild weather, but the whole is packed and surfaced with fern fronds during frosty weather.

And what, you may well ask, is this performance in aid of? Some gardeners have a particular affinity for New Zealand plants and to them explanations will be superfluous. The 3-in.-long leaf is very tough and leathery (putting up with any amount of wind) green on top; but the margins, undersides, leaf stalks and young stems are all a pale fawn-grey. The leaf is oval but with a slightly undulating margin. It is immensely satisfying; I can say no more. *S. elaeagnifolius buchananii* is constructed on the same principles but is dwarf and remarkably hardy. My plant is five years old from a cutting and barely a foot tall by 15 in. across but it will become wide-spreading in time.* A solid little bush with rounded, 1½-in.-long leathery leaves, the same colour as the last but without the undulating margin.

Some of the best **Taxus** cultivars at the Bedgebury National Pinetum are either unlabelled or else the same label does duty for entirely different plants.

The dark green of the Common Yew itself, *T. baccata*, grown either as hedge or tree, is in the top flight as a background to paler colours. There is a natural example of this in King's Wood, the largest wood of wild yews extant, in the South Downs of West Sussex, where the trees are interspersed with whitebeams, *Sorbus aria*, whose foliage is pure silver when unfolding in spring. 'Nature has shown us the way', one is tempted to remark, albeit teleologically. Another natural team gives us Old Man's Beard (*Clematis vitalba*) flinging its trails through yew.

The more compact and upright habit of the Irish Yew, *T.b.* 'Fastigiata', whether clipped or unclipped, is often better suited to a garden context where marked accents are required. The usual mistake is to plant a couple (as a lead-in to a vista) too closely. They grow slowly, but very large in time. There is a golden form of the Irish yew, *T.b.* 'Fastigiata Aureo-marginata', and this has given rise to Standishii, which makes a small column and never goes beyond its bounds. It is a bright colour.

* On the contrary, it died last summer.

There are many golden or more or less golden yews of bushy habit, associating well with junipers as a large feature in or at the edge of a wide expanse of lawn. *T.b.* 'Elegantissima' would be the right choice for the majority of medium-sized gardens. The young leaves are yellow throughout but become green in the centre of the bush. In another good one, Semperaurea, the tips of the leaves are bright yellow, becoming green at the base. It will grow 6 ft. tall by 12 ft. across, in time.

The only **Thuja** I feel impelled to include is *T. occidentalis* 'Rheingold', and that has been sufficiently described in Chapter 4 (p. 55).

Funny how the conifers come in clusters. I must return to **Tsuga** again for a moment in order to bring in *T. canadensis pendula*. It is a weeping *bush*. The leaves are arranged in a double comb, like a yew's, but are very short and neat and glaucous underneath, which makes a pretty blue and green combination on the drooping shoots and branches. This shrub grows vast in time, only 7 ft. tall but 15 ft. across. It looks humpy like Eyore after he'd been standing in the snow. No one could own a plant without loving it.

Of the **viburnums**, *Viburnum davidii* has been described (p. 55). It takes a large shrubbery or lawn to accommodate *V. rhytidophyllum* because you need a group of it so as to get the handsome crops of red berries, in August, changing to black. It grows 15 ft. tall and has large ovate-lanceolate leaves, rather like a rhododendron's but round-ended and glossy green on top, the surface elaborately patterned with veins in low relief. This is an excellent tree-shrub at its best, with its leaves standing out proudly, but they too often assume a hang-dog droop, especially if growing in shade.

The laurustinus, *V. tinus*, has a variegated form which is said to be good. I have not seen it. The leaves are a lighter green than usual, edged in cream. It is quite slow growing and one is advised not to take its hardiness for granted.

Both the greater and the lesser **periwinkles**, *Vinca major* and *V. minor*, have variegated cultivars. Usually, their flowers are blue (mauve, really). They are shade-tolerant but develop their brightest colouring (and flower far more freely) in a good light. The lesser make the more efficient ground cover, as they root wherever they touch the ground. The greater root only at the tips but make the more interesting, bumpy plants, their larger leaf (usually in two shades of green with a cream margin) making more impact. It is heart-shaped, 1½ in. long by 1¾ in. broad.

A free-for-all ground cover can be made using *Pachysandra terminalis*, a large-leaved ivy and any of the variegated periwinkles.

The worst thing about the majority of **Weigela** cultivars is their coarse, oval leaf. There are two principal exceptions, in both of which the leaf is relatively small and, although ovate, comes to a sharp, tapering point.

The purple-leaved *W. florida* 'Foliis Purpureis' grows only 4 ft. tall and needs full sun if the colouring is to be definite; not wan and muddy, as usually seen. Its flowers are a muddy mauvish shade. I had always disliked this shrub until, recently, I saw it *massed* in a sunny position behind a large patch (not yet flowering, for it was July) of *Sedum* 'Autumn Joy'.

W. florida 'Variegata' is a plant I have grown up with and always liked. It is described in Chapter 4 (p. 57). Although variegated, it makes a surprisingly effective background to bronze flowers and foliage.

Finally, **Yucca**. These exotic-looking evergreens are seldom planted without a strong desire for their handsome branched spikes of waxy white flowers. Their sombre foliage, arranged like a formalised vegetable explosion in the stiff-leaved *Y. gloriosa*, has great architectural significance. Gertrude Jekyll used them as an end-piece to one section of her principal flower border. Lutyens used them to mark the four corners of a semi-formal garden at Dixter, where I live and was born, but my mother was naturally alarmed by their sharp points (this being the stiff *Y. gloriosa*) on her children's account, and they were scrapped.

This species has a variegated counterpart of much less vigour but the same stiff habit. The leaves are cream and pale green along the centre, normal green at the margins. And the flabby-leaved *Y. filamentosa* has a very nice variegated form also, with streaks of primrose yellow, pale and mid-green throughout the leaf, but with most of the yellow near the centre. Stocks are not easily located, for they are slow of increase.

CHAPTER 6

Wall Shrubs and Climbers

*

THERE is all too little wall space in most of our gardens, even if
we allow ourselves to include interwoven fencing in the definition.
We shall not want to give it all over to foliage, but we should
certainly allow a heavy bias towards plants whose leaves will
give us pleasure for months, if not all the year. (All the year
pleasure is perhaps a trifle self-defeating, as we may, through
familiarity, cease to notice the object of it.) Thus, the bold leaves
of *Vitis coignetiae* even without any bonus of flowers is likely to
hold us in better stead than the potato climber, *Solanum crispum*,
which blooms profusely for a few weeks but is essentially spine-
less and amorphous, as becomes only too clearly apparent once
the flowers have fallen.

One of the most effective uses for wall plants of a well defined
foliar pattern is at the back of a border. Whenever you can afford
the space, allow a narrow 2 ft. (or 3 ft. if you can) border against
the wall, then a 3 ft. service path and then will come the back of
the mixed border itself, which will be viewed from its front side.
By this method, the back-of-the-border contents will not get
drawn, through the proximity of the dark wall face, while for
their part the wall shrubs will remain furnished right down to
ground level where they, too, will be receiving light that would
be denied them if the border itself reached right back to the wall.
This is, of course, an old and well tried device. Gertrude Jekyll
made use of it behind her principal flower borders.

Again if space allows, the service path can be widened to
become more than a merely functional feature. Given a width of
5 ft. (but that's asking quite a lot, I know) you could enjoy the
wall shrubs at close range, when you felt so inclined, without
receiving a shower bath from your waist downwards as you
swished past the (generally) water-laden, overhanging foliage.

The main point, however, is to be able to view them and yet be pleasantly conscious of them as a background, from across the front of your main border. You may be some 20 ft. away, so a bold foliage pattern will make the most of the situation.

The genus **Actinidia** belongs to its own family of *Actinidiaceae*. It comprises a group of deciduous twining climbers from East Asia. The best known species in British gardens is *A. kolomikta*. It is absolutely hardy, like all its brethren, but is none the less apt to be tricky. The point of this plant is that its heart-shaped leaves, which are purplish on their first appearance, can then develop vivid pink and pure white bands. Working from the tip backwards, you will first get a white area, then pink and then (if any of the leaf remains) green. However, plants sometimes fail to perform and nobody can really tell you why, though it seems necessary to give it a reasonably light position. Again, it sometimes seems to have little will to live, and this has been my experience with it, to date. but I'm sure it's only a question of finding the right place and I intend to keep on trying, because it really is worth it.

 A. kolomitka can climb to the top of a two-storey building or of a fruit tree, but another way I've seen it used, in Sweden, is as a 4–5-ft.-high but wide-spreading shrub in an open position. Given the space, this is a pleasing treatment for several plants that are normally sited against walls or trees: *Hydrangea petiolaris*, for instance, and *Solanum crispum*.

 The Chinese Gooseberry, *A. chinensis*, has terrific vigour and is a splendid foliage plant with large, hairy, broadly cordate leaves, 7 or 8 in. long by 5 or 7 in. wide. It has a disarmingly dégagé manner of flinging its tentacle-like shoots around and hanging them out from their supports. It flowers freely and charmingly at midsummer with $1\frac{1}{2}$-in.-wide saucers that are whitish on opening but soon change to biscuit. Fruits are borne only if you have male and female plants. One *A. chinensis* is about as much as most people can cope with in their gardens and so its fruiting potential, though said to be luscious, generally goes by default.

 Of *A. arguta*, seen from a distance, you can exclaim 'what a nice pattern of foliage that wall-shrub makes!' The leaves stand out like a curtain of greenery yet each retains its individuality; heart shaped at the base but drawn out to a fine point and of a lustrous green. *A. melanandra* has lanceolate leaves with red petioles and young stems. Its clusters of small white, pendulous flowers are nothing much to look at but smell of lemons.

Akebia quinata is a twining climber that I am pleased to meet again in your garden but would never bother about in my own. Its palmate leaves are distinctively composed of (usually) five rounded and well separated leaflets. The small, 3-sepalled, chocolate-coloured flowers in spring are interesting without being showy but they are spicily scented. This is a vigorous shrub and takes up quite a lot of space.

With its finely cut, silver-grey foliage, **Artemisia arborescens** is one of the prettiest of the wormwood tribe and it is shrubby. Grown in a border, it admirably offsets most flower colours and will be about 3 or 4 ft. tall itself. But you cannot expect it to be winter-hardy, unless your soil is light and the position sheltered. Really this is at its best against a wall, where it will run up to 8 ft. but must be allowed to bulge forwards 2 or 3 ft. It can be pruned back to the wall each spring.

Azara microphylla is a pretty enough evergreen with glossy foliage reminiscent of something between box and *Lonicera nitida* arranged on upright, plume-like branches. But one really grows it for its flowers which, although insignificant, hidden away on the undersides of the branches and consisting principally of yellow stamens, are yet so beguilingly scented of vanilla that you catch this mouth-watering aroma on the wind at a considerable distance. In April, that is.

Azara microphylla 'Variegata' flowers as freely, but is, when thriving, one of the most beautiful of all variegated shrubs: so light and graceful that it could take off at any moment. The leaves are broadly edged in cream-yellow. You see this shrub at its best in Ireland, where it grows 20 ft. tall. Alas, it is not nearly as hardy as the green prototype and must have a very warm wall in most gardens.

The only **Clematis** that any sensible person would grow more for its leaves than for its flowers is *C. cirrhosa* (often known as *C. calycina* or *C. balearica*). It is evergreen and its leaves, though quite small, are rather charming – only an inch or two long, usually trifoliate but boldly toothed additionally. They are smooth on top but positively glossy beneath. In winter, the top side becomes bronzed, especially on the margins. The plant will run up to 15 ft. and is quite vigorous but not all that hardy and if its foliage and flower buds are not to be damaged in winter, it must have a sheltered wall. Given shelter, the aspect can be north as soon as south.

I have just been out to look at my specimen and find that its first two blooms are already, on 29th January, fully out. Their season lasts till April. They have little or no scent in the open at this season, but if brought indoors, immediately exhale a distinct and pleasing fragrance in which vanilla seems to be the main ingredient. The flowers have 4 sepals and are bell-shaped, quite small and insignificant, about an inch across at the mouth. The sepals are very pale green, freckled inside the bell with a dusting of purple dots.

C. cirrhosa var. *balearica* has much more finely divided and fern-like leaves. This, too, is good without striving to be so (as does *C. armandii*) and then not making it.

Of the legume fraternity, **Coronilla glauca** is a loose, unkempt sort of shrub, but carrying its heads of warm-scented yellow flowers whenever the weather allows from autumn onwards, with a climax in spring. A bush should be clipped over several times in the growing season. It is fairly hardy as a free-standing shrub (when, however, it will need a permanent stake) but is safer against a wall. Its glaucous pinnate foliage makes a pleasant setting for the flowers. No more. In *C. glauca* 'Variegata', however, the foliage is the main thing. Each leaflet has so broad a cream margin that there is more of this colour than of green. The flowers contribute nothing much to such a lively setting, as may be imagined, but they do no harm. As usual, the variegated form is less hardy than the type-plant, and it must be given a sunny wall, where it may run up to 4 or 5 ft., if not unduly checked in winter.

The reader must try not to become restive on discovering that quite a proportion of the shrubs I suggest for walls are very much on the borderlines of hardiness. The main idea with any wall (or so it seems to me) is to give us the opportunity for trying such plants. The richest rewards are seldom won without risks being taken. If, to you, a loss is a disaster and a personal affront, you can always play safe with forsythia and winter jasmine. But I feel sure this is not the case or you would never have read thus far.

With this apologia I lead into another semi-hardy genus from the southern hemisphere. You see the Tasmanian **Drimys aromatica** (now *D. lanceolata*) a lot in Irish gardens. There is a hedge of it at Mount Stewart in County Down. So it is not too dicy as a wall shrub in the South-East of England, for instance. You could liken it to a much refined version of the strawberry tree, *Arbutus unedo*. The evergreen foliage is oblanceolate, that is to say long and narrow but broadest at the rounded tips. The young stems, leaf stalks and main veins are red. It is a comely shrub, but must be expected to bush out 2 or 3 ft. from the wall against which it is grown. The plant is aromatic, as will be discovered on bruising it. Whether, in muggy weather, it is capable of exhaling an aroma without being bullied, I cannot say.

D. colorata (correctly *Pseudowintera colorata*) from New Zealand, is tenderer still and far less vigorous, cowering at a height of one or two feet, as I have seen it. Give it a cool, damp spot against a shaded wall unless you live somewhere on our western seaboard. Its leaf is shaped, in this case, like *Elaeagnus pungens*. But it is a pale, yellow-green with reddish purple margins and the stems are dark brown. Altogether a remarkable study in unexpected contrasts.

The **loquat**, *Eriobotrya japonica*, is undoubtedly a handsome piece of evergreen wall furniture and so much hardier than is generally supposed that its successful cultivation can win you far greater admiration than you deserve. The R.H.S. Dictionary twice refers to its 'noble foliage'. The tough, oval leaves are indeed large and declamatory, up to a foot long, green on top, greyish underneath, rough textured. I suppose I have been put off the plant from too frequently seeing it as a scrubby tree in warmer countries where it is grown for its fruit. It is a coarse thing. I like some coarse plants but can't warm to this one.

Particularly where you have a high wall, not unduly studded

with windows, a wide variety of **Eucalyptus** can make a hand-some and unusual feature. They will be allowed to grow so high and then be pruned back each spring to a framework of branches trained against the wall. In this way, juvenile foliage will be permanently retained and its glaucous colouring makes a lively contrast to red brick. *E. gunnii* will fill the bill as effectively as almost any, though I should be tempted to use the less hardy *E. perriniana* (see p. 27) in such a favourable situation.

I mentioned the climbing propensities of **Euonymus fortunei** (syn. *E. radicans*) and its variegated forms in the last chapter.

Which brings us to the daunting subject of the ivies, of the genus **Hedera**, most of them being derived from our common Wild Ivy, *H. helix*. The subject is daunting because there are not only a great many varieties in cultivation but there are about three times the number of synonyms. Even if you have made a speciality of ivies, as did Margery Fish, for instance, it is easy to lose your way. A count-up reveals that I have only nine different kinds in my garden (not counting the wilding), which is a meagre assortment.

Ivies can be used in a great many different ways: on walls, of course and on trees, which they don't really damage at all. If a tree succumbs under an ivy, the chances are it would have done so anyway. The ivy's strong stems will have prevented it from blowing over years earlier. Ivies are good ground cover, both in sun and in shade and they can also be used to scramble around the base and lower branches of deciduous shrubs, providing winter interest where there would otherwise be none. There need never be a fear of them getting above themselves and smothering every-thing within reach, because you can choose your varieties for vigour according to how much work you want them to do. Some are quite weak and will even need encouraging.

One of the most important uses for ivies, not yet mentioned, is as house plants. Because they are used this way, many people get the idea that the more popular pot types must be tender. In fact, however, most are perfectly hardy; so hardy that the severest winter weather has no effect on their foliage either at the time or subsequently. Many varieties, in fact, take on attractive purplish or pink tints in winter.

19. *Iris pallida* 'Variegata' sells on sight, and small wonder.

20. At its brightest in spring, *Iris pseudacorus* 'Variegata' can be grown in very wet places or under water.

I will deal first with two of the handsomest large-leaved ivies. *H. colchica* 'Dentato-variegata' is extremely robust and hardy. As with many ivies, its leaves vary a great deal in size, shape and colouring. They are on the coarse side and not exquisitely shaped by any means; often nearly 6 in. long and almost as wide, roughly triangular with wavy (but not toothed) margins. The colouring is excellent, in about three shades of green with a very uneven cream-coloured margin. Some leaves are cream all over. The general effect is bold and striking. I have one plant on a 9 ft. north wall *behind* a specimen of its near relation, *Fatsia japonica*. Plain green against variegated makes a change from variegated against green. Incidentally, the crushed leaves of this ivy have a pleasing and sweet aroma.

I am often asked, by amateur gardeners, for suggestions on what to plant against a north wall that will be colourful for a long season. Most flowers have a short season; even the winter jasmine will be making a real show for only a short stretch. I try them with this ivy but usually fail to convince. There are still many gardeners for whom ivies are inevitably dreary. This, I believe, will pass. Certainly *H. colchica* 'Dentato-variegata' is gay and smiling and for 12 months in the year, at that. It flowers in December and then looks charming with a frill of small leaves surrounding each inflorescence. Excellent for cutting, both in this condition and for its long, leafy trails.

The leaves of *H. canariensis* 'Variegata' (alias Gloire de Marengo) are large but only half the size of the last. The plant is much more elegant but not so tough. In an exposed position, as I have it growing up a pole as a vertical feature in my Long Border, its leaves and younger shoots can be destroyed in a hard winter, but the old wood remains unaffected and the plant will have recovered by mid-summer. There is a particular freshness in this one's variegation: blue green and bay green in the leaf centre but almost white at the margin. In winter, the margin often turns pinkish purple, and so do the leaf stalks.

H. hibernica, the Irish Ivy, is sometimes treated as a species, sometimes as a variety of *H. helix*. It is efficient and strong-growing ground cover under trees but is made for business rather than pleasure: the sort of plant I might recommend someone else to grow but that I wouldn't touch myself.

Now we arrive at the cultivars of *H. helix*. Some of these have an excellent leaf shape with sharp points. Sagittifolia, for instance, has an elongated central tongue and two short sharp lobes set well back on either side. Several more are like this and they make a good pattern of foliage. By contrast, Cristata is shapeless because the whole leaf margin is crimped and frilly like parsley foliage.

Glacier is one of the most effective of the moderately vigorous cultivars, with a glaucous leaf outlined with a very thin silver line. It furnishes and nicely subdues a red brick wall up to 4 ft. or so. Silver Queen is another of this kind but much less vigorous and distinctly sparse in habit with long gaps between its leaves. The white leaf margin turns pink in winter. I have had it in a pot for years; when it looks tired and gangling indoors, I cut it back and put it out to strengthen up. There it is at this moment and happens to have started climbing a shrub rose. It is totally non-aggressive. Tricolor (alias Elegantissima or Marginata Rubra) is similar but with a more distinct cream margin and an even more marked habit of turning pink in winter.

Of those with yellow variegation, Buttercup varies with the season, being yellow throughout the leaf in summer and in sun. I have not grown this. Margery Fish said it was particularly satisfactory in shade but Graham Thomas recommends full sun for the brightest colouring. I am very fond of Angularis Aurea (alias Aureo-variegata) myself although it has a reputation for reverting to plain green. There are two ways of looking at this (and the same applies to other gold-leaved shrubs like *Euonymus japonica*). You can either consider it as a golden shrub that is constantly going green, curse it; or you can think of it as a green shrub that is constantly delighting you by throwing golden shoots, bless it. Given a sunny position, Angularis Aurea will never let you down completely and the proportion of gold to green – the one forming a setting for the other – is just right in my eyes.

One of the most striking and popular of the moderately vigorous yellow-variegated ivies is Gold Heart, often known as Jubilee. For a long time, its leaves may be tiny but can grow to a fair size, 2 or 3 in. across and they have a pale lemon flash in the centre of a green surround. You can grow this one on a north wall and still get the benefit of its typical colouring, but in very dark places it does lose it. Also, shoots do revert.

Many of the ivies, especially the more vigorous ones, have two kinds of leaves and shoots. The vegetative condition is invariable at ground level; also on vertical surfaces for as long as the plant is invading new territory. Strand-like, self-clinging shoots are made and the leaves are as lobed as they ever will be. Once the ivy has got to the top of a wall, tree, post or other vertical support, however, its shoots become short-jointed and non-clinging; more densely crowded with leaves having no lobes whatever. These sorts of shoots can be most useful in flower arrangements as a complement to the long trails (as I said of *H. colchica* 'D-v.'). If you propagate an ivy from its mature, adult wood, you get a shrubby non-climbing plant, and it can be grown as such in a border, though it will probably need a stake.

There is a sweetie called *H. helix* 'Conglomerata' (and a similar one called Congesta) that never climbs but makes a sprawling 2 ft. shrub of great character. The lower leaves in the centre of the bush may be 2 in. across, deep green with all the veins picked out in pale green. The stiff young shoots rise vertically or obliquely. They are clothed in minute leaves in their lower reaches and with nothing at all at the top, where they stick up like candles. It is what is snobbishly known as a connoisseur's plant (each of us is a connoisseur in his own valuation) and could never achieve a wide acclaim by the rabble.

I shall have to reserve my main gush of admiration for **Helichrysum petiolatum** when discussing tender plants (p. 160). Should you happen to site it against a wall where it can thread its way through the branches of a climbing rose or ceanothus, for instance, it will hoist itself up 8 ft. or more and may even survive the winter now and again. In that case you will prune away its withered tips in spring, and off it will go again. It is a plant you cannot have too much of; everything it does is right and there are so many ways in which it can be grown.

I have recently acquired *Jasminum officinale* 'Aureo-variegatum', which is a variegated form of the summer jasmine with the scented white flowers. This form has dark green leaves strikingly mottled and blotched with yellow. It makes a particularly bold foliage effect, with leaves of more than their usual size, if the shrub is pruned back pretty hard every spring. You won't get many flowers this way but you will get the best of the plant's main asset.

Lonicera is the genus of the honeysuckles but it sets a fairly elementary trap that gardeners spring early in their careers by being sometimes climbing with long tubular flowers; sometimes an altogether un-honeysuckle-like shrub with short-tubed flowers. Of the former, *L. japonica* 'Aureo-reticulata' is a moderately vigorous plant whose green leaves are netted with golden variegation along the veins. This is especially popular with flower arrangers in search of trailing material for pedestal arrangements. Except in a hot summer, the flowering of *L.j.* 'Aureo-reticulata' is pretty meagre. Give it a sunny wall or balustrade.

L. implexa makes a change. When I first saw a plant, before its flowering season, I had no idea what it could be and wondered if it were some abstruse euphorbia. The leaves are in opposite pairs and stemless. Towards the tips of the shoots, they join to make a disc, (rather like *Eucalyptus perriniana*). Though green on top, they are glaucous underneath. Both in their colouring and in their arrangement they make a distinct impression. The flowers, it must be confessed, are not memorable. This shrub is well adapted for clothing the lower part of a wall where somebody else's legs have gone bare. It is by no means rampant, seldom more than 5 or 6 ft. tall.

L. splendida is far more glaucous than this and stands out as a blue wall feature at some distance. It is an exciting species, the more so as you never know till you have tried, whether it will thrive or just look unhappy, year by year. Hillier calls it fastidious. Its tastes are worth cultivating. When suited, this is as vigorous as our native woodbine. Its hardiness is scarcely in question: it thrives at Crathes Castle near Aberdeen. This honeysuckle flowers pleasantly in subdued tones of yellow, purple and red.

I had not intended to include **Magnolia grandiflora**, as it is with flowers in mind that we plant it. However, I feel I must mention its excellent evergreen foliage, in passing, so glossy on the upper surface. On the undersides, it can have a rust-coloured indumentum in some cultivars, notably Ferrugineum. The shrub is wasted if you cannot allow it plenty of space and have to be for ever curbing it. Remember that it is a tree by nature. Lacking sufficient wall space, grow it as a free-standing bush. I have discussed **mahonias** already, too, but would remind the reader that *Mahonia lomariifolia* benefits from wall protection and deserves to be near the top of one's list of candidates for such cosy mural lay-by's as may be available, whether facing west, south or east.

Nandina domestica is another shrub requiring protection. Mine is not near a wall but would be better, I suspect, if it were. Sun is not necessary to it, however. It is a curious plant, related to *Berberis* but having something of the look of a bamboo, except when carrying its panicles of demure white flowers in autumn. The evergreen leaves are very large, when you come to analyse them, but do not give a large impression since they are doubly pinnate and overlap to such an extent that you cannot see where one leaf begins and another ends. The leaflets are glossy, lanceolate, one or two inches long, elegantly tapering and a pretty copper colour when young. The general impression is of a refined mop. As usually seen, the shrub is about 4 ft. tall.

Many daisy bushes, of the genus **Olearia**, have interesting foliage and there is an astonishing diversity of leaf form, but the only one I want to recommend here, specifically as a wall foliage shrub is *O. zennorensis*. It is a hybrid but, curiously, not mentioned by the R.H.S. Dictionary. Hilliers list it, however. The evergreen leaves are lanceolate, about 4 in. long by ½ in. wide grey-green and regularly toothed along their margins like a crocodile's jaw. Very fetching.

Parthenocissus is the genus of climbers, largely self-supporting, that have often been referred, in the past, to *Ampelopsis* or to *Vitis* and are commonly known as Virginia Creepers. The most widely planted, and seen, typically, against 3- or 4-storeyed Victorian red brick buildings whose very chimney pots may be enveloped, is *P. tricuspidata* (syn. *Ampelopsis veitchii* or *Vitis inconstans*). I detest this plant, which I associate with the gloomier aspects of boarding school life. Its large, shiny, three-pointed leaves are coarse and change to brilliant carmine tints in early autumn which are quite repulsive in their normal context. I don't think this creeper is being planted as much as it used to be, though I can't think why.

Having got that *bête noire* off my chest, I can highly recommend any and all of the rest, within this genus. The true Virginia Creeper is *Parthenocissus quinquefolia* – well named as to its specific epithet, since the palmate leaves are usually divided, finger-wise, into five leaflets. I know one that drapes a garage, or car port, rather. Its shoots of the current season hang over the port entrance almost down to the ground and swish aside like an Indian bead curtain, when the car goes in or out. This creeper, again, is self-clinging when it has something to cling to. Its foliage changes to magnificent orange and red shades in early autumn. They may already have reached their brightness by mid-September. Some people object to this early evidence of approaching winter. Perhaps it gives them premonitory twinges of frost bite in their extremities.

P. inserta is similar except that it doesn't cling to the flat surfaces with adhesive discs but has tendrils, like a vine, and needs to get them round something. It is first rate, then, for climbing up a tree, as it might be an old yew, and would associate well in autumn against this background, with the fluffy white seed heads of *Clematis vitalba* (Old Man's Beard).

But the prettiest in this group must surely be *P. henryana* (usually sold as *Vitis henryana*). It has plenty of vigour but the leaves are smaller and neater than the others', with 3 or 5 leaflets. The plant is self-clinging. but sometimes takes a year or two to get the hang of this. If grown against a sunless wall, the leaves are prettily marbled, in summer, the area next the veins being picked out in a pale, silvery green. But it thrives in sun or in shade and colours agreeably in autumn. Where a wall has concrete footings, it will grow happily in a large tub or trough, butted against the wall. Again, it may be used as ground cover.

I have been in two minds about whether to include **Pileostegia viburnoides**, because its 6-in.-long leathery oval leaves have little that's outstanding about them except their red stalks. But it is a self-clinging evergreen climber, and there are few such, apart from the ivies. Furthermore it flowers charmingly in September, with a froth of white blossom. Also, I like the habit of the plant and the way its branches stand out from a wall once they have reached the adult stage. It needs no sun and will run up to 25 ft. or more. This is a close relation of the climbing hydrangea which, however, is deciduous.

Piptanthus laburnifolius (syn. *P. nepalensis*) also deserves mention, although principally a flowering shrub. It is more or less evergreen, but its largest leaves are shed in winter. These are trifoliate, dark green, the leaflets up to 6 in. long and therefore striking. Although hardy in much of the country as a free-standing bush, it is excellent trained to a wall and requires little or no sun. It makes vigorous young stems from the base and these are a dark blue-green and polished. Its height is 8 ft. by rather more across, when trained. The clusters of substantial yellow pea flowers are carried for six weeks from the end of April. Easily raised from seed.

I dealt with the **pittosporums** in Chapter 3 (p. 34). **Senecio leucostachys** was described in the last chapter (p. 102) but, apropos of walls, I must mention that it can climb through other shrubs to a considerable height: 12 ft. at least. In this it resembles *Helichrysum petiolatum* but the senecio is hardier.

Lastly, then, the true grape vines of the genus **Vitis**. They all have ornamentally lobed foliage but it seems to be one of the sad facts of vine life that the most luscious-fruiting cultivars have the least ornamentally sculpted leaves.

The most spectacular of all vines, *V. coignetiae*, anyway makes no pretence at distinction in this department. Its leaves are discreetly lobed and are of a generally rounded outline, rough-textured. But this climber is built on the largest scale, having the vigour to reach the tops of the tallest trees. Its leaves are up to a foot long and nearly as wide and they should take on the most brilliant crimson tints in autumn. There are, however, various seedling stocks of this vine in commerce, some of which are poor colourers. Make this point to the nurseryman from whom you are buying a plant. If he says: 'well, we propagate vegetatively from our own stock plant and it always colours magnificently', you can relax.

Many gardeners, on hearing what a vigorous climber like this or *Clematis montana* or *Polygonum baldschuanicum* is capable of, exclaim 'Whoopee!', scrape a tiny dust hollow out of some ghastly piece of couch-infested turf, tread the young plant in, spatter it with a tablespoon of water and then wait expectantly for the advertised Jack-and-the-Beanstalk results. Not surprisingly (to me at least) nothing happens. You simply must give the plant a decent start. The soil at the foot of a tree (if that is the chosen site) is often in a state of exhaustion: full of tree roots and dust dry. You will need to excavate a large hole, say 18 in. deep and 3 or 4 ft. across, fill it with good top soil from elsewhere and keep your young plant free of encroaching weeds and thoroughly watered – 2 or 3 gallons at a time – in dry spells, until it is growing strongly and obviously established. If excavation is too much like hard work, you can start the plant in a large bottomless box, filled with good soil and set against the trunk on ground that has been just sufficiently broken up (with a pick, if need be) for it to grow out from the box and into the ground, in a short while. Watering will need to be even more conscientious. A third and even better idea, where the tree's shape allows it, is to plant your vine just outside some low, outer branches and train it (with string) on to them rather than up the trunk itself. On the outside of the tree, roots will be easier to cope with when preparing a position and there will be more light, which will again help your youngster.

A danger, here, is that the tree may have whippy branches and be in a windy position. It may then be difficult for the vine to make initial contact with a constantly moving host. If grown on a wall, it should be a large wall, to suit *V. coignetiae*. A wall over-hung by trees will also (wind permitting) suggest the possibility of climbing it from the wall up on to the trees. If a similar vine but with a smaller leaf would look more appropriate in the space available, then I suggest *V. davidii*.

V. flexuosa has slender stems and a restrained habit with glossy leaves, not prominently lobed, however. It looks well scrambling at or near ground level.

There is a purple-leaved form of the grape vine, *V. vinifera* 'Purpurea' that is highly ornamental, though you must not expect it to cover a great area and it should be given a cosy wall by way of encouragement. Its deeply lobed and shallowly scalloped leaves are red at first becoming purple at maturity. I have never grown this myself but met a specimen in the car park at Bedgebury Pinetum in the autumn of 1970, this park being on the site of an old walled garden whose walls still support some noteworthy plants. The purple vine was looking doubly luscious, just then, through being liberally hung with small bunches of black grapes. As the place was seething with visitors, it might have struck me as odd that the grapes hadn't been eaten. Without stopping to consider such niceties I popped a fruit in my mouth. This was a mistake. It was almost as bitter as a sloe and I realised, too late, that the blackness of the grapes had nothing to do, as it normally would, with their ripeness but was just another manifestation of the dark pigment with which the entire plant was impregnated.

CHAPTER 7

Herbaceous Plants for Mixed Borders

*

I FIND it very easy, once I get going, to forget exactly what it was I said I should be writing about when I was starting a chapter. In this case I mean to discuss the sort of hardy foliage plants that could take their place in a bed or border with shrubs, bedding out plants etc. I shall, I hope, concentrate on the principal ingredients, again, leaving such out-of-place oddments as the giant *Gunnera manicata* to a final chapter.

There is something vaguely repulsive about the word herbaceous. My one-time botany lecturer used to tell his first-year students that 'the herbaceous border is not to be confused with the vegetarian lodger'. Even without any such mistake in identity, many gardeners nowadays refuse to grow herbaceous plants. They will grow hostas and Japanese anemones and astilbes (or astileebs, as one often hears them called); that's all right but herbaceous plants, no. They are too troublesome: outdated relics of gracious living, hordes of servants and all that rubbish from the bad old past.

There are many herbaceous plants I love (and so, come to that, do you). I never think of them as such. I like them individually, regardless of categories. But categorise one must, at any rate for the convenience of constructing chapters in a book, so there we are. I will introduce you to my team, plant by plant, and they will insinuate themselves into your good graces by sheer force of charm. You'll forget the clumsy word herbaceous altogether.

Acaenas are 'poor relations of the rose', to quote a New Zealand book about its wild flowers. Leave out the 'poor', and I'm ready to agree. However, it needs to be understood that numbered among the New Zealand acaenas are some weeds (weeds in their native habitat, anyway) whose burr seed heads get into your socks and work through to your ankles. This is an aggravating habit, but it is the New Zealanders' problem, not ours.

Here we have a useful group of evergreen grovellers. Some, like *Acaena novae-zelandiae*, with colourful carmine red burrs, or *A. buchananii*, with a neat, compact habit and dusky leaves, are so ground-hugging as to be more especially useful in paving cracks. Others make a little more height. It is difficult to be sure of their correct names since they are in a state of confusion. One that I have most often met as *A*. 'Coerulea' or *A. ascendens* (both names certainly invalid) has quite tiny glaucous pinnate foliage borne on longish scrambling stems that can rise into and intermingle with any foot- or 18-in.-tall plant or shrub they happen to be near. Grow it among miniature roses, for instance, and you will soon come to appreciate that this is no poor relation.

A larger-leaved and more robustly growing cultivar, but still with glaucous pinnate foliage, was given me as Blue Haze. Above ground it has a somewhat tufted but also trailing habit, about a foot tall and it spreads by underground rhizomes. This is bold enough to make an effective group and I like it very much, though I have not had it for long.

When we come to discuss **Acanthus**, are we thinking more in terms of the famous acanthus leaf or of those stately spikes of sinister hooded flowers? If the former, then I think *A. mollis* 'Laterifolius' has it. The leaves may not be as heavily cut as in other species, but they are particularly large and shining and bright green. Flowering, however, is a toss-up. Sometimes they will, sometimes they won't and I have never been able to relate their performance to seasonal factors.

A. spinosus has a more finely cut, darker green and spikier leaf altogether. It is a regular flowerer. I rather fancy a third species, *A. longifolius*, myself. Its leaves are not heavily embroidered but pinnatifid. Flowering is profuse, the stems self-supporting, about 3 to 3½ ft. tall (they can rise to an inconveniently toppling 6 ft. in *A. spinosus*).

Like several other fleshy-rooted plants that increase by root cuttings, acanthus dislike being moved, are slow to settle down, but once established, are difficult to eradicate. If I tell you to site them carefully so as to be sure of not wanting to move them again at some future date, I must also add that I have never succeeded in following my own advice.

Ajugas are low carpeters – at least the forms of *Ajuga reptans*, our native bugle, are. They find their way into every book on ground cover, though in fact they let the weeds through and these have to be picked out by hand. Multicolor (alias Rainbow) is the only one I grow. At present (February) its leaves are nearly all a very dark purple, enlivened by a metallic sheen, and this is how Atropurpurea (or Purpurea) always looks. Multicolor, however, breaks out into fascinating blotches and mottling in pink, purple and creamy yellow. A few leaves show this even now but it is more marked in summer. Both this and Atropurpurea should have a sunny position to bring out the full richness of their colouring, and a stodgy clay soil like mine suits them to perfection. Variegata has a pale leaf in green and off-white and this does very well in shade. It is not as vigorous as the others. All have spikes of blue labiate flowers for a short time in May, and these are not to be despised.

One never met **Alchemilla mollis** until twenty years ago. Now it is in every self-respecting garden and is especially beloved of flower arrangers. Although deciduous, this really does cover the ground and suppress all weeds as do the hostas. Its leaves are like an umbrella turned inside out and they are hairy, holding raindrops in their centre, but with a light-reflecting air bubble trapped underneath, that winks and sparkles with contagious glee. The panicles of tiny lime green flowers appear in late spring and early summer, about 2 ft. tall but collapsing when weighted by rain. Eventually, in July, they turn brownish. If I can get around to it, I raze the plants with a knife at this stage and they reclothe themselves with fresh young foliage, though at a lower level.

If not cut down, *A. mollis* seeds itself all over the place, sometimes just where you want it but could never have planted it, in a crack; sometimes just where you don't want it. Sun or shade suit it equally.

Anaphalis are greys and want sun, therefore. They are mildly invasive, spreading underground by rhizomes. They have corymbose heads of small white everlasting flowers. Being very easily grown they can be overdone and are then just boring: especially *A. margaritacea*. The leaves in *A. triplinervis* are larger and more positive, ovate-lanceolate. The plant is only 2 ft. tall and has a good dense habit. In a way I prefer *A. yedoensis* to either of the others, but it is awkward to manage, growing 3 ft. tall and inclined to flop. Also it runs to such an extent that I find it advisable, among other groups of plants, to lift and re-set it every autumn. This disturbance also has the effect of reducing its stature during the next growing season. The greyish leaves have a much paler grey margin.

The **artemisias** are all but one of them foliage plants, if they are anything at all. Their leaves are usually grey and much dissected and they inhabit that no man's land between shrub and herbaceous plant. Why do people call them artemeesias, I often wonder? The i of Artemis should surely be short.

Artemisias like parched soils and the best of drainage. Many will do all right on my clay but are not as pale as they might be. Others, like *Artemisia nutans*, which are on the borderlines of hardiness at the best of times, are quite distinctly on the wrong side of the border with me.

The truest shrub is that old cottage garden favourite *A. abrotanum*, which I was brought up to call Old Man, but you may have known as Southernwood or Ladslove. If kept neat by hard pruning each winter, it is a comely 3 ft. shrub with a very distinctive aroma (not, I am happy to say, of old men). The leaves are filigree and grey-green. If they were only more grey than green instead of the other way about, this would be a tip-top plant.

I have dealt with *A. arborescens* (p. 109) as a wall plant. *A. absinthium*, the true wormwood, is sub-shrubby and not very exciting, though the 3 ft. Lambrook Silver is a good form of it that I've not grown. A lowlier shrub within the genus never seems to have had its name settled for it – *A. splendens*, *A. discolor*, and *A. canescens* are only three of the impossibilities. It is a sprawling, 1½-ft.-tall shrub that can be kept in order by pruning. The filigree grey leaves are twisted and particularly concentrated near the tips of the shoots in a sort of spider's web whorl. Sometimes their colouring and texture reminds me of certain lichens. It is a fascinating plant but I have yet to see it really effectively used in the garden. Perhaps with self-sown tiny-flowered violas rambling through it?

Although only 5 or 6 in. tall, *A. pedemontana* is really shrubby: a miserable sight in winter but densely filigree silver in its summer dress. It is considerably more reliable than *A. schmidtii* 'Nana', which I otherwise prefer. This has very similar foliage to the last in a low, 5 in. hummock, and it makes no bones about being truly herbaceous. In spring, it sprouts again from silver buds at ground level. These are often pecked out by sparrows, who are mad on grey plants in spring. Plants often survive the winter only to fail at the next fence.

The felted leaves of *A. stelleriana* are fairly substantial. They are reminiscent of *Senecio cineraria*. The plant grows to about 2 ft., when in flower. I got rid of mine in a rage, because I thought it was wrongly named. By the time I discovered that it was right and I was wrong, it was too late.

A. pontica is a dim grey but made light by the extremely fine cut of its anyway small leaves. It is truly herbaceous, with stiff wiry stems to 18 in. or 2 ft. and they are carried in such a dense forest that weeds never get among them. This is mildly invasive, by rhizomes, but easily controlled. So, too, is *A. ludoviciana*. John Raven, in *A Botanist's Garden*, points out that although this is given separate specific status, in the R.H.S. Dictionary of Gardening, from *A. palmeri*, the two as found in commerce appear to be identical and this relieves my mind, as I could never make out what differences I should be able to see. It has a silver-grey felted leaf and was included in the Chapter 4 border (p. 53).

The arum of arums, for foliage, is *Arum italicum* 'Pictum'. Ask any flower arranger. It has arrow-shaped leaves. The largest are about 10 in. long now, in winter, but they will get larger yet. The background colouring is dark green, over which is marked a pale green reticulated pattern that follows every vein and terminates within a quarter inch of the margin in a perfectly defined hem.

Apart from drum-sticks of orange berries, the plant is dormant from June to September. From then on, new foliage keeps on appearing. Frosty weather can damage it but more soon comes.

Plants are at their lushest in spring, being some 2 ft. tall then and carrying typical lords-and-ladies inflorescences.

The plant is excellent in a moist, shady border but not too dark, otherwise the marbling won't stand out so well. Sun is acceptable too, as long as the moisture is there. For once, slugs are no problem.

If you buy plants, they may be seedlings, and seedlings seldom show any marbling until their second year: increasingly thereafter. Bide your time, awhile, before shrieking out that you have been sold a pup. It may, on the contrary, be an ugly duckling with splendid prospects.

Gertrude Jekyll can never have known this plant. But she rightly valued our native *A. maculatum* which grows with us whether we want it or not – in country gardens, anyway. In *Wood and Garden* she tells us: 'When the first Daffodils are out and suitable greenery is not abundant in the garden (for it does not do to cut their own blades), I bring home handfuls of the wild Arum leaves, so common in roadside hedges, grasping the whole plant close to the ground; then a steady pull breaks it away from the tuber, and you have a fine long-stalked sheaf of leafage held together by its own underground stems. This should be prepared like the Lent Hellebores, by putting it deep in water for a time. I always think the Trumpet Daffodils look better with this than with any other kind of foliage.'

The name *A. maculatum* indicates spotting and, indeed, the wild arum's leaves can be sprinkled with purple spots. I wish they were more often and more liberally. Mostly they are plain green. Some plantsman might select us a well-spotted strain.

Bergenias were great favourites with Miss Jekyll, although in her day they were known as megascas (with a short second syllable). Some huge clumps of the one that is especially associated with her, *Bergenia cordifolia* 'Purpurea', were planted in this garden when it was first made, around 1912. There they (two of them, anyway) have remained undisturbed ever since. They are 100% efficient ground coverers and have required no attention from that day to this. I loathe them. Sheer inertia and the fact that they do a job so efficiently, have so far prevented me from taking action. The reader should be warned that this is often what happens with ground cover plants. They save us work but without giving any positive pleasure in return. We may tell ourselves that we quite like them but that is merely face-saving and to excuse ourselves for leaving them, as we might for leaving the television on when no-one is looking at it. 'It's bad for the apparatus to keep turning it on and off', we say. 'Mene mene tekel upharsin', as the hand wrote on Belshazzar's wall.

B. *cordifolia* has large, orbicular leaves measuring 9 in. each way and in winter they take on a liverish purple flush. They are leathery without the pleasant feel of leather. Their flowers, in April, are a villainous magenta on red stalks but I actually don't mind them at all. The plant can look very presentable, not in a huge patch, like we have it, but sandwiched between the edge of a border and something taller than itself behind, under whose skirts the bergenia can investigate.

Miss Jekyll had it in front of yuccas and it came over a low stone ledge, about 15 in. high, that made the corner of her border at this point. It looks just right in the photographs.

Another bergenia that presents itself flatteringly on a ledge is the really beautiful B. *ciliata*. It has large green leaves 8 in. by 6 wide, in summer, which are mostly replaced by quite tiny 3-in.-long leaves in winter. The whole green leaf surface, as also the leaf stalks, are covered with hairs. The plant holds itself well and flowers prettily in spring. Pale pink.

Ballawley's great cabbage-leaves flop all over the place. They are perfectly smooth and glossy green in summer, changing in winter to liver on top but beetroot underneath, about 8 to 10 in. long and 6 in. across. The leaf stalks are rather too long and the leaves can be snapped off if grown in a windy place. The flowers, in April, are a vivid, clean magenta.

21. ABOVE, *Hosta crispula* has the boldest variegation of all the plantain lilies and will retain it into autumn if grown in moist shade. As I have it here, backed by Solomon's Seals, its margins presently get scorched. Photographed in early June. BELOW. *Hosta plantaginea grandiflora* is probably grown more for its white, scented flowers that come in autumn, than for its leaves, but the latter retain a remarkably fresh and spring-like colouring throughout the entire growing season and they present themselves well.

Perhaps the smartest bergenia leaf (apart from *B. ciliata*) is owned by *B. purpurescens*, which used to be known as *B. delavayi* and *B. beesiana*. This leaf is neat, not floppy, and held stiffly in an oblique to upright plane. The leaf blade is 5 in. long by 3 in. wide, purple in winter. The flowers come on a tall, branching inflorescence and are a clean, reddish-purple shade. This is by no means a ground coverer, though it will make a good patch. I have interplanted mine with small bulbs.

The leaves of *B. crassifolia*, *B. schmidtii* and of handsome-flowering cultivars like Morgenrote, Abendglut and Silberlicht are boring at best and really dreadful at their worst (now, February).

Bergenias can be grown in sun or in shade but flower more freely in a fairly light position, where they also develop their exquisite liverish complexions to apoplectic perfection.

Cerastium tomentosum, called Snow-in-Summer, is so invasive that it is difficult to know how to prevent the servant from

22. ABOVE LEFT, young foliage and old on *Rhododendron sinogrande* at Inverewe in north-west Scotland. Complete protection from wind is essential, otherwise the leaf stalks snap off. A mild, moist climate is preferred but the species can also be grown successfully in the dry south-east of England. RIGHT, *Cornus alternifolia* 'Argentea' froths most delicately, and yet this dogwood has a firm structure built up in horizontal layers. MIDDLE LEFT, the lime green of *Alchemilla mollis* offset by a purple-leaved cultivar of the Venetian sumach *Cotinus coggygria* (syn. *Rhus cotinus*). The latter can be pruned, in winter, to keep it low while the former can be cut back as its flowers fade, allowing a fresh crop of shell-leaves to develop. RIGHT, lime green and purple again in an unusual association at Ladham House, Goudhurst, Kent. This time the shell leaves belong to *Tellima grandiflora* and are evergreen. The flower racemes are in marked contrast to the rich purple rose foliage of the well-known floribunda, Rosemary Rose, here used as a mixed border ingredient. BELOW LEFT, the the brilliant yellow green of parsley makes a mossy foreground to the glaucous dome of Jackman's Blue Rue. The smell of these two strongly aromatic plants is in equally marked antithesis. RIGHT, the dark spots that liberally bespatter most forms of *Orchis maculata* show up best in the young foliage, but it can be seen what a fine border plant this wilding makes when given its chance.

becoming master. And yet one cannot help admiring the plant, making a rug of palest grey foliage sprinkled with white stitchwort flowers in late spring. The answer, I fear, must generally be to look for something similar but more politely behaved. The variety *C.t. columnae* will answer pretty well. Its habit is much more restrained; its shoots and foliage are like the type-plant in miniature and almost dead white. An open, sunny position will produce the densest and whitest growth.

The common edible seakale, **Crambe maritima**, is seldom used for ornament, but this was another Jekyll plant, growing at one end of her large flower border where the main planting was of hoary and glaucous foliage; yucca, seakale, *Cineraria maritima* (now *Senecio cineraria*), rue, *Elymus arenarius* (blue lyme grass), santolina and *Stachys lanata*. 'The front of the border has some important foliage giving a distinct blue effect; prominent among it Sea Kale. The flower-stems are cut hard back in the earlier summer, and it is now in handsome fresh leaf.' That was in August. Seakale flowers in late May with a great white cumulus cloud of honey-scented blossom, about 2 ft. high. The glaucous leaves are cabbagy and retain their freshness and good colouring until the first autumn frost.

One ornamental vegetable follows another. The Globe Artichoke, **Cynara scolymus**, should either be grown for eating or simply to look at: not for both at once. Gardeners with limited space are tempted to plant this in a flower border and then cut off the edible heads when right for eating, which is usually in July, just when the border should be looking its fullest and most luxuriant. It wouldn't be so bad if they would remove the entire flower stalk to the ground, but no; they wait for the side shoots as well.

Neither are the most ornamental globe artichokes the best for eating or *vice versa*. The type producing the flower heads with purple bracts wins for looks. Actually the cardoon, *Cynara cardunculus*, is an altogether more important looking and effective plant. Its grey foliage is longer (4 or 5 ft.) and more deeply cut. The inflorescences branch more and the flower heads are spikier, which improves their looks though not their handling properties. However, this is an enormous and unwieldy plant, growing 8 ft.

tall and requiring hefty stakes and tying material. Treated entirely as a foliage plant, you can cut out the flowering spikes as soon as they appear and the plant will cease to be any sort of a problem except for its propensity to swamp neighbours with its foliage. You will have to learn how near it is safe to plant to it. I suggest allowing 5 ft. for lower plants. A shrub, as it might be *Gleditsia triacanthos* 'Sunburst', which I have planted next my cardoons, will rise above them and can go a little closer if you are sure of watching that it's not overlaid in the first couple of years while still a baby.

Cardoons are reputedly not altogether hardy. My experience, at least with the strain I grow, is that once established it is absolutely hardy. I have had the same group at the back of my border for more than 20 years and I never protect it. Plant in spring.

The plant I have of **Eryngium agavifolium** came to me from Robert Poland of Brook House Nursery, Ardingly, Haywards Heath, Sussex and is a beautiful thing which I can recommend to anyone that finds the sea holly tribe fascinating. There is an evergreen group hailing from Central and South America, of which this is one (from the Argentine). The leaves and their arrangement are far more like a bromeliad's than an agave. They form a pineapple-like rosette but are slenderer with long but fine mock spines along the margins. The leaves curve over and back on themselves. They are about 2 ft. long and sea green. The branching inflorescences rise to 3½ ft. or so and are handsome, each head being large enough to make its mark, although green. *E. bromellifolium*, of gardens, is the same thing.

One I have known and grown for longer and which is my favourite of the evergreen group, is *E. pandanifolium*. It comes from Uruguay. This does make a very large plant with multiple crowns of 6-ft.-long sword leaves. The spines along their margins are short but sharp and it is advisable to wear gloves when the job of pulling old dead ones out, comes round, which it does in spring and autumn. The inflorescence does not show itself much till August but then grows to 8 ft. and is at its best throughout the autumn. Mine still looked splendid – massive yet poised and graceful – till mid-December, when the first hard frosts collapsed the flowering stems and withered the tips of most of the leaves.

The plant will look a bit of a shambles till late spring, when the young foliage is appearing and I have cleared away the old débris. Each inflorescence consists of a large quantity – perhaps a couple of hundred – tiny, half-inch-long, cone-shaped flower heads. When actually flowering they are a soft dove mauve; by no means showy but the sum effect is beautiful indeed. Seed ripens in early December, but only after a hot summer and an open autumn, as in 1969, '70 and '71. Sown the next spring in a cold frame, it germinates freely. Seedlings will be large enough to plant out the following spring.

The R.H.S. Dictionary calls this plant half hardy but it is much less tender than it looks. The only time I nearly lost my stock was in 1962–63, and even then I found a few live bits to start me off again. Once established the plant becomes so voluminous that the ground underneath it is always bone dry, even on my clay soil, and I believe this to be its principal safeguard, in frosty weather. I have never protected my group in any way. It will certainly take 20 degrees Fahrenheit of frost.

Of the hardy eryngiums that disappear in winter, *E. variifolium* grows only 2 ft. tall and very stiffly. Its leaves are green-and-white-variegated. I can't get wholly enthusiastic about this.

The herbaceous spurges can be quickly disposed of. *Euphorbia sikkimensis* is at its most beautiful in February and March when its ruby red shoots are just becoming active at the 6–12 in. level. This species does well in shade but its young shoots will be more intensely coloured if grown in an open situation, preferably so that they can be admired with back-lighting from the sun. Actually this is an awkward plant to accommodate satisfactorily in the garden. It later grows to 6 ft. at least and must be efficiently supported if included in a border, otherwise it will look a mess and get in the way of its neighbours. Most gardeners will be wise to forget about it.

The Cypress Spurge, *E. cyparissias*, can be a bit of a weed if you plant it without appreciating that it is a runner. I have it in the cracks of a path where it abuts on a wall and it is no trouble. It grows only a foot tall with slender, upright shoots clothed with narrow, glaucous foliage distinctly evocative of some conifer. The light green inflorescences are discreetly charming and the plant takes on gay tints in autumn before disappearing for the winter. If you collect spurges, you will want *E. dulcis*. It does little more throughout the summer than fill up space at the 1 ft. level, but performs a star turn for several weeks in autumn by colouring a warm (not hot) shade of orange-red.

E. myrsinites is technically shrubby, I suppose, though no more likely to be classified as such than is aubretia. It makes prostrate vegetative shoots each year from the base of the plant, on which it flowers in the following spring. After seeding, these shoots die. Its glaucous foliage is retained throughout the winter and again has coniferous intimations, this time of the monkey puzzle. This is a good plant for a sunny ledge or bank. It does not like shade. *E. biglandulosa* is not unlike. The Plantsmen call it 'the unparalleled aristocrat among spurges'. I have not grown it but from seeing it at Wisley noted its 1½ ft. height and that its leaves were coarser, less glaucous and not so closely arranged as in *E. myrsinites*. An inferior thing, in fact, but I have not seen its 'flat, golden (flower) heads in spring'.

I think I had better deal with **ferns** in a separate chapter because, although they are all foliage plants, many are quite unsuited to border life.

I have only lately been given the variegated **strawberry**, which is a sport from the cultivated, fruit-bearing *Fragaria vesca*. I cannot find it in any of my reference books or plant catalogues, so let's call it *F. vesca* 'Variegata'. Forget about fruit. It may have some but the sort of places where you'll want to grow it will make protection against birds quite impracticable. The leaves are varyingly, but often, heavily splashed with white. The splashings are not zoned; they may occur anywhere on any leaflet. The sum impact is gay, even frivolous and it lasts right through the winter. Young leaves show least variegation; it becomes bold as they mature. This appears to be rather a successful ground-coverer. It even seems to be coping with my arch-enemy, *Oxalis purpurata*. I have it at the foot of shrubs in a sunny spot but it does its stuff quite well even in their denser shade.

The natural habitat of **Glyceria maxima** 'Variegata' (alias *G. aquatica* 'Foliis-variegatis') is under water. It is a familiar ornamental of ponds where the first leaves to appear on the surface in spring are pink, but as they rise 2 or 3 ft. above it they reveal their typically bold green and white variegation (bolder and more effective than the comparable Gardeners' Garters, *Phalaris arundinacea* 'Picta'). It is an invasive plant and none too easily controlled when it has the free range of a natural pond's muddy bottom. I was just beginning to worry about what to do, when we were plagued by water voles, which completely destroyed my colony and the gardeners' garters to boot.

G. maxima 'Variegata' is a valuable border or bedding plant and remains smart right through till autumn. Here it is easy as well as wise to lift your clumps annually and re-set just a few pieces for the nest season's display.

Follows another grass, **Helictotrichon sempervirens** (syn. *Avena candida*), whose stiff steely blue foliage is arranged on a 15-in.-tall, porcupine-like hump. Its habitual air of importance relaxes, in May, when flowering stems rise to 3½ ft. and arch gracefully at their tips. Later, they should be cut away. This plant is not quite as happy on my heavy soil as I could wish. Chunks tend to rot away: it should never be monkeyed around with in autumn. It looks uncommonly well as a feature breaking an expanse of paving. A sunny position and free drainage will ensure the bluest leaf colouring and the most vigorous growth, but you should always comb through your plants with your fingers, each spring, so as to extract unsightly accumulations of dead stems and leaves.

And so we arrive at the august and fashionable genus **Hosta**, erstwhile *Funkia*. What can Lloyd say about it that has not already been said many times over? I suppose it might help to try and keep its members in perspective. For hostas have lately achieved apotheosis of a sacred-cow-like nature. They are so easy to grow, so ground-covering, so weed-suppressing, so indispensable to flower arrangers, so many things to so many people, that the fact of their having faults also and of not being the be-all and end-all of herbaceous plants in the garden, is apt to be forgotten.

Hostas are the 'leibspeis' – the favourite diet of slugs. When slugs favour a pinnate-leaved plant, the damage passes largely unnoticed. If they make a cut-leaved plant even more cut than normal, it may even be an improvement. But when a solid leaf like the hosta's is chewed up, nothing but ill can come of it. Another point about hostas (abetted by slugs) is that many go into an early decline: by the beginning of September they may already be quite repulsive and spoiling your autumn border.

However, their many virtues are real enough and I should be foolish to belittle them. One that is not always appreciated is that many hostas will thrive in a soil that is not specially water-retentive at all. And some, again, are actually better in full sun than in the shade that others prefer. In fact there is a wide variety of hostas to choose for a wide variety of situations.

Some of the green-leaved types are more essentially flowering than foliage plants. I shall not need to do more than mention *H. rectifolia*, *H. lancifolia* and *H. ventricosa*.

Of those (the majority) that are grown principally for their leaves, some make their main contribution by leaf colouring, many by leaf variegation and some by sheer size of leaf. Even those with moderately sized leaves tend to be heavyweights in the vegetable world, with a solidity that draws the eye and makes them valuable as points of focus.

The naming of hostas is extremely confusing. There is hope that it will become less so, because much useful sorting out has lately been done by the R.H.S. and more particularly by Christopher Brickell, director of the gardens at Wisley. But nomenclature is still and will long remain in a state of flux, and the fact that you know the right name (right at this moment) for the hosta you want is no guarantee that the plant so-named in a nursery catalogue will refer to the same thing.

If you want the largest possible leaf combined with the most glaucous colouring, go for *Hosta sieboldiana elegans*. (It is not so long since we were told to call this *H. glauca*, but it has gone back again.) The leaves are heart-shaped, blunt-tipped, nearly a foot across each way, in a vigorous plant, and with an attractively cross-rippled surface like a sandy beach at low tide. One does not necessarily yearn for a huge leaf. Equally attractive in its way and half the size but just as blue is *H. tokudama* (which I first had as *H. fortunei* but has also been grown in its time as *H. sieboldiana* and *H. glauca*). The flowers in neither of these hostas are of much account: borne on stumpy, crowded spikes and a washy non-colour. Be warned that many stocks of hostas are infected with virus diseases, which reduce their vigour and may cause a kind of pseudo-variegation of the leaves in two or more shades of green. This is particularly noticeable in *H. sieboldiana* and *H.s. elegans* (the former is less glaucous than the variety).

H. elata is closely related to *H. sieboldiana* and also has the largest of leaves, held on long stalks and with wavy margins, but it is not glaucous.

H. sieboldii must not be confused with *H. sieboldiana* (though of course it will be). The former is the plant we used to know as *H. albomarginata*. The white edge to its leaf is so narrow that you have to look closely to see it. This is nearly related to *H. lancifolia* and has a pretty habit but is best regarded, in the main, as a flowering plant.

H. crispula is the handsomest and most striking of the variegated hostas with large leaves: broad yet drawn to sharp points, green with a wide white margin. Young plants have miserable, quite untypical foliage and may wrongly persuade you that the nursery has supplied the wrong thing. This hosta looks ravishing when its leaves first unfold, in spring. Later, their margins are apt to become baked and papery, if exposed to sun. Some plants I have nestling beneath a *Fatsia japonica* remain in pristine condition right into September, however.

Thomas Hogg is a name used for several different hostas. Correctly it is applied to one with fairly narrow leaves in two shades of green and edged with white. It is not very exciting.

Surely far and away the best of the small-leaved variegated hostas is *H. undulata* var. *undulata*, as it should be known, but is more often, for brevity, called simply *H. undulata*. It is a low plant with narrow, pointed leaves that are very much twisted, because there is more cream-white in them than green. The green is mainly concentrated in a narrow margin but also in central streaks. In too shady a position, there will be too much green but in too much sun the leaf gets scorched. Shade but not dark shade is the recipe. *H. undulata* var. *unvittata* (also known as *H.u. medio-variegata*) is charming, too. It has a much broader and richer green margin, with a white centre to the leaf, and the foliage is not twisted.

The name of *H. fortunei* 'Albopicta' remains as we have always inappropriately known it. There is no white here at all. The broad but pointed leaves start a delicious soft yellow, in spring, edged in pale green. This is their big moment. Later they become green all over. *H.f.* 'Aurea' is pale yellow throughout the leaf, in spring.

H. ventricosa has a well variegated sport, *H.v.* 'Variegata', in which the typical heart-shaped plantain leaf has a broad yellow margin. This hasn't settled down with me yet but I think it will be good and if its flowers are up to the species' standard – racemes of violet-coloured bells – they will be worth having too. The only other one with worth-while flowers of those mentioned is *H. undulata*, with loose racemes of mauve funnels.

The flowers of *H. plantaginea* are, perhaps, its more particular attraction, but I must include this species (already mentioned in Chapter 4, p. 57) on account of its fresh yellow-green foliage. The flowers come late, not before September and seldom complete their season before cold nights or excessive damp intervene. This is a plant for a sunny position and it should probably be considered only for its foliage in the less sunny parts of these islands. Newly planted specimens are especially late in making flower buds so don't let that worry you; they'll be earlier the next year. *H. plantaginea* 'Grandiflora' is the variety most often (if not always) grown and offered, even if listed as *H. plantaginea* plain. What the difference between these two should be, I cannot say. The 1969 Supplement to the R.H.S. Dictionary says that var. *grandiflora* 'has broad perianth segments and broadly cordate leaf blades', whereas Christopher Brickell, in the R.H.S. Journal Vol. 93 (1968) p. 370, tells us exactly the opposite. Var. *grandiflora* 'differs in the narrower more elongated perianth lobes (broad ovate in the type) and the usually longer pointed, elongated foliage'.

There is a hybrid hosta with one of those loathsome folksy names, Honeybells (yes, it comes from the U.S.) that has *H. plantaginea* as one parent and inherits its scent and foliage. The flowers are white, pencilled violet. I think I shall have to swallow my disgust and get it. If the reader is wondering what the honey has to do with, we are in the same boat. The scent is of that heavy quality that is put forth only in the evening and at night and attracts moths, not bees. It has not the scent of honey. Neither does the flower look like any honey that I've ever seen – white with violet streaks. Certainly not.

The **iris**'s sword-leaves are basically a good shape and a strong contrast to broad, horizontally aligned foliage like the hosta's. Much iris foliage, and more especially in the popular bearded types, goes off nastily soon after the plants' June flowering. The old blue-flowered *Iris pallida dalmatica* retains most of its glaucous leaf colouring through the growing season.

By and large, however, it is to the irises with variegated foliage that we must look for this plant's principal contribution as it touches our subject. Strange to say, not one of them is mentioned in the Dictionary of Gardening.

The green-and-white-striped variety of our native *I. foetidissima* is outstanding because, first, it belongs to a bold 2 ft. plant; second because it is evergreen and third because it is happiest in shade and the variegation looms up particularly well in this context. The variegated *I. japonica* is also evergreen and shade loving. The leaf fans are held in an oblique plane and rise to no great height although the leaves themselves are 15 in. long. They usually have a broad cream-white strip on one side, up to the centre, and are green (in two shades) on the other. Plants increase rapidly by their exploratory rhizomes and they really need dividing and re-setting every other year at least, if the boldest foliage effect is to be obtained.

I. pallida has at least two variegated forms: a yellow, which I have seen only in Bowles's corner at Wisley, and a white which I have and love. The green is glaucous, as in *I. pallida* itself. This is deciduous, making 2-ft.-tall fans if grown on good soil. It is readily increased from the eyes along its rhizomes. 'Sells on sight' is the laconic descriptive comment against this plant in a well-known wholesale catalogue. Small wonder.

The under-water *I. laevigata* has a variegated form which I have only just been given and have not had the chance to assess while our own Wild Flag, *I. pseudacorus*, which is also a water plant, has a primrose-yellow-and-green variegated sport which is at its best when the young leaves appear in spring. Later, they change to green in the same way as *Hosta fortunei* 'Albopicta'.

Honours may be said to be equally divided between flowers and foliage in **Kirengeshoma palmata**, a member of the saxifrage family from Japan. The majority of Japanese plants are calcifuge; this one can take a certain amount of lime if the ground is made humus-rich and moist. It thrives in shade but, in the cooler parts of Britain, needs all the sun that's going, to make it flower before the end of the growing season.

The leaves are unusual in a herbaceous plant, being palmately lobed rather like a poinsettia's. They are set against black stems. The flowers start opening in early September, with me; about an inch long and shaped a little like a shuttlecock, but slightly irregular. Their colouring is soft, pale yellow. This is a plant that people do notice, although it is not showy. It is, *par excellence*, a subject for the foliage border, where its flowers will not be metaphorically killed by showy neighbours. I made the mistake of planting mine in front of a bright yellow Black-Eyed-Susan, *Rudbeckia* 'Goldsturm', and the kirengeshoma became practically invisible.

It grows about 2 ft. tall with me but almost double this height in the damper climate of Scotland.

Kniphofia caulescens, which was included in the plan in Chapter 4 (p. 55) is hardy anywhere in Britain *if* it has the right growing conditions: that is to say, extremely sharp drainage. It makes an exciting and unusual feature in the middle of a gravel walk at Crathes Castle, near Aberdeen. I planted it in one of my borders without thought or preparations, and the stodgy soil did for it in the first winter. *K. caulescens* carries typical pokers in September but its glaucous foliage is its outstanding feature. *K. northiae* is larger-leaved still, but plain green. Again, its foliage is arranged in rosettes but they are too coarse to give much pleasure.

The **dead-nettles** are useful (those that aren't weeds) and mildly pleasing though not in the front rank for excitement. But anyway, if a meal consisted entirely of oysters, caviar and pâté de foie gras, a bit of plain bread would eventually make a welcome relief.

Lamium maculatum has a green leaf – purplish in winter – with a white central flash. This is its nature and no aberration: it does not 'revert'. Its habit is to make a loose mat and it flowers gaily in spring being unashamedly magenta. There is an albino form and another, Salmoneum, with pale salmony pink flowers. Also the golden-leaved *L.m.* 'Aureum' (still with the white central flash). This is a diminutive plant and no sort of ground-coverer, but deserving a special place. Its colouring is brilliant in spring.

L. galeobdolon 'Variegatum' (or *Galeobdolon luteum* 'Variegatum') seems to be a form of our native Archangel, but this does not revert either and it comes true from seed, so perhaps it will turn out to be a species after all. It is an efficient ground-cover plant, yes, but a rampageous thug in the wrong place and not to be trusted in polite society. Its mottled leaves are prettily marbled in two shades of green. The spikes of yellow flowers appear briefly in spring. This plant spreads mainly by overground runners, which root at every node. It is useful for covering any awkward piece of ground, and more particularly in shade, though the patterning of its foliage is more distinct if a fair amount of light is available. It will even cope with dry shade.

I feel like going straight into another group of labiate thugs, the mints, but must make a brief alphabetical pause with the golden-leaved form of **Creeping Jenny**, *Lysimachia nummularia* 'Aurea'. It is well adapted to shade, but not too deep if you want a bright leaf colouring. The plant creeps about at ground level and is ideally suited, it seems to me, for linking the units in a group of ferns. It has the usual yellow flowers, in July, and they are charming.

L. ephemerum is a very different loosestrife – a 3 ft. border plant, notable for its ultra-smooth, grey-green foliage. There are spikes of whitish flowers in August, but the leaf's the thing. This is a trouble-free plant that has only lately achieved popularity, of a limited sort.

I advise the gardener herb-enthusiast to embrace each new mint that comes his way (friends are always ready to part with bits) cautiously. Many of them spread like lightning and are awkward to deal with when they get under or in between stones (as in a path or dry wall) or into the crowns of neighbouring plants that don't like being disturbed as you will have to, if matters are to be sorted out. Arthur Hellyer wrote of *Mentha gentilis* 'Aurea', recently, that he had never deliberately introduced a plant to his garden that had so quickly become a formidably invasive weed. The same with me. I have set about ridding myself of it but this will take time. The foliage, in case you're interested, is fairly small for a mint, oval, green with gold markings and the plant is not too tall: 18 in. or so. The trouble with these kinds of mints is that they soon get tired of growing where you wanted them to (dying out through congestion) but have an insatiable appetite for pastures new. They continually need re-planting.

One of the prettiest of the vigorous ones (I have just introduced it and am keeping my fingers crossed and eyes skinned) is Bowles's Grey-Leaved Mint. About 3½ ft. tall, it makes a splendid patch of grey and when its spikes of mauve flowers are out in July it looks like some veronica.

The Apple Mint, *M. rotundifolia*, with its round woolly leaves, is pleasant enough to look at though better to eat. However, *M.r.* 'Variegata' is extremely fresh and pretty and quite diminutive – only a foot tall, its green leaves liberally splashed with white. Some shoots come white all over. Others, on reverting to plain green, still look nothing like the apple mint and I suspect that they are not really connected after all. Like other culinary mints this variegated one is subject to rust disease, and this was what spoilt and nearly exterminated my stock.

One can never have too much of the little creeping peppermint, *M. requienii*. Some people mistake it for the redoubtable *Helxine soleirolii* or Mind-Your-Own-Business, but *M. requienii* is innocent of any kind of nastiness. And it smells delicious, when bruised. It has tiny leaves and a creeping habit like pearlwort (*Sagina procumbens*), with which it is nearly always associated. In sun, it flowers freely – tiny mauve things – but really it is happiest in damp shade. If you are a *laissez-faire* gardener with a shady piece of lawn that you don't treat with weed-killers, this is an ideal spot to introduce the creeping peppermint. As you tread and mow, a pungent waft from the plant will vie with the smell of oil and petrol fumes. And it is a useful pavement crack plant in awkward, shady places, Not fully hardy, however. Plant in spring. If the winter is hard, some of your stock will die out but will soon be replaced by self-sown seedlings.

The last species tempted me to stray from my purpose of discussing border plants, but I can return to the charge, pennons flying, with an indispensable genus of grasses: *Miscanthus*, formerly known as *Eulalia*. They are of a tufted, clump-forming habit, tall or very tall and upstanding but with recurved leaf tips that give them the appearance of a foliar fountain. To appreciate them as they deserve, they should be allowed to rise head and shoulders above their neighbours. A 7 ft. miscanthus should ideally have nothing higher than 4 ft. near it. These grasses have the quality and usefulness of bamboos but differ in that they die to the ground in winter. Their old stems and leaves change to a beautiful pale fawn colouring in autumn and early winter, but moult heavily in the new year and must be cut down then.

M. sacchariflorus is the giant of the genus, growing 12 ft. high when established. It does spread, slowly, by short rhizomes and, like other rhizomatous grasses, moves or divides badly in autumn; well in spring. The leaves are an inch or so wide and plain green but outward curving. This makes a stately feature. It stands up to a lot of wind in the sense of being self-supporting but its leaves can get torn to ribbons by a summer gale. If you can be bothered to strip its tired, lower leaves in late summer, the plant's general appearance is certainly improved. There are no flowers.

M. sinensis has a number of excellent cultivars of which I know and grow three. *Zebrinus*, the Zebra Grass, has green leaves with yellow cross-banding. We have already met it twice (p. 16 and p. 54). It grows 7 ft. tall in shade but develops a more marked variegation and is slightly less tall in sun. Its flowers, as with the other cultivars to be described, come in October – a sort of inverted cat-o'-nine-tails arrangement (only there are up to a score of them to a bunch), each tail crinkled with self-conscious regularity, like a newly permed coiffure. The colour is at first a lustrous coppery purple, soon changing to fluffy whiteness and pretty for use indoors with other deads.

M.s. 'Gracillimus' has narrow green leaves with a pale medial vein giving it a silvered look. It is, indeed, very graceful. *M.s.* 'Variegatus', sometimes listed as Foliis Striatis, has bold longitudinal variegation in cream and green. A fine plant, growing to 5 or 6 ft.; slightly less than the others.

The Golden **Marjoram**, *Origanum vulgare* 'Aureum' was in our plan (p. 52). It is at its freshest and brightest in spring but retains a pretty good colour throughout the summer. The leaves are arranged along their shoots in a neat rosette formation that gives a positive texture to the clump as a whole. Divide your plants in early spring, if you want to increase them.

Phalaris arundinacea 'Picta' is the old-fashioned Ribbon Grass or Gardener's Garters. The leaf blades are longitudinally striped in green and white. "Like *Miscanthus sinensis* 'Variegatus'?" you might ask. Not at all like, because this plant is a runner, not a clump-former. It makes colonies, and although not difficult to control, it has the slight stigma of a weed rather than the stamp of a hero. Don't let me put you off it, though. It has considerable charm, especially in spring and early summer. Later, when its full height of 4 ft. has been reached, it is inclined to flop around and become unsightly. You can grow it under water, for a change; no flopping there.

This plant reminds me of a claim, made by a keen gardening friend, that ornamental grasses in general exert a kind of attraction on other, weed grasses, which become embedded in their crowns or colonies and are well-nigh impossible to extract. That this happens is undeniable: my own Gardener's Garters has a grass-like sedge in it that I have never been able to eliminate. But there is no occult force at work. It is simply that grass or grass-like weeds, when they do happen to seed themselves near one of their ornamental brethren, pass unnoticed in the first instance, by reason of their similarity with the host plant. By the time you have noticed that couch or creeping soft grass or whatever, has got in, you're too late. The interlocking mesh of grass friend with grass foe defies disentanglement.

There may be room for a big chap like the ornamental **rhubarb** (all rhubarbs are, in fact, ornamental) *Rheum palmatum*, in a large border, if you can place it in the centre of an island or at the back of a one-sider, in such a way that the gap it leaves in later summer, when the bulk of its foliage dies away, passes unnoticed. This species has deeply toothed leaves, even more jagged in its variety *R.p. tanguticum*. In a good clone, the leaf, especially in youth, is flushed red and looks marvellous with the sun shining through it.

The typical rhubarb inflorescence is red, also, rising to 5 or 6 ft. It is also a fine plant for the wild garden or stream-side.

Rodgersias could be baby rheums, but in fact they belong to the saxifrage family and are a most beautiful genus of foliage plants. Being deciduous helps them avoid that leathery coarseness that is evident in their cousins the bergenias.

Their young leaves, in spring, are unbelievably fresh: so tender, indeed, as to be easily blackened by late frosts, but this does not matter any more than a frost on bracken. Within days, the strong root and rhizome system is ready with a fresh crop. Rodgersias are as efficient ground cover as hostas. Likewise, only more so, they enjoy moist conditions. The two types of plant look well together. Some shade is an advantage, especially to *Rodgersia tabularis*, whose great platter leaves can scorch in the June sun. This species has disc-shaped leaves and is a fresh and tender green, most of all when young. The others tend towards bronzed complexions, markedly so in R. *podophylla*, with a palmate leaf whose leaflets are shaped like a webbed foot. R. *aesculifolia*, as its name suggests, has a leaf like a horse chestnut's. None of these three species flower particularly freely; when they do, it is with a white, paniculate inflorescence like an astilbe's.

R. *pinnata* is a variable species; the fact of its leaves being pinnate rather than palmate is not always obvious. In one form, the leaves are green and the flowers white. But there are gradations in which the flowers are dusky pink even verging on red, and the darker the flower the darker also are the leaves, especially in their young state. I had a beautiful pink form from Maurice

23. Adjacent portions of the same piece of my garden. ABOVE, the vigorous *Canna indica* 'Purpurea' with its large plain leaves contrasts well with the glaucous pinnate foliage of *Melianthus major*, though the latter, as here shown, is a good deal smaller than is typical (I had been taking cuttings). This canna does not flower effectively and some gardeners prefer to remove its inflorescences as they appear. BELOW, another form of the grass, *Miscanthus sinensis*. This one, Variegatus, has pale longitudinal stripes and grows only 4 or 5 ft. tall, which is rather less than Zebrinus and Gracillimus. To right front, *Helichrysum splendidum* (see Plate 6).

Mason. It flowers freely on 3½ ft. stems and then contrives to be as charming and colourful (though gradually becoming darker) after flowering as it is at the time. The plant is a good do-er and spreads by underground rhizomes. Darkest of all is R.*p.* 'Superba', but it is slow to make headway.

There are several **saxifrages** for general garden use that might be described as foliage plants. *Saxifraga stolonifera* has long been grown (as *S. sarmentosa*) for ground cover under greenhouse staging. It has accumulated a number of popular names of which Mother of Thousands is the favourite. Considering how hardy and accommodating it is, growing happily in dark places under evergreen shrubs where you would be unlikely to think of planting anything at all, I cannot imagine why we don't see more of it. The leaves are evergreen, borne in loose rosettes; fleshy, almost round, marbled with pale green along the veins and dark in between. The plant spreads by overground runners, with plantlets at the ends. It flowers on 1 ft. sprays in June and looks quite different from London Pride (*S. umbrosa*), with which one might excusably compare it, in that the flowers are zygomorphic, with 3 short upper petals and 2 longer lower ones. There is a variegated form, Tricolor, in pink, green and white, but this, alas, is neither as vigorous nor as hardy and is best cherished in a pot.

Similar to *S. stolonifera*, almost if not quite as hardy and more excitingly coloured is *S. cuscutiformis*. The areas between the pale green veining are in this case purple and the leaf undersides and stalks are a bright reddish purple. I must admit, however, that at this moment in midwinter, *S. stolonifera* is looking the more relaxed and effective plant. The specific epithet *cuscutiformis* refers to the pinkish purple, thread-like runners which are similar in appearance to the stems of dodder, *Cuscuta*, a genus of parasitic plants of which we have two native species.

The glossy, rounded leaves of *S. fortunei* are deciduous and borne on clump-forming plants. They are typically a nondescript

24. The young foliage of *Rhododendron hodgsonii* (photographed in late June) has a silvery sheen on it. Given shelter and moisture, this species makes a magnificent tree-shrub and is always a pleasure to look at regardless of what flowers it may produce.

brownish colour underneath, but vivid purple in Wada's Variety. A foaming mass of irregularly shaped white flowers makes a welcome appearance in October. They are more freely and effectively borne on the type-plant, which has greater vigour than Wada's form. A cool shady place for this one.

There is a variegated London Pride: *S. umbrosa* 'Variegata' or 'Variegata Aurea', with yellow spots on the leaves, which are evergreen, borne in dense rosettes like the type-plant. Sometimes this is attractive, sometimes repulsive, and I have yet to find out or make up my mind why it veers between these two conditions and how to prevent the unattractive alternative. I fancy that sun promotes an unhealthy, jaundiced cast and that light shade will encourage a deeper green background against which yellow spots stand out acceptably.

The variegated **Figwort** is usually referred to *Scrophularia nodosa* but should undoubtedly be ascribed to *S. aquatica*. The ovate leaves have wavy margins which are deeply variegated in cream and/or white. The plant grows 3 or 4 ft. tall in a season, branching vigorously. The flowering shoots need to be pinched out as they form, since they have no kind of merit and detract from the foliage.

This is a difficult plant to assess. It can look fine or it can look a fright and in both cases it may be perfectly healthy, for it is easily pleased on any reasonably moist soil, in sun or in shade. Obviously it tends to look its best in spring and early summer, before any inclination to run to flower becomes insistent, but in an open position by a stream I have seen it still in prime condition in September. Pests certainly make heavy inroads on its complexion: notably capsid bugs and the mullein shark caterpillar, but probably slugs are every bit as damaging as either, in the long run. The plant dies back in winter to a basal tuft of large evergreen leaves.

The **sedums** or stonecrops are succulents. Hardy plants with fleshy leaves being the exception rather than the rule, they contribute a kind of foliage that we shall not find elsewhere.

The first plant I have it in mind to discuss is sometimes called *Sedum spectabile* 'Variegatum', sometimes *S. telephium* 'Variegatum'. Perhaps it has a bit in it of both species. Its leaves are streaked in pale blue-green and cream. I like it at close range but consider its colouring too indeterminate to constitute a highlight. Neither do the pale pink flower heads help. With its glaucous leaves and flower buds, the old ice plant, *S. spectabile* itself, has far more to contribute, in a border, before ever it flowers. This is a stiff plant and incongruous in one's and two's. It needs massing in a large setting and then looks like a pink floral eiderdown at the height of its August-September season. It has become fashionable in certain quarters to decry its pink flower colouring as crude, so let me here record that I enjoy it. Bees and butterflies flock to this species.

I have described the purple-leaved *Sedum maximum* 'Atropurpureum' (p. 53) and will only add that slugs can make a visual mess of its foliage.

S. sieboldii is usually seen as a small, trailing pot plant on a window sill, but it is hardy (the variegated sport, less so). Its leaves are glaucous with purplish red margins and they are arranged in threes to form circles round the stems. Each stem grows about 6 in. long so this is really a rock garden or ledge plant.

S. rosea, Rose Root (often listed as *S. rhodiola*), is large enough to take its place at the edge of a border. It has the look of a spurge, being not unlike *Euphorbia myrsinites* in its glaucous leaf colouring and yellow terminal flower heads. But the habit is arching rather than prostrate. The plant is dioecious but for looks when flowering there's little to choose between males and females. This is one of our most attractive wild flowers, usually sited on dramatic rock ledges; often on sea cliffs in association with thrift (*Arenaria maritima*) but also on base-rich mountains together with the vivid blue *Myosotis alpestris* and the pink cushions of *Silene acaulis*.

Now that gardeners have become grass-conscious, a stream of new ornamental species and varieties is reaching us and bids fair to continue to do so for many years. They are not really new, in most cases, but because of a sharpened eye in their direction, they are being much more freely circulated.

Such is *Spartina pectinata* 'Aureo-marginata' (or *S. michauxiana* 'Aureo-marginata'). Its height, when established, ranges between 4 and 6 ft. It is stately and self-supporting with ribbon-like leaves striped yellow along the margins and mid-rib; green in between. It spreads by rhizomes and wants watching.

Stachys lanata is a very old favourite among the greys, extensively used for edging. Lamb's Lugs is one of its popular names; I won't run through the rest. Its oval leaves are thickly felted. It is a worthy plant that I find a little boring. In early summer it begins to run up to flower and the young stems are beautiful, though their height may be unwelcome. They subsequently become dishevelled, gawky and stemmy and have to be removed. However there is a clone called Silver Carpet which doesn't flower, or very little.

S. lanata needs frequent division and re-planting, to keep it looking smart – every year, for preference; every other at least. It is subject to mildew (especially in the Silver Carpet clone) and this can make the foliage unsightly just when it should be looking its whitest.

Tellima grandiflora has been socially acclaimed through the flower arrangers' movement. Here is yet another member of the saxifrage family, its nearest relative, I suppose, being the heuchera, but it is a far more obliging and easily pleased plant. Its mound of basal rounded leaves with scalloped margins is evergreen, taking on bronzed tints in winter and positively purple in the clone called Purpurea. Slender stems of green flowers are borne at the 2 ft. level in May and June. The plant is modest to a fault. You might crush an acre of it beneath the soles of your unheeding feet, before realising what carnage you had wrought.

CHAPTER 8

Ferns

*

GARDENING books quite frequently, nowadays, include a chapter on ferns, and although Graham Thomas in *Plants for Ground-Cover* starts his, discouragingly, with the bald statement 'Ferns are out of fashion', I think there is plenty of evidence that they are coming back. It is true that ferns don't flower in the ordinary sense, although their spore-bearing fronds have a decorative harmony that is appreciated by flower arrangers (on which see *Garden Foliage for Flower Arrangement* by Sybil Emberton). Lack of flowers, however, is no deterrent to the gardener whose tastes have reached out beyond the gay colours of the florists' dahlias and gladioli.

The ferns' great strength lies not so much in their colouring – any other leaves may be as fresh – as in their form: the delicate and sometimes intricate patterns created by a pinnately divided leaf. And these leaves or fronds, as we also know them, are often borne in a circle about the growing point of the parent rhizome, which is in itself a congenial and orderly arrangement. Others make a carpet of fronds, a sward, a feather-bed as inviting, in its way, as any bank where the wild thyme blows.

Ferns are good shade plants. Some enjoy sun as well, prefer it even, but most reach their maximum luxuriance in moist shade. Because of the moisture factor, they do better in the humid climate of the west and north of these islands than in the comparatively arid east. But we too can make most of them happy by enriching their soil with water-holding humus and by irrigating them if need be.

Some ferns grow excellently under trees. Others grow even better in shade that is cast by trees without actually being under their drip. A border under a north wall is good in the same way. Many can take their place in mixed borders such as we have already discussed and shall be considering again. You can (and this makes for ease of cultivation) give over an entire border to ferns but I don't fancy this idea myself: contrasts in form (as it might be of ferns with bergenias) are more effective.

The clump-forming ferns – athyriums, dryopteris, polystichums – have such a beautiful and regular habit, that neighbouring plants should never be allowed to jostle them. You can ensure this by arranging that they stand (like certain grasses I mentioned, such as *Miscanthus*) head and shoulders above the surrounding vegetation. There may, of course, be tall shrubs or trees above them, but in their own layer you will concentrate on lowly companions such as winter aconites, violets, crocuses and snowdrops; lilies-of-the-valley, lungworts (*Pulmonaria*), Creeping Jenny, cyclamen, *Hacquetia epipactis* (ha! you weren't expecting that) and primroses. Anything on their own level like Solomon's Seal or candelabra primulas, hellebores, *Danaë racemosa* or sarcococcas – will compete, not merely in a physical sense but visually, for your attention.

Some of the small ferns can be happily accommodated in the cracks of retaining walls or in the cracks of ordinary mortared walls whose mortar is crumbling (but they will probably have to sow themselves in these, as deliberate planting is difficult); also in paving cracks and in the risers of garden steps. And I am sorry to say that the moist and shaded side of a rock garden, abhorrent a garden feature though this usually is, may prove the happiest spot, both visually and culturally, for some of the lower, mat-forming ferns.

Boggy ground, pond- or stream-side will suit certain ferns that do not insist (as most do) on sharp drainage. Let us start there. The pond-side fern to beat all others is *Osmunda regalis*. It is a native, sorely depleted by collectors. I was thrilled on 'discovering' my first wild colony along both banks of a short piece of river connecting two lochs in north-west Scotland. I later learned that the habitat was, as I might have guessed, well known to everyone within many miles' radius. The colony, sad to say, is steadily wasting – not through human agency direct but through repeated nibbling by sheep.

On good soil (it must be lime-free) with its toes in water, the royal fern will grow 4 ft. tall easily and not just in the rain-soaked west. Old colonies by the lake at Scotney Castle, in Kent, are as large as any I have seen. You should not plant this (or any other) fern so that its crown is covered with water at any time in the year. I made this mistake and my plant just existed without progressing until I moved it up on to the bank above my pond. There was a certain amount of shade from trees and scrub above the osmundas I found wild, but this fern is perfectly happy in a fully exposed position. Its enormous sterile leaves are bipinnate and there are separate spore-bearing leaves that unfold 'into lacy scrolls and arabesques', as Sybil Emberton describes them.

The lakeside osmunda clumps at Scotney are in effective association with two ferns that I will take next because they, too, are as happy in sun as in shade, provided there is plenty of moisture available. I doubt if *Onoclea sensibilis* would do in a stagnant bog but it will grow in very wet turf where there is some movement in the water. It comes from North America and is absolutely hardy but is called the Sensitive Fern, as Reginald Kaye tells us in his book *Hardy Ferns* (indispensable to any enthusiast), because its fronds wither away at the first suspicion of frost. This is a vigorous runner and better, therefore, in a semi-wild setting than in a border where the appearance of its fronds here, there and everywhere may be a bit of a nuisance. The fronds are borne singly and are of two kinds: the sterile ones are the more conspicuous, upright, pinnate, about 2 ft. tall and a very fresh green. The pinnae are quite broad but with deeply indented margins.

The Shuttlecock or Ostrich Feather Fern, *Matteuccia struthiopteris* (often met as *Struthiopteris germanica*) is as freely running, its branching rhizomes just below the soil surface, but its showy sterile fronds are carried in a ring like the feathers in a shuttlecock. At maturity, one set of fronds is inclined to overlap and have its design masked by another, but their separate identity is most distinct in spring, before they are full-grown. These leaves are lacy and may be 5 ft. tall but are more usually about 3 ft. The stiff fertile fronds arise inside the ring of sterile ones and are scarcely noticed in summer but come into their own in winter when they stand up erect though dead by now but handsome in a field of snow, whereas the rest of the foliage has withered completely away.

If it has insufficient moisture in the growing season, this fern begins to look distressed with browning of its fronds, long before autumn's arrival.

Both the last two ferns need plenty of space in which to make large colonies. I will move on to two colonisers on a smaller scale: the Oak Fern, *Gymnocarpium* (*Thelypteris*) *dryopteris* and the Beech Fern *Thelypteris phegopteris*. Both are natives, commonly found in mountainous districts and calcifuge. Both, on a suitably moist and humus-rich soil, will run about and make a delightful sward of fronds at the 1 ft. level. Neither, as far as I can see, has the slightest leaf resemblance to oak or beech.

The Oak Fern, in the wild, is usually in a shaded spot, as by a steep-sided burn or among large scree boulders. I have established it under *Buddleia alternifolia*, with plenty of peat incorporated and I hand-water it a good deal in the summer. It is quite happy though rather on the dwarf side. Its leaves are broadly triangular but thrice divided and the freshest green imaginable. The beech fern grows with me in a soggy border next (and shaded by) the spreading *Fuchsia exoniensis*. Its pinnate fronds are more narrowly triangular than the last and they settle down, in early middle age, to a lack-lustre shade of green but this is a pretty thing, all the same.

Blechnum tabulare from the Falkland Islands and Tierra del Fuego is our first evergreen to come under review, and I have therefore been able to help myself to a sample from the winter garden. I introduce it here because, again, it is a runner and makes a carpet with its dark green, leathery fronds (copper-coloured when young). They are once pinnate only and the margins of the pinnae are waved and turned under so that their upper surfaces are convex and rippling. The rachis (or leaf stalk) is grooved and hollow and tends to get kinked when it has been weighted by snow.

This fern is tolerant of many conditions but will be only 15 in. or so tall in sun and ordinary soil, whereas in moist shade it may rise to 4 ft.; 2 ft. is fairly average, a colony's potential height being reduced by the oblique angle at which the fronds are held.

Blechnum penna-marina, from New Zealand, is diminutive, its sterile fronds barely two inches long and held obliquely or horizontal. They are pinnate and the stumpy pinnae have rounded tips. The slender fertile fronds are twice as long and rise vertically. With their bronzed colouring, they make a marked contrast. *B. penna-marina* runs. I have it growing round a *Cyclamen neapolitanum* at the edge of a lawn and it has blended with the grass in the turf. It is worth a special place like a stone sink.

Adiantum venustum, my last professional runner, belongs to the genus of maidenhair ferns but unlike many maidenhairs is perfectly hardy. It forms a carpet of the most elegant, much branched fronds, only 6 in. or less, tall. The stems are like thin black wire; the leaflets equilaterally triangular, except that the distal side of the triangle, which is the end of the leaflet, is slightly rounded. This species is barely evergreen; the fronds are still alive in February, as I write, but charmingly bronzed. It was a woodland plant as I have seen it in the wild (Kashmir).

The other adiantum that I grow in my garden is *A. pedatum*, from North America. This is deciduous, more or less clump-forming though its range does gradually increase by rhizome activity; about a foot tall or more in a damp climate. It is a ravishing beauty with black stems that open into an arc on which pinnate blades are distributed fanwise – much the same arrangement as in *Helleborus foetidus*. The plant is hardy but must have shade and moisture. The delicate-textured leaves are easily burnt.

Come to think of it, there is another runner that I must hurriedly smuggle in: dear old polypody, *Polypodium vulgare*, one of the commonest of all our native ferns. I feel rather hurt on its behalf that John Raven, in *A Botanist's Garden* stigmatises it as 'the most undistinguished of all British ferns'! I love it. It has such a pretty way of growing, whether rather sparsely on a tree butt or branch, or in a great curtain as I have it on a certain shady wall. I can't be sure it was never planted but I'm pretty certain it just came, and worked its way down the wall face from an original position on top. If it weren't in such a shaded position, I would include a photograph of it as it is now, in February, looking splendidly evergreen. In April and May it does admittedly become tatty as the old fronds slowly wither.

The leaf blades are rather more than a foot long, simply pinnatifid, with large rusty spore patches (sori) making a pattern on the undersides. There are many garden varieties of polypody, with variously elaborated designs, and they are often beautiful, especially the crested forms.

I would hazard that, next to bracken, *Blechnum spicant* is the commonest fern in the British Isles, although found only in acid soil. But it is still worth bringing into the garden. Like other blechnums, it is evergreen and it has separate and distinct fertile and sterile fronds. The habit of the plant is more or less clumpy; it may be quite dwarf in open situations, or 18 in. and 2 ft. tall in damp woodland. The pinnate barren fronds are like a larger version of *B. penna-marina*, outward spreading, while the stiff but slender fertile, spore-bearing fronds rise in the centre of the clump in telling contrast. If you can site this on a low ledge which is yet moist and, for preference shady, it will display its charms to perfection.

The commonest woodland ferns are the Lady and the Male. Both have countless cultivars with variously crested, subdivided, reduced or enlarged fronds; some good, some unbalanced or distorted. One wants to develop a critical eye, in respect of these, and to remember that ferns in general must retain elegance and poise. Without these qualities they are nothing, however clever and intricate their design.

Dryopteris filix-mas is the common Male Fern, particularly beautiful when its fronds are unfurling in May and June, but remaining in good fettle until finally withered in mid-December. The fronds are arranged in a circle about the crowns of thick rhizomes, and rise to 3 or 3½ ft. This fern seeds itself all over the garden and one has to be firm. Nearly related and with a similar bipinnate leaf is *D. borreri* (another native), but it has a stiffer frond of greater substance and is habitually evergreen. Grown side by side with *D. filix-mas* in a dry spot, however, I find that it has markedly less vigour.

D. dilatata (or *D. austriaca*) grows naturally in my garden and is much more elegant than most of its tribe, with broad, spreading triangular fronds and narrow pinnules offset by dark stems. One position it has chosen for itself is particularly happy: between the back of a garden seat and the yew hedge behind it.

The Lady Fern, *Athyrium filix-femina*, is always graceful, with broad lacy fronds that arch outwards so that their tips often touch the ground. It grows 2 or 3 ft. high and is a common wild plant. This is deciduous.

Then the Shield ferns: natives again, more in the west but also round us. *Polystichum aculeatum*, the Hard Shield Fern, and *P. setiferum*, the Soft Shield Fern, have given rise to some of the best of all cultivars for garden use. In particular I recommend *P.a.* 'Bevis'. To quote Mr Kaye, who sets it in a class by itself, 'the graceful fronds have elongated divisions of a silky texture, the pinnae near the frond tip curving together to form a tail'. This grows about 3 ft. tall and, like other polystichums, is evergreen.

In the *P. setiferum* group, I should recommend starting with Acutilobum and with one of the plumose types. *P.s.* 'Acutilobum' (or 'Proliferum') has elongated, obliquely held fronds, often with a slight twist to them, bipinnate, the pinnules hard in texture and sharp in outline but with spaces between them that make up a perforated frond. It is lined with bulbils along the central rachis. Pin a frond down on a box of soil in a close frame, and you will get a score of babies.

So too with the plumose soft shield fern I have, *P.s.* 'Plumoso-divisilobum', in which the broad fronds are so much divided as to create bright green, mossy platforms. If you can perch these *P. setiferum* cultivars up a bit, it helps a lot in setting them off. A border margin is sometimes built up with a few courses of narrow stones, for instance, and if this is crowned with a polystichum you will have a feature to delight you on every day of the year.

I wrote earlier that ferns are less effective when herded together than when set apart with, or above, plants having a different type of leaf form. The exception to this is the Hart's-tongue, *Phyllitis scolopendrium*, whose simple, undivided strap-leaves are so markedly different from all other ferns that they cannot help but contrast with them.

Once you have hart's-tongues in your garden, they will be everywhere, and very welcome at that. When they grow in a damp border, their fronds are 2½ ft. long and lush, but they will also appear in cracks in old walls and be quite tiny plants there. I'm not so keen on the crested hart's-tongues but there are two very beautiful old cultivars in which the entirety of the leaf has not been sacrificed. *P.s.* 'Undulatum' has gently waved margins while in *P.s.* 'Crispum' they are more tightly pleated and crimped.

To end this chapter, let us take a look at some small ferns that are especially suitable for growing in vertical cracks – in addition to polypody and the hart's-tongue.

The steps in our garden are in some places built up with tiles, laid flat, in others with narrow stones. Neither material is cemented and both form an ideally cool root run in which the maidenhair and black spleenworts, *Asplenium trichomanes* and *A. adiantum-nigrum*, have established. Both are evergreen. The former has bipinnate leaves, but the tufted habit and black stems of the once-pinnate *A. adiantum-nigrum* makes it the more telling plant. It often grows in the rotten plaster of old walls, flattening itself against the wall face in star-fish style. Another spleenwort that colonises old walls is wall rue, *A. ruta-muraria*, but this is one that you'll either inherit or not. It would be difficult to establish in cold blood.

Rusty Back, *Ceterach officinarum*, also grows in our steps, though sparingly. It likes a moister climate. Its leaves are simply pinnate, very rounded and entirely covered on their undersides with a rust of brown scales. In periods of drought, the leaves shrivel away and the plant virtually disappears, but returns to life with the advent of better (wetter) days.

The Holly Fern, *Polystichum lonchitis*, is quite different from members of the genus already described. It has a 9-in.-long, evergreen pinnate leaf of harsh texture, but often with a subtle curve or double curve to it. The leaflet margins are toothed and I suppose this is where the somewhat far-fetched comparison with holly comes in. The leaves are borne in a loose rosette and the plant is at its best in a cool, vertical, wall crack. It is calcicole.

The Parsley Fern is calcifuge, however, otherwise I would try it in a wall too. It looks a bit silly at the front of a border, as I have it now. This is *Cryptogramma crispa*. It naturally grows in scree and looks extremely fetching like that, and well named, having the fresh green of parsley as well as the crimped foliage. This is a deciduous fern, about 6 in. tall and upright growing but able to creep a bit with its rhizomes.

CHAPTER 9

Mobiles and Ephemerals

*

WE now come to the main ingredients among garden impermanencies. These are the plants that will elicit an interested enquiry from visitors to my garden, swiftly followed by a disappointed 'Oh, it's an annual is it?', or 'If it's not hardy it's no good to me.' After continual repetition, I get bored and disappointed myself with this sort of reaction. One finally has the impression that no gardeners any longer have a greenhouse or a cold frame even, and that none of them know how to sow a seed. 'I haven't the time' or, more impersonally, 'of course one hasn't the time, nowadays' is the way they put it, although Saturdays as well as Sundays are non-work days for most of society and there are longer holidays and more leisure than ever before.

Often, where annuals, biennials and tender perennials are concerned, it's really a question not so much of time involved but of knowing what to do; how and when to do it.

But why be bothered anyway, when there are so many good shrubs and hardy plants available – far more than we can ever hope to grow? Well, there is a special kind of luxuriance about many tender plants. It is this very lushness that makes them tender. But they have a professional aptitude for making summer seem summery. If we always want to be reminded that we are at Latitude 52 degrees, not so very far from the North Pole, then we can surround ourselves with heathers, whose spartan needle leaves appear capable of enduring whatever blizzards the ice gods care to unleash.

However, there are times in summer when the wind drops; when morning mist disperses in steam as the sun breaks through and you can almost hear the vegetable world stretching itself complaisantly and basking with pleasure. At such times (and at all others) I can gladly dispense with heather – there is plenty on the moors at no great distance if I want it. Flowers like gazanias, that visibly respond to and communicate an infectious delight in the panoply of summer; foliage of fragile, clammy texture that will obviously be dashed to tatters under the conditions that obtain for most of the year, but that is now, at least and at last, free to indulge in a natural and uninhibited luxuriance: these are the companions of my choice in the dog days.

Some of the annuals and biennials I shall mention are of a much tougher fibre: they raise fewer problems and offer minor rewards.

Tropical bedding as practised in London, in spas and at seaside resorts is probably the most repulsive manifestation of the 'parks and gardens' mentality. None of us, individually, can afford to do it (only collectively, as ratepayers) but none, I should hope, would want to. It is almost invariably a fussy mess with far too much incident, too many colours, too many variegated foliage plants, too small groups or spots of any one kind.

In our own gardens, all we need to do is to include a few of the most telling ingredients and work patches (generous patches, if need be) of them in among the hardies. The fact that they have to be removed at the end of the season need not distress us. Rather should we think, on autumn's arrival and as we make our next year's plans, how pleasant it is that we can do everything differently on each future occasion and experiment happily with our mobiles without the necessity for any greater upheaval than we any way expect as we set about our tasks of renewal and removal each spring and autumn.

I shall not take this section alphabetically, but shall break it down so as to consider, first, the perennials, then biennials and lastly annuals, or perennials normally treated as annuals.

Dahlias and cannas can be taken together as both are tender perennials that are stored in winter, in a dormant state.

The great drawback to most dahlias is their clumsy and undistinguished foliage. But there is one exception: Bishop of Llandaff. I remember the dahlia breeder, Mr Harry Stredwick, telling me that he didn't think it was a dahlia at all, and he said this with disgust. Properties that recommend it to one kind of gardener are just those properties that condemn it to another. Its foliage is purple and so cut up as to look like a fern's. The flowers are semi-single and red. There are other dahlias with bronzed leaves but this, by itself, is not good enough. One must have form as well. Bishop of Llandaff has a robust constitution. It carries virus diseases but is not crippled by them. It makes huge tubers and there are no overwintering problems in any cool, frost-free place. You can raise it from seed and then sort out the seedlings for those you like best.

The best cannas for foliage are also bronze-leaved. It is difficult to run down exactly what one wants, here. In the days when they sold tender bedding perennials, Hillier's used to list an ideal variety called Egandale. Alas, I lost it through carelessness in the 1963 winter. Its leaves, instead of being broadly ovate and lax, were spikily lanceolate and upward pointing. Its red flowers were tiny and of no consequence. This eliminated any kind of disappointment in advance, because large-flowered cannas are fragile and very much at the mercy of the season. Egandale was always dependable and strong-growing, to 6 ft. However, there is a canna clone going around – they call it *Canna indica* 'Purpurea' at Kew – that is near the wild type and has good purple leaves, though broader than Egandale's. It is vigorous and increases rapidly. I am thinking of growing it as a background to white Japanese anemones, next summer.

Of the large-flowered, purple-leaved types, two of the best are Wyoming, with apricot-orange flowers, and the red King Humbert.

Cannas perennate by their fleshy rhizomes and the safest way to overwinter them, I find, is by boxing them up in old potting soil, putting them in a cool frost-free chamber, like a cellar, and watering just once a week, so as to prevent the rhizomes from shrivelling. You can transport them bodily, boxes and all, to a greenhouse in spring, to start them growing. Even a cold frame will do (it has to, with me), but then I shouldn't move them into it till April. The great thing, at this stage, is not to over-water. Until there is strong root action, cannas can't take a lot of moisture; it just rots them.

Next to consider a fistful of perennials that are normally overwintered by rooting cuttings from the old plants, in autumn, and bringing these through the cold months under frost-protected glass.

I have already expatiated on *Senecio leucostachys* with other shrubby members of its genus (see p. 102). Similar in having grey foliage and a rambling habit is *Helichrysum petiolatum*, which I should designate the most valuable of all grey foliage plants, notwithstanding its lack of hardiness. Planted on the level, it will spread 2 or 3 ft. in every direction in the course of a growing season, threading its way through the stems of neighbouring plants. Planted in a tub, trough or window box, it will cascade over the edge (breaking the hard line of its container's rim) and then flow outwards. Wind may twist its branches in this exposed position, but scarcely ever breaks them. If you want this versatile plant to achieve height, put a cane in the soil near its middle and tie a shoot to this. As the shoot grows, keep on clipping it to the cane with stem ties. This way it will grow 3 or 4 ft. tall and will make horizontal side-branches like a little tree.

The felted white leaves are heart-shaped, about an inch across and long, but smaller on old plants than on young. Some people keep their old plants through the winter but young stock is more vigorous and takes up far less storage space. I take my cuttings in the second half of October, about 8 to a 3½ in. pot. When they have rooted, in an unheated cold frame, I transfer the pot to my greenhouse which is heated only just enough to exclude frost. Cuttings of these tender plants come through the winter much better if left in the pots they were struck in, than if potted separately as soon as they have rooted. And, of course, they occupy 7 or 8 times less of the valuable space on your greenhouse bench. In late March, I do at last pot them off in John Innes No. 2 compost and the weather is then warm enough to allow them to go straight into a cold frame. They are ready for use in their summer quarters in May. There is now a very attractive pale yellow-leaved form of *H. petiolatum* in circulation. Its one disadvantage is that the leaves may scorch if it is allowed to go short of water in hot weather. This can happen to the grey type-plant, too, but shows less.

H. microphyllum has much tinier leaves, closely set on lax stems.

25. ABOVE, the Shuttlecock or Ostrich Feather fern, *Matteuccia struthiopteris*, is deciduous.   BELOW, the evergreen *Polystichum setiferum* 'Acutilobum' is one of many beautiful cultivated forms of our native shield ferns.

26. Two striking but tender foliage plants for bedding out. ABOVE, *Coprosma repens* 'Variegata'.   BELOW, the strongly aromatic *Plectranthus coleoides* 'Variegatus', of a trailing habit.

One gives it the same treatment as *H. petiolatum*, although it is a shade hardier. It is apt to look a little lost in a mixed border planting, though I do use it this way, but it is excellent in ornamental pots and tubs.

The most beautiful of grey leaves – I would back them against all comers – are worn by *Centaurea gymnocarpa*. They are bipinnatifid, nearly a foot long when mature and 3½ in. across, marvellously lacy and carried in very loose rosettes that yet retain just sufficient identity to give the plant a purposeful and self-possessed air. As it happens, my old plants have overwintered exceptionally well to date (St Valentine's Day) and I have a handsome leaf sample before me, but hardiness is not to be relied upon. Always take a potful of cuttings, in September, just in case. They will overwinter safely in a cold frame.

This is a chunky shrub, really, and not a rambler – about 2 ft. high and a little more across. In public gardens you see it misused as a dot plant in a molten waste of scarlet salvias. I suggest grouping three in a triangle at the front of your mixed border. I often have the little pink penstemon Evelyn next to mine.

The centaurea's flowers are mauve thistly things and totally unacceptable, to borrow a trades union phrase. They appear in late spring and early summer. If the shoots bearing them are conscientiously removed, the centaurea eventually decides that it prefers life as a foliage plant after all, and behaves like one for the rest of the year.

Some seed firms offer this and I once raised a batch of seedlings, but they ran to flower forthwith and refused to settle down in the required manner. Better, in this respect, is *C. rutifolia*, more often offered as *C. candidissima*. It is reasonably hardy on light soil and more effective in its second year than in its first. The leaves are grey and pinnatifid but not so elegant as *C. gymnocarpa*.

From grey to blue. Sea green, really. The foliage plant I dote on more than any (at least, when I'm thinking about it) is *Melianthus major*. It is a shrub and, if not cut down by frost (in Cornwall, for instance) can grow 10 ft. tall. Used for bedding out or as a plant that gets cut to the ground in winter but will spring up from the base, one can expect it to reach to 4 ft. by the autumn. The pinnate leaves are about a foot long, but can be more and the leaflets are handsomely toothed. The plant has such distinction as to win universal admiration.

Nowadays, I leave my old stock outside and cover the ground with a thick layer of male fern fronds, in December, using the old melianthus stems as a fixing. Young shoots come up from below ground level fairly late in spring. I also take cuttings in autumn, and these, planted out in spring, will be more forward and make taller plants than old stock left in the garden.

Cuttings can be taken from the fleshy terminal shoots on strongly growing plants, made in August or September, but this does spoil the look of the plants from which they were taken. You can very often find some shoots from low down, even from below ground level, appearing in the autumn, and these make first rate cutting material.

There is a glaucous-leaved grass, *Arundo donax*, whose white-striped form, Versicolor (alias variegata), is twice as beautiful but, alas, twice as tender. Its ribbon leaves are widely spaced on an upright stem (to 3 ft. usually), broad at the base but tapering finely. The white striping is very broad and bold. This plant likes thoroughly wet conditions in the growing season but the safest course, in autumn, is to lift it bodily, with as little root disturbance as possible. Box (or pot) it up and keep it on the dry side in a greenhouse. Propagation can be by division in spring, but this is tricky and if not done carefully (and I'm not sure what carefully means in this case) may lead to loss of your entire stock (as has happened to mine). On the other hand, old stems not infrequently branch in a surprisingly un-grass-like manner and you can use the side-shoots as cuttings.

The tropical bedding that is practised in many public gardens includes a wealth of variegated plants of a peculiarly fidgety and, in the aggregate, repulsive kind. Virus-infected abutilons (of the mallow tribe) with a hectic mottling in green and yellow, are among the worst offenders. From one such source, however, I have received a plant I do like: a variegated form of the Mexican Cigar Plant, *Cuphea ignea* (syn. *C. platycentra*). The lanceolate leaves are mottled green and yellow, here too, and I shouldn't be surprised if a virus were the cause, but the leaves being small, the effect is quite pretty and there are plenty of the usual cigar flowers: ½ in.-long scarlet tubes 'charred' at the mouth in black and white. The plant grows 15 or 18 in. tall and has a relaxed and diffuse habit, mixing pleasantly with *Senecio leucostachys* and *Helichrysum microphyllum*.

Another good parks plant is *Plectranthus coleoides* 'Variegatus'. I suspect that this one has got around only recently. I had never seen it until 1970, and it is not included even in the latest supplement to the R.H.S. Dictionary. It is a trailing plant not unlike the trailing variegated ground ivy, *Glechoma* (*Nepeta*) *hederacea* 'Variegata', that is used in hanging baskets. But the shoots in the plectranthus are more substantial and the 2-inch-wide, heart-shaped leaves with crenate margins are thick: green in the middle with a broad, bold white margin. This is excellent both for bedding and for pot-work.

There are a number of zonal pelargoniums (which are the bedding 'geraniums') with variegated foliage that are the staple diet for summer bedding purposes in all public gardens. They are often jumbled up together and a less appetising hodge-podge would be hard to conceive. One of the nastiest is called Henry Cox, having multi-coloured leaves in zones of yellow, green, bronze and red, and brick-coloured flowers for good measure: thoroughly restless. For my money I would back Caroline Schmidt. Its habit is taller, less dumpy, than most. Small double, cherry red flowers are set against green leaves with a broad white margin. One often wishes, with these jazzy-leaved pelargoniums, that they would foreswear flowers altogether. This has actually happened in the case of Mme Salléron, whose green leaves are silver-edged. Its habit is squat, which makes it suitable for edging – but not on my recommendation.

By contrast *Pelargonium tomentosum*, with a strong peppermint scent when bruised, has an exploratory habit and will grow 4 ft. across in a season. Its large, woolly green leaves are basically heart-shaped but with wavy margins. It is nice to grow, for instance, at the foot of a clematis, in summer, or to lap over the ramp of steps on a bank.

P. crispum could hardly present a greater contrast: stiffly vertical in habit (usually 18 in. or 2 ft. tall but there is no upper limit to the height of a pelargonium) with serried ranks of small, crimped leaves which are green-and-yellow-variegated in the popular cultivar Variegatum.

The true geraniums, or cranesbills, are mainly hardy perennials and all have pretty leaves, without exception. There is one I must bring in here: *Geranium maderense* (previously lumped under the omnibus title *G. palmatum*), this being tender except in Cornwall, the Scillies and Ireland. It was described definitively (until someone proves him to be wrong) by P. F. Yeo in the R.H.S. Journal, Vol. 95 (1970) p. 413. This plant is curious as well as beautiful. It makes a rosette of foliage on a thick, woody stem up to 2 ft. tall. Each leaf, on my plants, is nearly a foot long and across, palmate, with five leaflets which are themselves bipinnatifid – deeply divided twice over, not quite back to the main veins. These leaves are borne on long petioles (15 in. or so) of a reddish colour and as the leaves die the petioles bend right back to the ground, forming a sort of wig-wam that helps support the plant's trunk. Dr Yeo observes: 'If it is desired to retain the biologically interesting feature of a stem supported by persistent petioles professional gardeners should on no account be allowed near the plant!', meaning that, in order to tidy the plant up, they are sure to remove these leaf remnants. I confess that, not realising what the plant was up to, I used to remove them myself, but then I am a professional gardener so what can you expect?

As a foliage plant, *G. maderense* makes a splendid tub specimen but is a little awkward to manage. The tub has to be found a frost-proof place in winter and, the plant being evergreen, cannot go into total darkness. Mine are at present in a cellar dimly lit by one cobwebby window. The larger the tub, the finer and more luxuriant the plant grows, and if the tub is very large, the plant will flower – profusely, with mauve-pink blossom, probably dying thereafter. It is easily and quickly raised from seed, if you can get seed. If not, the plant in its vegetative state will produce occasional small shoots from its trunk, and these are easily rooted as cuttings in a frame. The Plantsmen list this.

Among the several plants that you never see except in public gardens and are then at a loss to name, are the iresines, a small group of tender foliage plants with brilliantly coloured leaves. *Iresine herbstii* has deep reddish purple foliage, very smooth, only

2 or 3 inches long and blunt at the tip, giving it a slightly un-balanced look. It has a cultivar Brilliantissima that is purple with beetroot red veins that associates beautifully with grey foliage plants like *Artemisia arborescens* (clipped and kept low). *I.h.* 'Aureo-reticulata' looks quite different, having red veins against a golden background. The other species, *I. lindenii* has pointed beetroot-red leaves. All are readily propagated from cuttings but need warmer overwintering conditions than I give them.

So, too, with the *Coleus blumei* hybrids. The best stocks have little propensity to flowering, which is a great advantage, but they must be carried through the winter under heated glass. If you cannot do this you may yet be satisfied with seed strains, growing them as annuals. These are mixtures in brilliant colours, many of them agreeable and developing their best tones if bedded in a partially shaded position. The seedlings are intolerant of chilly spring weather and if they cannot be given heat, sowing should be delayed until early May, and planting out till the second half of June. The brilliance of their patterned foliage, often edged with a green hem stitch, is almost unbelievable in a plant that can be grown outside. Coleus offer plenty of scope for the indulgence of vulgar tastes. On my own terms, I like them very much and if you think I'm vulgar I shall not argue the point.

There are still a few tender perennials I should like to intro-duce. They scarcely ever get written about but may be seen at Kew gardens, where some imaginative and adventurous bedding out is at last being practised under the direction of Mr Brian Halliwell*. He is not content with clichés and is not enamoured of gaudy effects or riots in colour.

I should like to see more of *Coprosma repens* 'Variegata' (if that be its correct name: *Coprosma* is a New Zealand genus and I cannot find this one mentioned in my books on New Zealand flowers). It has a very clean, shining, almost orbicular leaf, green in the centre with a broad white margin (another cultivar has the margin yellow). Superficially it reminds me of a variegated form of *Euonymus japonicus*, but its texture is soft and its habit prostrate. This overwinters easily under barely frost-free conditions. *Polygonum lanigerum* is notoriously tricky to bring through from

---

* Alas! he has now been transferred to another department.

one season to another and ready to rot away at every stage in its propagation. I have not lost my rooted cuttings, taken last August, yet, but am only in February. It has lanceolate, 8-to-10 in.-long, silkily grey leaves on a sprawling plant and, especially considering that it belongs to a genus which I cannot warm to, I find it distinctly and surprisingly alluring.

I had never thought of using the popular house plant, *Setcreasea purpurea*, for summer bedding until I saw it thus at Kew with a yellow gazania. Setcreasea has fleshy, purple leaves and a prostrate habit. It is an obviously close relative of the tradescantias. And then a begonia, that I have not met except at Kew (and certainly not in reference books or catalogues), but which is used both inside and out, there. This is Cleopatra, of tufted habit, easily increased by division and with green, hairy, frilled leaves marked with purple. But its colouring is constantly changing with the season and according to whether you grow it in sun or in shade. It had been bedded out for the summer with *Achillea* 'Moonshine', a hardy plant with grey filigree foliage and corymbs of yellow flowers at 2½ ft. Early in the season, the begonia bore a generous crop of its small white flowers, then settled down as a background to the achillea.

Eucalyptus are perennials, but for bedding purposes they are treated as biennials. The species generally used in public places is *Eucalyptus globulus*. Its juvenile leaves are of a telling glaucous hue and they are quite large, broad at the base; coarser than one might wish but undeniably striking and looking well with purple-leaved *Ricinus*. This is raised from seed, like all the genus, but seed sown in spring doesn't give you a big enough plant in the same season. You should sow in July for the following year. Pot your seedlings off individually (3½ in.) in early autumn and overwinter under frost-free glass. Planted out in May, they will make rapid strides and attain 8 ft. by the end of the season, when they should be discarded (for most of us they are not hardy, anyway). *E. gunnii* has prettier juvenile leaves and, although not so fast growing, could be treated in the same way. And so, no doubt, could other species. It is a question of experimenting and of obtaining fresh, viable seed.

Moving on to biennials, the mullein, *Verbascum bombyciferum* is also listed as *V. broussa* or as Silver Spire. It is the mullein with the whitest felting of its bold, ovate-lanceolate leaves, these being borne in a handsome basal rosette, about 2 ft. tall. When it runs up to flower, it grows to 6 ft. at least and then dies. This is naturally a biennial but if seed is sown in early spring and the young plants given generous treatment, they will behave as annuals, which is not what you want, bearing in mind that the yellow-flowered candelabrums, though pleasant enough, are less striking than the unflowered leaf rosettes. On the other hand, if you pinch out the flowering shoots as soon as they appear, the plant can last for several years, but will probably succumb to mildew. The most sensible treatment, I think, is to sow in a pot in early June, bring on the young seedlings quickly and without a check (prick out first, then plant out) and enjoy them in your borders in late summer and autumn. After that you can either get rid of them and start again the next year, or overwinter them in situ and allow them to flower the next year, or overwinter them and remove the flowering shoots as they develop the next year. If the plants are not to be allowed to flower, they can be sited near a border's margin, where the foliage can be best seen and most appreciated. If they are eventually to flower, however, they will have to go further in.

The simple mullein leaf contrasts excellently with everything that's fussy or filigree like santolinas or the majority of artemisias.

Although friends keep giving me their seeds, I have so far resisted growing the popular onopordons – *Onopordon acanthium* and *O. arabicum* – because they are so vilely prickly in all their parts. Therein, admittedly, lies a part of their attraction – the spines look handsome and I enjoy seeing them in any friends' gardens.

Thompson & Morgan list these two species as hardy perennials but, like the mullein just described, they far oftener behave as biennials and the R.H.S. Dictionary, which originally gave *O. acanthium* as a perennial, corrects this to 'biennial and mono-carpic' in the Supplement. *O. arabicum* is, correctly, *O. nervosum*, a 'woolly biennial' (Supplement).

Well then, they self-sow abundantly and at first make a loose basal rosette of large, grey or white thistle leaves. The handsomest stage is reached prior to flowering in late spring, when the plant rises to 6 or 8 ft., branching widely with winged stems which are themselves cruelly (but ornamentally) spiny and large grey thistle heads, the size of a cardoon's. As the plant begins to run to seed, which is already its condition in July, it turns a dirty colour and becomes increasingly hideous – another reason why I don't grow it. Of course you can and should root it out but you are left with a large late summer and autumn gap.

Silybum marianum, Our Lady's Milk Thistle, is another freely self-sowing thistly plant that I shall recommend you to grow so that I can see it in your garden. Its thistle leaves have large white splashes on them against a glossy green background. You get the finest foliage from autumn-sown (or self-sown) seedlings, although it will behave like an annual if sown in spring. The plant is excessively spiny. It grows 2 or 3 ft. tall, only, and carries miserable little purple thistle heads. From then on it is not worth a place.

The Caper Spurge (which is poisonous and *not* an edible caper; merely looks like one, please note), *Euphorbia lathyrus*, completes my troika of handsome biennials that I have no intention of introducing into my garden. If a weed be a plant growing in the wrong place, this inevitably becomes a weed, for it has a far reaching method of seed dispersal. I shall always remember sitting in a summer house in Margery Fish's Somerset garden one sunny autumn afternoon (I believe I was making penstemon cuttings). The tiled roof was continually bombarded by ripe caper spurge seeds that nearby plants were ejecting with a terrific release of energy. Each seed that came my way pinged on to the roof above me and then rattled a noisy, bouncing descent.

E. lathyrus looks pleasant enough when flowering but is at its smartest in its first year, when each plant consists of one sturdy vertical stem clothed in dark green, linear-lanceolate foliage, arranged in four ranks, to form a perfect cross. It is said to ward off moles but there is not a shred of evidence that it does. I prefer more reliable if less picturesque methods.

Ricinus communis 'Gibsonii', the purple-leaved form of the true castor oil, is a tender perennial – a small tree, even – that we grow as an annual in this country. It is a splendid plant when grouped. The leaves are palmate, with seven divisions and are quite a foot across, probably a good bit more (I have only a photograph to remind me, at this winter season); rich purple, glabrous with a dull sheen. Stems and petioles are reddish. A degree or two more or less of summer warmth makes all the difference to the performance of this plant. As I have no heated glass I do not sow it till April, in a cold frame, potting the seedlings off individually into 5 in. paper containers, thereafter, prior to planting them out. In a good season they will be 7 or 8 ft. tall by October and impart a marvellous flamboyance.

The green-leaved type-plant is much more vigorous but not worth growing. Some seed merchants put out a badly selected strain of Gibsonii in which a proportion of the plants come green. The answer is to change your supplier.

In complete foliar contrast to this is maize, which is a broad-leaved annual grass. Some maize strains have ornamental foliage but these again are more or less badly selected. One strain of *Zea mays*, hopefully called Quadricolor, more often than not turns out to have perfectly dull, plain green leaves instead of being handsomely striped with cream, carmine, purple and green. Some firms do have better strains than others but to an extent you will have to do your own selecting. Grow the plants on, in pots, until they are large enough to give you some idea of their true colours. Plant out only the best – or pot them on into 8 in. pots and use them to stand around in strategic places where they will make a foil for *Lilium henryi*, for instance – also potted.

Z.m. 'Gracillima Variegata' can be extremely pretty with green and white stripes and leaves that are less coarse and a habit less robust than the last. It grows to 3 ft. or so (as against 5 ft. in Quadricolor) but again you must select your seedlings for their stripes.

The Summer Cypress, sometimes called Burning Bush on account of the hectic magenta-purple colouring it assumes in autumn, is an annual much abused in general usage. This is *Kochia scoparia* (syn. *K. trichophylla* and often sold as *K. childsii*), an unlikely member of the Spinach family. It makes a perfect oval-shaped 2 to 3 ft. bush, clothed all summer with narrow leaves of the freshest imaginable green. I find it useful between groups of gay front-line perennials to make an occasional and isolated exclamation mark. This fresh green shade is, after all, both rare and valuable, once spring is past. Plants are more often lined out like a military platoon in some small front garden, which does neither the plant nor anyone else any credit. Seeds, when viable, germinate in a matter of 3 days but they are not infrequently dud.

Orach, *Atriplex hortensis*, is another pleasing foliage plant in the *Chenopodiaceae* but this really does look like spinach and can be eaten as a vegetable in the same way. There are at least two seed strains in cultivation, but I am not sure what their proper names should be. It's the sort of plant you get seeds of from a friend and after that it sows itself, though without ever becoming a nuisance. One strain has purple leaves and stems, the other has them carmine and the latter is the more exciting and effective. The plant runs up to 6 ft. and is perhaps at its prettiest in late summer when the terminal panicles of flattened seed pods (of the same colouring as the rest of the plant) are developing but not yet ripe. At this juncture, however, your plants become top-heavy and need discreetly staking with short canes to stop them swerving over.

Talking of bad germination, I heard of no less than four different people, myself included, whose *Perilla* seed failed in 1971. Perillas are labiates with bold nettle-leaves, growing 2–3 ft. tall and always in a purple-coloured form. They are given various names, of which Nankinensis is the commonest. There was a well grown, well set-up patch at Wisley in 1971 calling itself *P. atropurpurea laciniata*. It contrasted handsomely with orange African marigolds in an adjacent patch.

Certain strains of certain vegetables make extremely decorative plants and can be grown for this purpose alone. Parsley, for instance. Its mossy foliage and bright green colouring makes you feel fresher just to look at it, and may be contrasted with, say, the blue-green of rue or the brilliant orange of dwarf tagetes: both are examples taken from life that I thought worth copying (and photographing).

There was a section of garden at Kew, recently, that was entirely devoted to bedding with ornamental herbs and vegetables. Among these I fancied a beet (offered by Carter's but no longer since they amalgamated with Dobie) called Flower Garden, with a svelte, deep purple leaf of willowy outline. Remember that slugs will spoil beet foliage. Then a Swiss Chard called Ruby (from Thompson & Morgan) but Dobie's Rhubarb Chard would probably be similar. The leaves are 2 ft. tall, crimped and basically green but with red veins and a terrific thick red midrib. Quite dramatic.

A well known lettuce called Salad Bowl makes the freshest imaginable edging – for a shortish season, that is, for no lettuce can be expected to remain pristine throughout the summer. This has frilly leaves of a strikingly bright pale green.

CHAPTER 10

Some Plans

*

1. *A shady border*

I shall have to make my own rules and conditions for the circumstances governing each plan, and in this instance we have a large,
shady, sheltered border on acid soil. Now, very often it is only
part of a border that is shaded and it is also true that only a few
gardeners will have as large a border as this to cope with whether
shaded or otherwise. But while I am dealing with this (and every
subsequent) theme, I need something to get my teeth into. If there
is any part of it that appeals to the reader, he can easily adapt that
to his own circumstances without needing to saddle himself with
the entire cabouche.

I am supposing that the border faces north and is backed by a
9-ft.-high wall, which also needs cover. Behind the wall are trees,
but they do not overhang much. In front of the border is a lawn
and, at the east end a path leading to a door in the wall. At its
other end the border, which is 18 yards long, takes a right-angled
turn and passes gradually into sunlight and out of our terms of
reference.

We can start at the border's definite end at the east. The beautiful
but slow growing Japanese maple of the golden foliage, is the
corner piece at the back here, and next to it a rhododendron
whose leaves are its main attraction with the warm rusty colouring
of their undersides. These two are seven feet apart, which will
look a lot at first and possibly not nearly enough later on. We
don't know how well either or both of them will do. Neither is
absolutely straightforward. If both flourish, one may have to be
removed, some day. Nothing is for ever.

Behind them, *Piptanthus laburnifolius*, which does not need a
wall but is easily trained to one. Its yellow blossom among the

large trifoliate leaves will make a good feature here for six weeks each spring.

Round the acer's frontage I suggest filling in with a harmless ground covering of woodruff – a native of alkaline woodland. It is a deciduous creeping plant, covered with pure white stars, in May, above fresh green foliage. Only 9 in. tall or thereabouts. More expensively one might choose *Cornus canadensis*, again deciduous and creeping at the same level. Each inch-wide inflorescence has four white bracts. The correct name for this is *Chamaepericlymenum canadense*, but few gardeners have yet got around to using it; I can't think why.

The corner will be distinctively marked by a line of the evergreen fern, *Polystichum setiferum* 'Plumoso-divisilobum'. Behind this, an orchis and a group of the greenhouse arum. Neither has been mentioned before because both are essentially flowering ingredients but with particularly good leaves.

Orchis maculata (or *O. fuchsii*) is our native spotted orchis, with heavily mottled foliage and substantial spikes of mauve flowers in June, rising to 2½ ft. It is an easily grown and effective plant but expensive to buy. Few nurserymen have ever thought of stocking and propagating it. You can, of course, dig up plants from the wild: they move very well. This is not a practice to be recommended because so much of our wild flora – and orchids in particular – has been decimated in just this way. Still, as it was how the orchis first entered my garden it seems only fair to mention and admit the fact. One can, after all, exercise discretion and refrain from being greedy when taking a plant from the wild, while also making sure that there really are plenty about and without any evidence of depletion to their numbers through other agencies.

O. maculata is so well established in our garden that it seeds everywhere (especially among irises and in paving cracks); quite possibly, some of its progeny have drifted back to the woods from which they originated, for the seed is very light. Roots also multiply rapidly when grown in a border and can soon be split up.

The greenhouse arum, *Zantedeschia aethiopica*, is a much hardier plant than is generally supposed. Take the precaution of planting

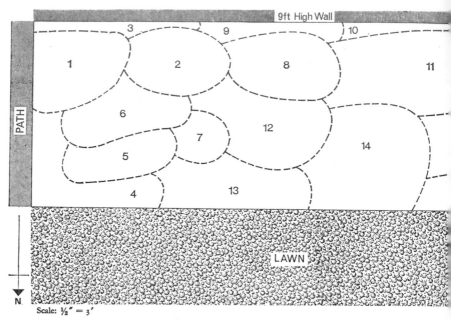

A SHADY BORDER

Contents in order of description:—

1. *Acer japonicum* 'Aureum' underplanted with *Asperula odorata* (woodruff) or *Cornus canadensis*
2. *Rhododendron arboreum* 'Sir Charles Lemon'
3. *Piptanthus laburnifolius*
4. *Polystichum setiferum* 'Plumoso-divisilobum'
5. *Orchis maculata*
6. *Zantedeschia aethiopica*
7. *Nandina domestica*
8. *Fatsia japonica*
9. *Hedera colchica* 'Dentato-variegata'
10. *Lonicera tellmanniana*
11. *Sambucus racemosa* 'Plumosa Aurea'
12. *Scrophularia aquatica* 'Variegata'
13. *Rodgersia podophylla*
14. *Hosta sieboldiana elegans*

it in spring and you can cover its roots and crowns with a layer of fern fronds in winter, if you like, so that frost cannot penetrate deeply. The dark green, spear-shaped leaves nobly offset the flowers' white spathes.

A plant of *Nandina domestica* will eventually fan out above its neighbours but I think we'll go to the back of the border again at this point. *Fatsia japonica* will make a large feature with its

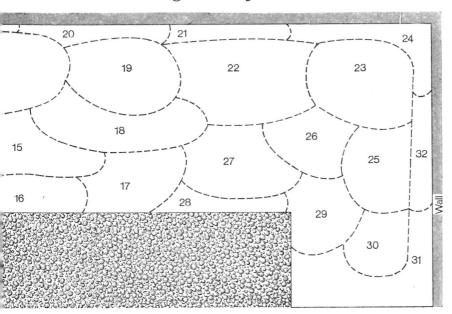

15. *Iris foetidissima* 'Variegata'
16. *Hosta undulata undulata*
17. *Danaë racemosa*
18. *Rhododendron concatenans*
19. *Hydrangea sargentiana*
20. *Pileostegia viburnoides*
21. *Lonicera tragophylla*
22. *Mahonia japonica*
23. *Rhododendron falconeri*

24. *Hydrangea petiolaris*
25. *Pieris formosa forrestii*
26. *Rodgersia tabularis*
27. *Blechnum tabulare*
28. *Hosta fortunei* 'Albo-picta'
29. *Rhododendron lepidostylum*
30. *Philadelphus coronarius* 'Aureus'
31. *Hedera colchica*
32. *Hedera canariensis* 'Variegata'

enormous evergreen fingered leaves and I fancy behind it (as I have in my own garden) the cheerfully variegated foliage of *Hedera colchica* 'Dentato-variegata'. Its leaves are not so small, either. *Lonicera tellmanniana*, to the right of this, will be able to send its trails through the ivy's branches. It is a scentless honeysuckle with glamorous apricot-orange flowers in June, and it prefers shade. Aphids can ruin its display, so watch out for them in May and spray betimes.

With the fatsia being so solid, we can give it rather frivolous neighbours. To its right, the golden cut-leaved elder, *Sambucus racemosa* 'Plumosa Aurea', cut back to a 3 or 4 ft. framework each winter. In front, the green-and-cream-variegated figwort, *Scrophularia aquatica* 'Variegata'.

Now for a bit more boldness. *Rodgersia podophylla* has palmately divided leaves but they are strongly patterned. Their colouring, especially in youth but again from midsummer onwards, is purplish and this will be well offset by the glaucous tones of *Hosta sieboldiana elegans*. It has huge, rounded leaves and the iris leaf form, being all spears, will make a suitable neighbour using the variegated *Iris foetidissima*, which is evergreen. *Hosta undulata* is variegated too, but pretty at a border's margin and sufficiently different from the iris to show up well against it.

Dark, rich, shining green plumes from *Danaë racemosa* and the glaucous young foliage of *Rhododendron concatenans* behind, its apricot bell-flowers coming in May. *Hydrangea sargentiana* behind this, I thought. It is a somewhat leggy plant but the rhododendron will grow up to hide that aspect of it. Its great, rounded, hairy leaves are exciting and unexpected, while the large lacecap inflorescences of pale mauve blossom are discreetly charming. We can put its climbing, evergreen relative *Pileostegia virburnoides* behind it on the wall, where it will foam with a lather of tiny white blossoms in September. And on its other side that other notably large-flowered but odourless honeysuckle, *Lonicera tragophylla*, this being pure yellow and always happiest in shade. It is a parent of *L. tellmanniana* and flowers at the same time. Its strands could be allowed to stray forward into *Mahonia japonica*, when the latter has made a fair-sized bush.

The mahonia, as I have said, is a must in every garden and if its scented, winter flowers are the main draw, at least its leaves are boldly pinnate and evergreen. We may eventually run into further space trouble here, because I have put *Rhododendron falconeri* in the corner. It is such a splendid shrub but if the site turns out to be as ideal as it seems, the mahonia will have to go, one day. On the other hand, if the rhododendron fails after all, for unpremeditated reasons (you never know with a pernickety thoroughbred), the mahonia itself will be able to take over most of the corner and the climbing *Hydrangea petiolaris*, in the angle, can bulk forwards quite

27. ABOVE, the water soldier, *Stratiotes aloides*, spends most of its life under water, rising to the surface only in summer. BELOW, the muscular foliage of *Gunnera manicata*, a plant happiest at the water's margin.

28. *Kochia*, called summer cypress, makes a vivid green incident in bed or border.

a bit. This is deciduous but has pleasant rufous stems in winter and carries white lacecap flowers in June.

The *Pieris* will, I take it, be sufficiently shaded from the sun, even at its high May declination (help will be needed from those trees behind the wall) to prevent scorching of its fabulous shrimp red young foliage. It will be in the same fighting context vis-à-vis the rhododendron as the mahonia. In front of these three, the pale green platter leaves of *Rodgersia tabularis*; the dark green pinnate fronds of *Blechnum tabulare*, a creeping fern, against which the pale butter-yellow young foliage of *Hosta fortunei* 'Albo-picta' will shine cheerfully in the spring.

Lastly, the extraordinarily bright blue foliage of the dwarf *Rhododendron lepidostylum* against the lime green of *Philadelphus coronarius* 'Aureus', which needs some shade, to prevent leaf scorch, but not so much as to fail to bring out its nice colouring. It will show up against a thoroughly dark green back-cloth in the large-leaved ivy *Hedera colchica* (not hitherto mentioned), on the left of which we have the prettily variegated Gloire de Marengo form of *Hedera canariensis* (*H.c.* 'Variegata').

Plants that will flower to some purpose in this border are: the arum and the orchis; *Rhododendron concatenans* and, later in the year, the hydrangea; *Mahonia japonica* from October to April, *Rhododendron falconeri* with white trusses in spring, but having a tendency to flowering biennially. The pieris is not altogether regular, either, but excellent when its white waxy bells do coincide with its young foliage; the mock orange, *Philadelphus coronarius* 'Aureus' is not showy but powerfully scented. On the walls, the two honeysuckles; the hydrangea, the related pileostegia; the piptanthus. But we have fielded a strong foliage side and no lack of colour will be felt from spring to autumn. There is plenty of evergreen substance, too.

2. *An open site with low, permanent contents*

This border adjoins a sitting-out area (on the other side of which is the house). The idea is to have an important bed near the house which can be enjoyed both from there and when sitting out, but to be able to look uninterruptedly across it at the garden beyond. Thus, nothing in it must be more than 2 or (at a pinch)

2½ ft. high, otherwise your chaise longue would need to be raised on stilts.

The border is 15 ft. across but its effective width is more because I am suggesting that it be framed in stone paving. Even on the lawn side, a 3 ft. paved margin, though not essential, will allow mat-forming plants to flow outwards and look very much at their ease.

The plants are mainly of a kind that will look presentable in winter as well as at other seasons, but there are some ordinary herbaceous plants as well. Once everything has knit together, there will be little upkeep. The site receives no shade. If winds are a problem, there is nothing here that will mind much. Hardiness will be no worry for half the gardeners in Britain. The other half might have to think again about the senecio, juniper, ballota, phormium, genista, santolina and anthemis. But I should give them a trial first, as they may well turn out to be all right after all. The soil I take to be average and reasonably drained. Except for the heather, it would not need to be acid.

I will discuss the border's contents in the order that I planned them. The solid, chunky *Senecio elaeagnifolius buchananii* will eventually fill the whole corner but it is slow growing so I have surrounded it at fairly close range with plants that will not interfere and can be dispensed with, finally. I reckon this to be a corner which people will tend to cut across so we want nothing (and that includes the senecio) that will spill over the paving here. They may stub their toes on the sheep's fescue but that won't hurt it. This, then, *Festuca ovina glauca*, is a hummocky, fine blue-leaved grass; evergreen but looking tired at winter's end. Split and replant it every other spring for best foliage effect. It is flanked on either side by the multicoloured bugle, which gives a mainly dark, purplish impression, especially in winter. Its stolons will soon make a mat, so you can economise on plant numbers at the start, if you want to.

Its leaves, and those of the senecio, are solid, so the acaena will make a contrast in every way, having an elegant, pinnate, pale blue leaf, all the year. Being a strong grower and as it spreads by underground stolons, you will have to watch out that this one does not interfere with our corner shrub.

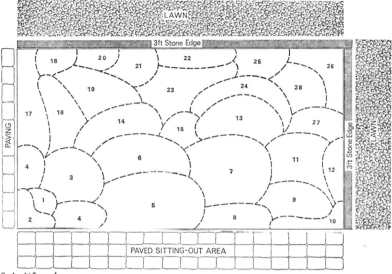

Scale: ½" = 4'

AN OPEN SITE WITH LOW PERMANENT CONTENTS

Contents in the order they are described:—

1. *Senecio elaeagnifolius buchananii*
2. *Festuca ovina glauca*
3. *Acaena* 'Blue Haze'
4. *Ajuga reptans* 'Multicolor'
5. *Juniperus conferta*
6. *Hebe* 'Waikiki'
7. *Euonymus fortunei* 'Silver Queen'
8. *Euphorbia myrsinites*
9. *Arum italicum* 'Pictum'
10. *Geranium renardii*
11. *Euphorbia amygdaloides* 'Purpurea'
12. *Pulmonaria saccharata*
13. *Pinus mugo pumilio*
14. *Ballota pseudodictamnus*
15. *Genista lydia*
16. *Hebe* 'Edinensis'
17. *Calluna vulgaris* 'Golden Feather'
18. *Phormium tenax alpinum* 'Purpureum'
19. *Ruta graveolens* 'Jackman's Blue Rue'
20. *Mentha rotundifolia* 'Variegata'
21. *Artemisia pontica*
22. *Helianthemum* 'Wisley Pink'
23. *Helictotrichon sempervirens*
24. *Hebe propinqua*
25. *Hebe albicans*
26. *Anthemis cupaniana*
27. *Santolina neapolitana*
28. *Eryngium bourgati*

Juniperus conferta will make a beautiful prostrate carpet, encroaching pleasantly on the patio – a bright pale green, yet with a dash of blue on the undersides of the leaves. It will show up against the 2 ft. *Hebe* 'Waikiki', whose colouring is a serious purple. Let me repeat once again, as I have used a number of them here, that the hebes are shrubby veronicas. Incidentally, you could plant 50 corms of the blue, autumn-flowering *Crocus speciosus* in the juniper patch and they would have a good chance of surviving even when they had to grow through the conifer's branches. Their leaves would look a little untidy in the spring, but they die off in May.

The euonymus will make an important feature, when it has got going: gay in green and cream with hints of purple in the winter. In front of it, the trailing, blue-leaved *Euphorbia myrsinites*. It has an almost animal-like quality and will crawl over the paving like some friendly caterpillar.

On the corner, arum and geranium will do a Cox and Box act, overlapping only in spring. The arum does not need shade, though often given it. With a season lasting from September to June, it leaves a gap for 3 summer months, apart from the bright orange clubs of its seed heads. Neighbours will help to fill the gap in but if you were still worried, you could interplant with some modest little number like the toad lily – one or other species of *Tricyrtis*, of slender habit to 2½ ft., eventually producing speckled, purplish flowers in autumn. *Geranium renardii* has leaves of the softest texture, a demurely grey shade of green and overlaid with a minute mosaic pattern of veins. You must draw your chair close up to it and have a peer in comfort.

I thought the strong, spiky habit and purple colouring of the wood spurge would look well behind the arum while the spotted-dog leaves of the lungwort (*Pulmonaria*), in two shades of green would spray out nicely at the edge. These leaves are ovate-lanceolate, with smooth edges, in complete contrast to the cranesbill's, which are round with crimped margins.

There usually comes a difficult point in every plan when you are stuck for what seems the right idea, and plant after plant comes up for review before the mind's eye like Banquo's ghost and all Banquo's royal descendants in Macbeth's uncomfortable vision.

In this case I had trouble in making up my mind what to put behind the Silver Queen euonymus. It must be plain – even dark – green, I early decided, which doesn't seem a very inhibiting proviso. In the end, it was this dwarf pine, of spreading habit but very low. Dwarf pines are extremely beautiful and full of character and this one has the additional merit of coning freely.

Behind *Hebe* 'Waikiki', the ever-grey *Ballota pseudodictamnus*; the purple would look well against the grey as would the grey against the purple from the other side. Rather than continue the ballota (which has a touch of the makeshift about it) right round to the pine, I have divided them with one plant of *Genista lydia*, which is not a foliage plant at all. But its down-curving, sickle-shaped branches give this broom an interesting texture. By the time it was large enough to meet the pine its life span would be near its end. It has brilliant yellow flowers in June and does look very well with the ballota, I know, as I have grown them together.

With a solid, plain green backing from *Hebe* 'Edinensis', I fancy a substantial patch of ling on the south corner (to which extent I eat the unkind words I wrote earlier). This one, Golden Feather, has a specially pleasing habit and well-furnished (not scraggy, as so often) shoots, quite apart from the excellent yellow colouring tinged with bronze at the tips in winter. The phormium's iris-like purple sword leaves will give a necessary firmness in this context. It is sometimes available from Washfield Nurseries, Hawkhurst, Kent, but if you can't get it, settle for one plant of a dwarf *Yucca* such as *Y. filamentosa* or *Y. flaccida*.

Jackman's Blue Rue crops up again, this time to offset the green of the hebe and the grey of the ballota. We can do with the movement (or fussiness) of a variegated plant in front of the rue: the elegant and non-invasive mint, said to be sport of the apple mint *Mentha rotundifolia*, though I find this hard to swallow. It is apple green and white. Its next neighbour, *Artemisia pontica*, of the finest grey filigree, is a bit invasive but easily checked. Its stiff wiry habit is strictly upright, but its wandering propensities will take it into the cracks of the paved edge, which you will like. However, I really want a mat-forming plant at this stage to lap wholeheartedly over the margin. *Helianthemum* 'Wisley Pink' is primarily a flowering plant but exceeding grey in the leaf and evergreen withal. It has great vigour and should be clipped over after flowering.

Behind this sun rose, the steely blue, porcupine hummocks of the grass, *Helictotrichon sempervirens*. Admittedly it rises to 4 ft. when flowering but you can see right through its stems, cutting them down in June when the display has finished.

Now I want a dignified and non-invasive fringe for the pine and have chosen *Hebe propinqua* which, with its scale-like leaves, looks something like a conifer itself. *H. albicans* will be in complete contrast; glaucous foliage and spikes of white flowers with dark stamens in early summer.

Finally, the fourth corner. *Anthemis cupaniana* is a coarse and fast growing mat-former but I want some cushions here and its finely dissected grey foliage is far from coarse. After its huge crop of white marguerite daisies, in May, all flowering stems need removing back to their point of origin. On heavy soil, this plant tends to die out in winter. The santolina will be grey again, at a higher level and the interesting spikiness of *Eryngium bourgati* will act as a stiffener, but you will have to watch out that the anthemis doesn't overlay it.

Of the 28 different kinds of plants used, 22 are evergreen. As you will have noted, twelve flower in a worthwhile manner including the two grasses, but here is a situation where the year-round interest and satisfaction of good foliage is of far greater importance than flowers.

3. *The same site as* (2), *but used for summer bedding*

However, there are more ways of killing a cat than by choking it with cream, as my father used to say, so let us consider a different treatment for this same site, using tender plants, or at any rate expendable material that we can light-heartedly discard at the end of the season (October–November) and follow with spring bulbs.

The worst trap one can fall into in respect of bedding is too much business, producing a spotty, confused end-product. As we are starting with a clean sheet at the beginning of each season, this is quite unnecessary. Everything can be planned beforehand, on paper, for broad and simple effects. No doubt a few ingredients

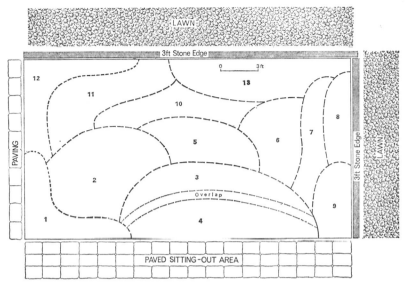

AN OPEN SITE USED FOR SUMMER BEDDING

Contents in the order they are described:—

1. *Senecio cineraria* 'Alice'
2. *Pelargonium* 'Caroline Schmidt'
3. *Petunia* 'Blue Lagoon'
4. *Helichrysum petiolatum*
5. *Chrysanthemum foeniculaceum*
6. *Artemisia arborescens*
7. *Glyceria maxima* 'Variegata'
8. *Verbena hybrida* 'Loveliness'
9. *Iresine lindenii*
10. *Kochia* 'Childsii'
11. *Helichrysum microphyllum* & Swiss Chard 'Ruby'
12. *Setcreasia purpurea* & *Dianthus* 'Queen of Hearts'
13. *Centaurea gymnocarpa*

will fail and substitutes have to be interpolated, but these need not destroy the simplicity of the plan. You must resist the temptation to bed everything out that has been overwintered under glass, for no better reason than because that is the easiest way to carry stock forward from one season to the next.

Again I start in the corner where we want no overspill with the compact, but frilly, grey-leaved *Senecio cineraria* 'Alice'. When propagating this, in early autumn, you may find that a lot of your cuttings get botrytis and rot away. As a precaution, dip the cuttings in Captan (a powder will do); use a very free-draining compost containing a large proportion (at least half) of grit and give the cuttings (albeit under glass) ventilation almost from the outset. If you find Alice difficult, use White Diamond, which is easier, probably because its leaves are simpler and hence hold the moisture less.

The senecio will make a firm foreground for a patch of the green-and-white-variegated *Pelargonium* 'Caroline Schmidt', which is also free of its double cerise flowers. Cerise and purple associate well: the petunia Blue Lagoon is really between mauve and purple, in depth and quality of colouring. In most situations, most petunias let you down in most English summers, sooner or later, because their blooms rot during a wet spell. As the rot (again caused by botrytis) once started is inclined to be self-perpetuating, it takes a long subsequent spell of fine weather to enable the plants to recover. This is not the case, however, with the majority of the blue and purple shades and I have noticed that Blue Lagoon (obtainable from Samuel Dobie of Chester) is particularly resistant to summer's vagaries. Furthermore, the blue and purple shades are the most fragrant, at night, so you will be able to enjoy their scent as you take your ease near by, of an evening.

Petunias, of course, are not foliage plants. Indeed their foliage is ugly, so we have in front of them the inestimable *Helichrysum petiolatum*: grey, with a spraying habit. I suggest allowing plants of the one and of the other to overlap (i.e. to be interplanted) where the two groups meet allowing two petunia plants for every helichrysum, since the latter is by far the more vigorous.

Behind the petunias, the 2 to 3 ft. *Chrysanthemum foeniculaceum* which I seem not to have mentioned yet. It is a soft and sappy shrub with pinnate foliage but of a solid deeply glaucous cast, overlaid with a sprinkling of small white marguerites.

Artemisia arborescens has a similar habit (a bit looser) and its pinnate leaves are finely divided also, but it is pale grey. For something quite different alongside: the spiky, green-and-cream-variegated grass, *Glyceria maxima* 'Variegata'. This makes a pleasant background for the sweetly scented, lavender-mauve bedding verbena called Loveliness. You propagate it from cuttings in the autumn. On the corner I should like the uprightly bushy, purple-leaved *Iresine lindenii*. You can stock yourself initially with this and other iresines from Thomas Butcher of Shirley, Croydon, Surrey. Subsequently you will take your own cuttings, but heated glass is necessary for overwintering.

On the other side of *Chrysanthemum foeniculaceum* I am suggesting a group of the distinct and blobby units formed by *Kochia* 'Childsii', which has been likened to a green busby. It is a fresh, yellow-green colour all through the summer and quite a different shade from anything else in our border.

Now a large mixed marginal planting of *Helichrysum microphyllum*, which is low and rambling and will make a carpet, with interjections by the 2-ft.-tall, red Swiss Chard, which goes by different names according to whom you buy your seed from. I would plant my chards 2 ft. apart. The helichrysum is silvery. You may have to prevent it, now and again, from smothering the chard.

On our last corner I should like another mixed planting. A low foundation will this time be formed by the purple, fleshy-leaved tradescantia called *Setcreasia purpurea*, the taller incidents by a bushy annual dianthus, about a foot high, of most brilliant red colouring, called Queen of Hearts. Plant these 15 in. apart. If you found the setcreasia awkward to manage, you might try the hardy annual pimpernel, *Anagallis linifolia*, sold variously as Phillipsii (Thompson & Morgan) and Coerulea (Butcher, Unwin, Dobie). It is a low sprawling plant covered with deep gentian-blue flowers that open out in any reasonably favourable weather right through from early summer till November.

Finally, to back these, *Centaurea gymnocarpa*, so often used as a dot plant in public gardens, but much prettier grouped, to my mind, though a fairly wide spacing between plants – say 18 in. – can be allowed so that their individuality may be enjoyed as well as their massed contribution. Depending on the age and stage of development of the plants at planting out time, they grow about 2 ft. tall and their long, silvery pinnate leaves are exceptionally elegant.

If we take an analytical view of this plan, we find that nine or ten of its components are purely for foliage; two more (the pelargonium and chrysanthemum) have a bonus of flowers and 3 or 4

Foliage Plants

are grown entirely for their flowers. To force oneself to use nothing but foliage would be gimmicky. Such flowers as we are allowing will look all the better for their foliar setting. There is a lot of silver and grey, here, practically no yellow. The green of *Kochia* 'Childsii' is on the yellow side; that's about all. The reds are all blue-reds (with the possible exception of the dianthus) and there are purples to match them.

It would be just as easy to strike a yellow balance, so let us do so, still using the same bed.

4. The same site as (2) and (3), using a yellow-biased summer bedding scheme

Starting on the same corner as before where, in contrast to most of the bed, our plants are required not to spill over the edge lest they be trodden on and bruised, the salvia–a form of common sage – makes compact bushes, variegated in green and gold. The grass behind them is striped in much the same colouring but is, of course, quite differently made. A clump-forming perennial that dies right down in winter, its leaves are narrowly strap-shaped and arch outwards at the tips. Its flower heads make a dark haze at 2½ ft. like a diaphanous cloud of tiny hovering insects. The plants can be moved in or out, as required, from a spare plot and, if they are sizeable clumps, can be spaced 2½ ft. or even 3 ft. apart.

Next along the margin, the yellow-variegated *Cuphea ignea* 'Variegata', which is easily overwintered as autumn-struck cuttings under conditions that are only just frost-free. It makes a pleasantly informal mass (meaning that it lacks form!) and its green-and-gold-mottled leaves are freely spangled with small scarlet tubular flowers. There is never a pause in their production. A firm background is called for and will be provided by the simple, felted heart-leaves of *Helichrysum petiolatum*, this time in its pale yellow form.

I should like a mixed planting, on the corner, to include the versatile *Begonia* 'Cleopatra' which I have already described (but don't ask me where to get it from). I think that well established plants of the 1½ to 2 ft. *Euphorbia niciciana*, moved in, like the molinia, from a spare plot, should make fit companions. Their acid yellow colouring and pale glaucous needle leaves will contrast

186

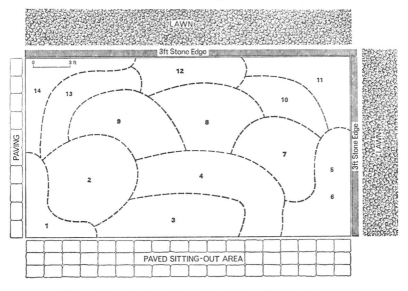

OPEN SITE USED FOR SUMMER BEDDING WITH
A YELLOW BIAS

In the order they are described:—

1. *Salvia officinalis* 'Icterina'
2. *Molinia caerulea* 'Variegata'
3. *Cuphea ignea* 'Variegata'
4. *Helichrysum petiolatum* 'Yellow Form'
5. *Begonia* 'Cleopatra'
6. *Euphorbia niciciana*
7. *Zea mays* 'Gracillima Variegata'
8. *Tagetes erecta* Orange African Marigold 2½ ft.
9. *Perilla atropurpurea* 'Laciniata'
10. *Kochia* 'Childsii'
11. *Fuchsia* 'Genii'
12. *Senecio leucostachys*
13. *Pelargonium* 'Maxim Kovaleski' & Pansy 'Lord Nelson'
14. *Fuchsia* 'Golden Treasure'

strikingly with the begonia's own fairly substantial heart-leaves in bronze and yellow-green.

The striped green-and-cream maize, spaced 2½ ft. apart, behind, will itself make an eloquent contrast in its setting. To finish off the centre of the bed, a juxtaposition of moderately but not too compact, orange African marigolds (*Tagetes erecta*), with the sombre purple heart-leaves of *Perilla atropurpurea* 'Laciniata' (somewhat enlivened, however, by their toothed margins), makes a handsome team.

I am including the highly stylised *Kochia* 'Childsii' again as a background for a hardy fuchsia that I fell for quite recently, with elegant yellow-green leaves and a good spreading habit. It does make a floral contribution in the autumn in the traditional fuchsia crimson and purple. This plan is otherwise devoid of grey but I do want a patch of it, in between my oranges and yellow-greens, in the form of my much beloved *Senecio leucostachys*, of the infiltrating habit.

The highlight of the last corner is the brilliant orange *Pelargonium* 'Maxim Kovaleski'. The pelargonium leaf is always well shaped but this has no pretensions as a foliage plant. The virtually non-flowering *Fuchsia* 'Golden Treasure' can make a foreground apron to it. And, as an extra thought, I have interplanted the pelargonium with a modest purple-flowered pansy (Lord Nelson, from Thompson & Morgan) that is perfectly well mannered and non-invasive but has the pleasant habit, like many pansies and violas, of growing up through neighbouring plants and flowering at their own level. There is another very long-flowering one called Blue Heaven that I have admired in a friend's garden and that might do the job as well, but I do rather fancy purple here, with the perilla being of that persuasion itself.

An analysis of this bed would give much the same balance of flowers and foliage as did the last. One extra point: provision should be made for keeping it well watered. The fuchsias and the helichrysum will burn if ever allowed to go dry in sunny weather. And anyway the plants will all benefit from a soaking from time to time, when rainfall is scant.

Perhaps I should add, at this point, that both bedding-out schemes and, indeed, all my plans are conjectural. They include ideas I have tried out but many more that I have not, and some of these would doubtless turn out, in practice, to need modification. You never can get a plan right first time and even when it is working from first to last it should be varied from year to year so that you can try out new plants and new ideas as they come to you.

5. *A mixed planting in a large island bed*

As a contrast to the fairly small scale on which we have for some time been concentrating, I now offer suggestions for a large, more or less elliptical island site in an open but not wind-battered position. The bed is about 40 ft. wide but I have included in it nothing that need grow much taller than 12 ft. In this way the plants will sit snugly in their environment and there will not be undue shading even on the bed's north side. I have used herbaceous and tender bedding plants as well as deciduous and evergreen shrubs, but if you didn't want to be bothered with bedding out it would be easy enough to substitute permanent (though not so lush) ingredients. The bed is surrounded by lawn, but I should have no hesitation about allowing plants to spill over on to the grass, where they felt so inclined, thereby breaking any hard formality of outline.

We start with a bold group of Adam's Needle, *Yucca gloriosa*, at the west end. The plants have stiff, dark green spear-leaves in rosette formation and will develop short, wrinkled trunks in course of time. And they should flower fairly regularly when established, with enormous, 4-to-5 ft.-long candelabrums of waxy white bells. Sometimes these develop too late in the autumn to flower properly. Since the plants are so sombrely coloured, they arc underplanted with a cheerful ground covering of green-and-primrose-variegated ivy. The variegated periwinkle, *Vinca major* 'Variegata' would do as well.

Additionally, a light and airy contrast will be gained by placing the Chilean bamboo, *Chusquea couleou*, behind. It will become, and indeed should be, the tallest and most striking feature at this end of the border. Still looking for contrasts, both to the yucca and to the bamboo, I have placed *Fatsia japonica*, with its huge, glossy, fingered leaves, alongside them: two plants that will grow together before long and make one unit. I have used the variegated form with white markings on the tips of its fingers. The plain green type-plant would look just as well but I used it in another plan and am aiming to include different ingredients for the sake of variety. In front of this, the intensely glaucous but fairly small leaved *Hosta tokudama*. It has a neat, determined air about it.

On the other side of yucca and bamboo, first a group of paulownia seedlings, grown and pruned for their enormous,

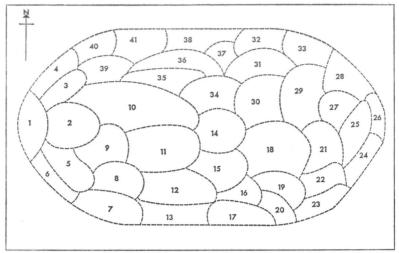

scale: $\frac{1}{2}'' = 5'$

A MIXED PLANTING IN A LARGE ISLAND BED

Contents in the order they are described:—

1. *Yucca gloriosa & Hedera colchica* 'Dentato-variegata'
2. *Chusquea couleou*
3. *Fatsia japonica* 'Variegata'
4. *Hosta tokudama*
5. *Paulownia tomentosa*
6. *Ligularia clivorum* 'Desdemona'
7. *Phlomis chrysophylla*
8. *Eryngium pandanifolium*
9. *Sambucus nigra* 'Aurea'
10. *Viburnum tinus*
11. *Hippophaë rhamnoides*
12. *Weigela florida* 'Foliis-purpureis'
13. *Sedum* 'Autumn Joy'
14. *Phyllostachys nigra* 'Henonis'
15. *Elaeagnus pungens* 'Maculata'
16. *Prunus laurocerasus* 'Otto Luyken'
17. *Bergenia* 'Ballawley'
18. *Griselinia littoralis*
19. *Rosa rubrifolia*
20. *Lonicera nitida* 'Baggesen's Golden'
21. *Ailanthus altissima*
22. *Canna indica* 'Purpurea'
23. *Melianthus major*
24. *Hosta plantaginea* 'Grandiflora'
25. *Prunus cistena*
26. *Potentilla* 'Elizabeth'
27. *Juniperus chinensis* 'Aurea'
28. *Salix repens argentea*
29. *Rhododendron campanulatum* 'Knap Hill'
30. *Berberis vulgaris* 'Atropurpurea'
31. *Rhododendron oreotrephes*
32. *Cotinus coggygria* 'Royal Purple'
33. *Fuchsia gracilis* 'Versicolor'
34. *Cornus alternifolia* 'Argentea'
35. *Eucalyptus globulus*
36. *Ricinus communis* 'Gibsonii'
37. *Miscanthus sinensis* 'Gracillimus'
38. *Anemone japonica* 'Alba'
39. *Ilex altaclarensis* 'Golden King'
40. *Polystichum aculeatum* 'Bevis'
41. *Rosa virginiana*

furry, heart-shaped leaves. They will be pruned to near ground level each spring and only one shoot allowed to develop subsequently, the others being rubbed out. In front, a flowering group of the 4 ft. hardy perennial, *Ligularia clivorum* 'Desdemona'. This does have excellent foliage, too, being almost orbicular; purple underneath, and purple on top, at first, but changing to dark green. Above all, however, I feel that we shall here appreciate the glowing orange of its daisies in July and August. They are borne on branching stems and are popular with butterflies.

Alongside this, the pale ever-grey foliage of *Phlomis chrysophylla* will show up to advantage, especially as this is a sunny position. If it carries its whorls of yellow, hooded flowers in June, and you don't like them, you can comfort yourself with the thought that there are not many of them and they are easily removed. If you do like them (I do), why then they're a welcome bonus. Behind this, the splendid and exotic *Eryngium pandanifolium*, with sea-green sword leaves. Let us hope that it will be hardy with you as it is with me. The inflorescences rise to 8 ft. in autumn and are very stately, though of subdued colouring.

To offset it by way of a background, I am suggesting the common Golden Elder, *Sambucus nigra* 'Aurea', whose coarsish foliage offers a subtle range of shades between green and gold. If this shrub grows too large, nothing could be easier than pruning it to the required size, and it is as hardy as nails (to coin a phrase).

It does, itself, benefit from a dark background. I am used to seeing it (with side lighting from a low sun) against a stormy sky in Scotland. We cannot be so sure of this accessory in England, and anyway I want an evergreen spine to my border: something solid and enduring the year through that will prevent us from seeing how large the bed is or what is growing on its other side. Hence my generous planting of the common laurustinus, *Viburnum tinus*. Once established (and you should really be content with buying small plants as large ones do not establish well) it billows rather like a dark cloud, and the foliage is on the leaden side of green. But the cloud lightens to rose and white, in autumn, as the pink buds open, in succession and whenever the weather is kind, right through till spring. Do not despise this shrub because it is common. If you refused to let me have it, I should substitute the almost (but not quite) equally familiar *Viburnum rhytidophyllum*, with large, elliptical, deeply wrinkled evergreen leaves. Its flowers, in spring, are too dirty a white for us to dwell upon, but the clusters of berries in August, first red and then black (with a striking mixture of red and black in between) make a fine display and it is only when you plant this species as a group that it fruits freely.

In front of the viburnums (whichever species has been decided on) I can now relax with a thicket of the deciduous, silver-leaved sea buckthorn, *Hippophaë rhamnoides*. One male in the centre, as pollinator, flanked by two wives on either side, carrying crops of translucent orange berries in autumn and winter. Actually, 5 plants is rather a lot in this space and you could make do with 2 ladies in front and the husband behind, forming an equilateral triangle.

Next I shall impose on you an association already adumbrated: the purple-leaved *Weigela florida* 'Foliis-purpureis' behind a planting of *Sedum* 'Autumn Joy', whose fleshy, fresh green leaves are good but whose main point is in its flat-headed inflorescences. These start opening in late August and are then pale pink, but they becom dearker and richer as they mature until a glowing ruby shade is achieved in October, and lasts till well into the next month. Established plants of this sedum tend to become too tall for the weight of their heads. They splay open untidily. I find it a simple matter to lift and replant them every autumn. Each clump is halved and one half is replaced in the same hole that it came out of (the other, discarded). In this way, its exuberance is checked; the plants' height is reduced in the next season and they remain self-supporting.

29. ABOVE, rocks are no longer much in evidence on the rock garden at Keillour Castle, in Perthshire, where this June scene is dominated by the brilliant young foliage of *Pieris formosa forrestii*. Its shrimp-red colouring often causes the beholder to think he is looking at blossom. BELOW, foliage in Maurice Mason's garden near King's Lynn in Norfolk. The central yellow shrub is a yew, *Taxus baccata* 'Semper-aurea', set about with a ground-work of plain and variegated-leaved ivies. Behind, a fountain of zebra grass, *Miscanthus sinensis* 'Zebrinus', whose yellowish bands show up against the light.

As a continuation of the vertebral evergreen idea, another plumy, clump-forming bamboo: *Phyllostachys nigra* 'Henonis'. The evergreenery of bamboos is inclined to become more than a little threadbare after frost bite in the new year, but their stems are always inspiring and they soon make a dense enough thicket not to be seen through.

By contrast, *Elaeagnus pungens* 'Maculata', which we shall site in front of it, looks a bit peculiar and indeterminate, in summer, when the miniature leaves borne on young shoots are a curious, brownish non-colour, but is at its most radiant in winter – positively brilliant when the sun comes out and intensifies its yellow variegation, but even on the dullest day it makes you feel better.

So busy and exciting a leaf demands the contrast of plain

30. ABOVE LEFT, forbidden fruit (see pp. 120-1); *Vitis vinifera* 'Purpurea', an ornamental, dark-leaved vine grown on an old brick wall at Bedgebury, where the National Pinetum has its car park. The fruits are for looks only. The plant is not very vigorous and deserves a snug position.   RIGHT, at Mount Usher, in County Wicklow, *Magnolia delavayi* makes a large free-standing bush or small tree, and carries its fragrant, waxy flowers freely (a glaucous flower bud is also visible, bottom right). Most of us grow this as an evergreen foliage plant, for which purpose it well deserves wall space, but may be grown 'unprotected' in protected town gardens.   MIDDLE LEFT. The grey flannel leaves of a number of mulleins are even more ornamental than their flowers, and this is particularly true of *Verbascum bombyciferum*. RIGHT, *Euphorbia myrsinites* in late summer. Later its young shoots all come down to the ground and carry their terminal, lime-green inflorescences in April.   BELOW LEFT, you don't always find the golden-leaved laburnum, *Laburnum anagyroides* 'Aureum', colouring as brightly as this specimen at Crathes Castle, which is furthermore seen to particular advantage against *Prunus cerasifera* 'Pissardii', the purple-leaved plum.   RIGHT, I am always photographing the golden, cut-leaved elder, *Sambucus racemosa*, 'Plumosa Aurea', and it was difficult to decide at which stage in its development to present it here. In this picture the young shoots, still coppery at the centre, are seen in early May; later they change to yellow all over; finally lime green, in July and August. Shade and moisture are the recipe for success with this shrub and a hardish pruning in winter.

neighbours, which it already has and which we will add to, in front of it, with a shiny, evergreen-leaved cherry laurel in a minor, dwarfish form, Otto Luyken. It is covered with candles of white blossom in spring. In front of that, at the border's margin again, *Bergenia* 'Ballawley'. Although evergreen, I find it difficult to remain in love with this plant the year through, and especially in winter, but it has its points and I like the unashamed magenta of its flowering panicles in spring. Some people are more enthusiastic about this plant than I am; others, less, so I should have a look or two at it before you buy.

Back to our evergreen vertebra (which describes a snaky twist at this end), the green of *Griselinia littoralis* is brighter and fresher than any other green to be found in the winter garden. A boskage of this. As a foreground to its plainness, I fancy the pinnate leaf and dusky purple colouring of *Rosa rubrifolia*, which additionally carries heavy crops of orange-red hips, at any rate in the south of Britain. The pale greenish-yellow of *Lonicera nitida* 'Baggesen's Golden' will be pleasing at the margin and goes well next the bergenia. I have them together in my Long Border.

Although it will look nothing in winter, I should like a lush and tropically flavoured planting now. First the Tree of Heaven, *Ailanthus altissima*, treated like the paulownia, as a hard-pruned shrub and trained to a single stem on each plant. Its pinnate leaves will be up to 3 ft. long by midsummer. Then the canna's purple but smooth and perfectly simple, undivided leaves, up to 6 ft. tall and in front of these, *Melianthus major*, whose height, if you leave the plants in situ so that they are levelled by frost each winter, will probably not exceed 4 ft. at the end of the season. Sea green, pinnate, oily smooth; undoubtedly the most beautiful leaf in the whole border.

I am continuing along the border's margin with the pale, yellow-green foliage of *Hosta plantaginea* 'Grandiflora'. Only 1½ or 2 ft. tall, it will contrast in almost every way with the canna and melianthus. Furthermore, it will enjoy its sunny position and should flower generously in the autumn. I want a dark background for it, which the offset cannas cannot altogether provide. Hence *Prunus cistena* in a group that can be pruned after flowering so as to keep it to a height of 3 or 4 ft. It is a very dark purple and I cannot resist imitating an example taken from the Northern Horticultural Society's garden at Harlow Car, of placing *Potentilla* 'Elizabeth' in front. This is a cultivar of the shrubby *P. fruticosa* and grown entirely for its pale yellow, cistus-like flowers, carried non-stop through summer and autumn. Unpruned shrubs grow 3 ft. tall, but it is better to cut them back a certain amount at least every other spring.

I want a feature at this end of the border and have chosen the golden form of the Chinese Juniper, *Juniperus chinensis* 'Aurea'. It will slowly rise to form an elegant but not too formal spire. A tree-shrub like this will need cherishing in its early years, in the vigorous and competitive context of a mixed border where many coarser elements will try to crowd it out. Damage can occur very quickly, by over-shading, and you should review the situation frequently during the summer, when thuggery reaches its peak. The juniper will make you impatient for progress in its early years but will gratify you later. You could, if impatience is your master, make the opposite kind of choice and plant a quick-growing column here: say, *Cupressus macrocarpa* 'Donard Gold' or 'Lutea', which would give you immediate pleasure and rapid growth but would present a problem before many years had passed.

Salix repens argentea has pretty little silvery leaves and a sprawling habit that is easily controlled by pruning. I am always inclined, in the case of willows that carry crops of pussies (but do buy males, with bright yellow catkins, if you can), to do my pruning in spring, after these have flowered, so as to make the most of every attainable asset. The silver foliage will here contrast with the yellow of juniper and potentilla.

Now a rhododendron. Since writing about *Rhododendron campanulatum* in the shrub chapter I have seen it growing wild in Kashmir. As expected, its leaf is always good: very pale on the underside when young but becoming bright rust brown in maturity. The few flower remnants, however, revealed this wilding to be an uninspired and washed out pink. So much better had it been pure white. However, the cultivar Knap Hill is an excellent shade of near blue and this rhododendron does not mind full exposure: there was nothing larger than itself in the wild, though cloud cover was admittedly pretty persistent. But then so it is in England.

I shall digress. R. *campanulatum*, where I saw it, was growing at about 10 or 11 thousand feet, on a steep hillside above the hill station of Gulmarg. It is in fascinating yet depressing country: beauty in decay is always saddening. Here there is such persistent over-grazing by sheep and cattle, that no palatable plant is capable of redeneration. Rhododendrons are not palatable, and old thickets were in reasonably good shape, but there wasn't a sign of a youngster anywhere. One felt that it was only a question of time before the remorseless tread of cattle's feet would wipe out nine-tenths of the native flora. And, quite evidently, nobody cares. To keep themselves alive is their sole, desperate concern.

A purple/blue/purple association should look well, if it works out as I intend. The purple-leaved form of *Berberis vulgaris* will stand out against the pale green of *Griselinia littoralis* (remember that this side of the border will be looked at from the north). In front of the berberis, *Rhododendron oreotrephes*, whose flowers are nothing to boast about but whose young foliage is verdigris. This is another case where protection will be needed in the early years against more aggressive neighbours. The purple sumach in front is easily controlled by winter pruning to prevent it growing more than 4 ft. tall. I think *Fuchsia gracilis* 'Versicolor' will fill in nicely between it and the silver willow. Its own colouring hovers between grey and pinky purple, while its red-and-purple flowers are not to be despised.

Variegation needs good backgrounds. The light green-and-white foliage of *Cornus alternifolia* 'Argentea' should show up well against bamboo and laurustinus. Watch that it isn't elbowed out.

Now for another splash around among the ephemerals: the glaucous, rounded (and, I fear, coarse) juvenile foliage of *Eucalyptus globulus* seedlings, behind the broad, glossy, palmate leaves of true castor oil, *Ricinus communis*, in its purple form, Gibsonii. The ricinus is inescapably tender, and even if the eucalyptus shows perennial tendencies, it will be wise to discard old plants in favour of the comelier young, replanted every late spring. The whole ricinus/eucalyptus area, as also the patch vacated by the cannas, can be planted up with tulips, each autumn. They will make their gay contribution in April and May and can subsequently be lifted and dried off, in early June, when the tender plants are ready to take their place.

A grassy fountain will be created by a single clump (it will soon grow 2 ft. across) of the 6 ft. grass, *Miscanthus sinensis* 'Gracillimus', but I am going to devote the front of the border at this point to a flower, pure and simple, the white Japanese anemone. You can have too much foliage just as (though more disastrously) you can have a congestion of flowers. This position, on the border's north side, will be quite shady, from midsummer onwards, and cries out for illumination by white flowers. What better than the anemone? It blooms at different levels, from 2 to 4 ft., and is out from early August till October. Its flowers, moreover, have a simplicity and fitness that devastate all artifice: a cupped bloom of 8 or so white petals surrounding a ring of yellow stamens, which themselves frame a green central button. We shall see them against reddish-purple castor oil foliage.

The holly, *Ilex altaclarensis* 'Golden King', is another slow grower in its early years, but too good to be passed over and we shall like it with its laurustinus background. In front, the elegant evergreen fern, *Polystichum aculeatum* 'Bevis', which will contrast, in summer, with the purposeful hosta, to which we have now returned. And I rather fancy a thicket of *Rosa virginiana* as our last ingredient. There is great warmth and vitality in this rose species with its red young stems and its glossy foliage that flares up so brilliantly and over a long period in autumn. Single pink briar flowers in July (of no great account) are followed by a handsome crop of small scarlet hips.

Last Foliar Fling

*

I know very well that in a few years' time (but I hope you won't read this before buying my book) I shall be wondering how I could have written so much rubbish. I have been working at this over two consecutive January–February seasons and even in the intervals between these two periods I gathered a frightening quantity of extra material and modified a great deal already written, from further experience.

I am making two points here: first, that I should have written a better book on foliage had I gone on thinking about it and collecting for it, for another 15 or 20 years, let us say. But then I might never have got it written. A compromise is essential and at least I have managed to record my warm and unchanging regard for many plants I have long cherished. Many others are comparatively new friends and I have probably over-enthused or else done them scant justice. And there are others not included at all that will be my friends of the future. Well, I apologise for their absence but it's nice to have them to look forward to.

Second point: having reached my second February it becomes imperative to have done by the end of the month. My editor is clamouring for the manuscript; my garden clamours for my attention and *Clematis*, now out of print, clamours to be re-written next winter (and probably the winter following).

Looking back on the plants I have discussed, I am aware of one particularly glaring omission: *Gunnera*. What happened was that, having dealt with trees, in the jejune manner of one who has not room to grow (and hence know) many, I decided to tackle the outstanding shrubs, herbaceous and bedding plants from the point of view of their use in mixed borders. Obviously a titchy little thing like the Creeping Peppermint, *Mentha requienii*, could never be so used, but it got in under the skirts of its bolder brethren. I then tried to show, in the plans, how to mix the ingredients in a border (Lloyd's notion of how, anyway). If you know the plants I'm talking about you will appreciate that this left out gunneras, which could only be included in a rather strange mixed border (they could, though, and I've half a mind to make the attempt). And it left out quite a number of water-loving foliage plants.

I've also omitted a few engaging weeds and some variegated plants that I could have worked in earlier, but was afraid to lest I got bogged down with excess matter. One last fling, then.

Waterside and Water Plants. First let me get *Gunnera manicata* off my chest. I have already written extensively on this majestic plant in *The Well-Tempered Garden* but am unlikely to be inhibited by that consideration. On the contrary I'm always delighted at any fresh opportunity for dwelling upon my special favourites.

I do, in this case, feel a tiny bit guilty about indulging myself because this gunnera is a giant: not merely the largest-leaved hardy foliage plant available but the bulkiest hardy herbaceous plant by any standard (except height). And so, even though it does not necessarily have to grow by the waterside – any damp spot will do, in sun or in shade – yet it will find a place in only a few gardens. After all, if yours is a small garden and you are a no-trouble gardener, you are unlikely to be the sort of person who would wish to draw attention to himself (as he undoubtedly would, attracting a stream of corney jokes) by filling half his total area with one gunnera plant. On the other hand, if you were a keen gardener with only a small area, you would certainly prefer to grow 200 alpines in the same space as one gunnera would fatly occupy. At present my gunneras, with their old leaves folded over and protecting their crowns, look like the last remains of some boneless wonder; an amoebic monster that dragged itself out of the pond to die on its banks. But the circle of etiolated turf round them shows that the diameter shaded by one plant in summer is 18 ft.

Still, more gardeners could find a suitable spot than do. The basic structure of the plant is as follows. Dormancy is visibly expressed, above ground, by enormous resting buds enclosed by scales of pinkish colouring. The plant begins to stretch itself in spring by simultaneously unfurling its first young leaves (there are plenty more in reserve in case these get frosted, as frequently happens) and pushing up its strange flowering stems which look like a cross between a vast fleshy fir cone and a fertility symbol. These inflorescences are at their most conspicuous in spring before the leaves are more than half expanded. When fully grown, the latter are up to 6 ft. across, kidney-shaped to circular in outline but with indented, frilly margins and a surface that rises to its subtending veins but falls between them. The leaf thus makes full use of its three-dimensional properties and is a miracle of lights and shades, especially when the sun is low and more especially still if grown by water so that sunlight is reflected off a gently rippling surface, on to the undersides of the gunnera's own leaves.

These leaves stand 6 ft. or so high (more, in shade) and are carried by stout, spiny stems. The leaf surface itself is rough to the touch and makes a grating sound as you pass your fingertips across it. The plant hails from south Brazil. I should love to see it in its native habitat; to see what animals its un-cuddly stems are warding off and whether anyone or anything makes use of its protective leafage to doze away the mid-day hours, shaded from sun, or to remain snugly dry in a tropical rain-storm.

There is a similar, but not so dramatic and ebullient species, called *G. tinctoria* (long known as *G. chilensis*) that must, I think, be frequently passed for *G. manicata*. It has an emaciated, hungry, Cassius-look about it.

G. manicata is not difficult to raise from seed. I was immensely flattered, two years ago, to find a self-sown seedling several yards away from the parent clump, but that was the first time in 40 years. Pick and dry off the seed heads in autumn, just before the first hard frosts. Sow thickly in a pot, in spring, but do not cover the pot with brown paper (as is normal with most spring-sown seeds) as full light seems to be necessary for germination. Even then, it is slow and uneven. I leave the pot on the open greenhouse bench. Seedlings germinate through the summer and autumn. They are tiny; I do not disturb them till the following spring. Prick out; finally pot off singly into 5 in. pots. The plants will be ready for their permanent quarters in the spring of the following year (2 years from sowing) and late spring is the right time to get them established. If there is still danger from a late frost, cover the young plant with a cloche. Even if planted by a pond, it will probably be some time before it can get its roots down to the water's level, so you must remember to water copiously. Establishing a young plant is the one tricky period, and you must not go into a trance.

Winters are seldom a problem in the south, but many gardeners in the midlands or north, who think they can't grow gunneras, could in fact do so if they would take a little extra trouble each late autumn. As well as folding its own leaves over the crowns, cover the plant with an old blanket (even a young blanket will serve) and cover this with a heavy sheet of polythene, kept in position round its margins by throwing earth on to them. Not a pretty arrangement, admittedly, but business-like and obviously there for a purpose and therefore acceptable from December to April.

From the southern tip of S. America, *Gunnera magellanica* is a surprising contrast but a pretty thing if you have the right place for it: damp, cultivated soil, where it won't get choked by weeds. It is a deciduous creeping plant with fresh green, kidney-shaped leaves and only a few inches high. Perfectly hardy.

The Water Saxifrage, *Peltiphyllum peltatum*, is another moisture-loving perennial with an umbrella- or mushroom-shaped leaf, this time of more-or-less circular outline but a frilly perimeter. It is deciduous. All you see of it in winter are its snaky rhizomes, much like a bearded iris's. Mine go right down into the water on one side of the colony, but up to a metalled road verge on the other. The latter site would seem to be dry, but I suppose the connecting root and rhizome links enable water to be drawn up to this high level.

In spring, pretty domed heads of pink flowers appear, borne on fleshy, pink stems which are a foot tall at flowering but extend afterwards. Flower colouring varies a good deal in different clones and can be washy in the less good ones. Then the leaves push up and make an efficient ground cover at the 3 to 4 ft. level – even up to 6 ft. in a moist climate. They brown off and become unsightly in early autumn in most gardens. At Inverewe, in N.W. Scotland, however, the spectacular planting of water saxifrage in a ditch all along the principal straight walk through the garden's centre, regularly takes on a marvellous flame and crimson colouring in autumn. This is a mystery because when these same plants are moved elsewhere, they die as drably as may be.

One method of treating a large boggy problem area that you didn't want the bother of draining would be to plant it with the Giant Butterburr, *Petasites japonicus giganteus*. Although deciduous, it is so rampantly agggressive (of 3-G status) that, to my knowledge, nothing else could compete successfully with it in this sort of position (where competitors are limited at the best of times). Its leaves are rounded, up to 4 ft. across and borne on 5 ft. stems. The plant conquers new territory by means of thick, exploratory rhizomes. This is the largest member of a genus that includes a number of similar, smaller possibilities, including the winter heliotrope, *P. fragrans*, whose sickly roadside scent I strongly associate with the daily winter walks I was obliged to take as a child. The petasites all flower, more or less wanly, in winter or early spring before their leaves appear.

Let us now descend from bog and brink into the water itself. I have already discussed *Glyceria* (pp. 133-4) and *Phalaris* (p. 143) because they are also good border plants; the variegated flag, *Iris pseudacorus* 'Variegata' and *I. laevigata* 'Variegata' (p. 138), because it was tidy to consider them with other like-minded irises.

The sweet flag, *Acorus calamus* 'Variegatus', with its cream-and-green-variegated spears, could easily be taken for an iris. Surprisingly it is an aroid. Its rhizomes spread happily in the mud beneath shallow water. Every part of the plant is fragrant, we are told; I keep forgetting to smell mine.

Another pretty spiky plant, quilled like a porcupine but with alternate bands in green and white, is the rush: *Scirpus tabernae-montanus* 'Zebrinus'. It rises 3 or 4 ft. out of the water and is hardy although it looks as though it might not be. Actually this belongs to the sedge family of *Cyperaceae* and another excellent plant to our purpose is the eponymous *Cyperus longus*, which turns out to be a somewhat rare but widely distributed native (I have just looked it up in my flora); indeed, the romantically named galingale. It belongs to a mainly tropical genus that includes the Egyptian papyrus. The eye-catching characteristic of this genus lies in their terminal leaves and inflorescences with spoke-like bracts, at the ends of long, bare stems. *C. longus* is no exception; a little disappointing at first, it gets into its stride when settled in. It grows a good 3 ft. out of the water and makes a dense colony, looking extremely untidy in winter but making good cover for birds.

C. alternifolius most certainly is tender and is grown for the most part as a window-sill or cool greenhouse plant – for which purpose, indeed, I use it myself and have warm feelings for it. The terminal mops of leaves and bracts are bright, shining green, some 2½ ft. high. It grows luxuriantly in a pond in summer. You can drop a pot of it into 3 or 4 inches of water, but as a pot is apt to blow over, it is really better to plant it into a deep box and submerge that.

My last choice from the vast and complex family of *Cyperaceae* is a form of the Great Pond-sedge, namely *Carex riparia* (or it may be *C. stricta* alias *C. elata*) in its yellow form, known as Bowles's Golden sedge. Its 2-ft.-long, flexible leaves are in one plane but ribbed, striped longitudinally with more gold than green. There is conflicting evidence on the correct name of this plant, alas, but it remains happily unconcerned and is perfectly amenable and especially gay in spring. You can get it from Treasures of Tenbury, Worcester.

Some water plants gain a living by floating permanently on the water's surface, their roots dangling below their foliage. Duckweed (spp. of *Lemna*) is typical but should never be introduced deliberately. Usually it arrives uninvited. You can get rid of it by introducing ducks but then you have the problem of getting rid of the ducks. I have no other constructive suggestion. Duckweed makes a green skin of vegetation on your pond, so that the water is invisible. Why it should take a hold on some ponds and not on others, I have yet to learn.

There are some tender, exotic floating aquatics that are for the summer only, and of these my favourite is the water hyacinth, *Eichhornia crassipes* (syn. *E. speciosa*) – a far worse water-weed in tropical countries than our humble duckweeds here, but in this country eichhornias need to be treated with tender affection and are not at all easy to overwinter unless you have well heated glass. They make clusters of buoyant, glossy green foliage, the leaf blade being roughly reniform, the stalk below it inflated and bulbous. You can just drop pieces into the pond, in spring, and allow them to float around. They grow more enthusiastically, however, if planted in a shallowly submerged pot or box. The leaves then make a dense carpet from which pieces occasionally break off and float away like ice from a decaying floe.

Then there are the submerged aquatics, which, if they rise to the surface at all, do no more than just break it. There is a coarseness about many of these which is not helped by the deposit of algae that masks the true colouring of their foliage for all the warmer months of the year. In winter, when a pond is at its clearest, they may come into their own – some of them.

The elodeas and potamogetons, although their leafy shoots are often rather beautiful, are generally far too rampant. To be able to see anything that's going on in your pond in summer, you may find yourself under the repeated obligation of fishing large quantities out. But this only makes it more congenial for what's left behind to go berserk once again.

And yet they are important for the health and welfare – for the general ecology of a pond. They push very necessary oxygen into the water and remove compounds of carbon. It is best to decide, after some study of the alternatives, which of them appeals to you the strongest and stick to that. One weed will generally be enough.

In a small pool, my own preference is for *Stratiotes aloides*, the Water Soldier. It is scarcely aggressive at all and makes attractive, spiky rosettes like an exotic star-fish or sea anemone, bronze-purple in colouring (when algae allow you to see its colour). In winter, however, it sinks and shrinks and becomes virtually invisible. Each star-fish makes babies at the ends of stolons, so that you get colonies in summer, at which time the tips of their leaves break the surface. Perry's of Enfield, Middlesex (who have long specialised in water plants) write of its 'rising to the surface during those summer months in which the flowers are produced'. Which is not the same, be it noted, as to say that flowers will be produced. I have never seen any.

In our larger 'natural' pond (originally dug out in the course of iron ore excavations) we have the Water Violet, *Hottonia palustris*. It found its way there before I came on the scene and has defied all attempts (my brother's, not mine) to eradicate it. Fortunately, I like this plant and can recommend it. Its pinnate leaves are finely dissected and are arranged in filigree rosettes of the brightest green colouring; brighter than any green in the winter garden, as I write, but greatly helped and enlivened when there is sunshine and, additionally, the brilliant red of a semi-torpid goldfish, seen against it. The hottonia makes billowing under-water clouds of greenery and is everywhere apparent except where the water-lilies grow. The latter are threadbare, now, but the water violet still keeps a respectful distance for it cannot abide being shaded, and the water lily pads, once they get going, are heavy shade-makers.

Why water *violet*? You may well ask. *Hottonia palustris* belongs to the Primulaceae and the relationship becomes plainer when it rises a foot above the water to flower, in May, just like a candelabra primula, in palest mauve. Actually, it reminds me most nearly of *Primula malacoides*. In a good year, the display is dazzling, but is followed by the plant's worst period, in July, when it becomes as murky as the water itself.

A Few More Weeds. From pond weeds to land weeds. . . . I shall not for long trifle with the reader's patience and sense of personal dignity on this theme, but I do feel that a few weeds deserve better than rejection with contumely.

Near to ground level we have the green mossy growth of *Helxine soleirolii*. It is a damp and spongy plant, especially happy in pavement cracks in a cool, moist, shaded position. Once in a lawn it will not easily be eliminated by selective weedkillers but this doesn't really matter; it does no harm there but it can be a competitive nuisance among more precious paving plants. However, there is a much prettier yellow-leaved form – lime green, really – that is also less robust. It has died on me and I shall have to try again. Helxine's popular name is Mind Your Own Business. It belongs to the stinging nettle family, *Urticaceae*, and bears a facial resemblance to another nettle relative, *Pilea*, used with astonishing want of imagination, in pots at the front of conservatory staging, to provide some sort of a vegetable foreground to banks of flowers in season.

The very word *Oxalis* is calculated to strike terror and dismay into the gardener's heart, much as is *Convolvulus* or *Epilobium*, but all three genera have gentlemanly exceptions. By my terms of reference I am here concerned only with *Oxalis* and with only one oxalis at that, namely *O. corniculata* 'Purpurea'. This is a charmer. It is essentially a plant for paving cracks and makes a soft hummock of its rich purple, trifoliate leaves, against which bright star-like yellow flowers are spangled. Another way this plant endears itself to me is as an irregular and unofficial edge-breaker in my rose garden. It must be watched here, as it grows up into the crutch of the less vigorous rose bushes. I am inclined to give the weed some latitude in this context but must admit that the rose, to me, is nothing more than a beautiful flower – not a shrine at which I feel obliged to worship. The oxalis is deciduous and vanishes from sight in winter. It spreads, in the main, by seeding. Sometimes its procumbent stems can root where they lie on the ground, but this is not so very usual. And a saving grace in the plant is that it does *not* make underground 'bulbs' (rhizomes, actually), which are the reason for *O. rubra* and others, becoming such a menace. *O. corniculata* 'Purpurea' is controllable.

The Common Plantain, *Plantago major*, has two attractive variants that I particularly associate with Margery Fish, through whom I came to know them. Rosularis is the Rose Plantain, whose inflorescence is changed into a tight rosette of green bracts. It looks like a green flower although it isn't really. The only trouble you will have with this plant, unless you do all your own gardening, is in preventing your friends, relations and employees from weeding it out. Then we have *P. major rubrifolia*, with dusky reddish purple foliage. This is another pretty plant for paving cracks. It does flower and seed itself around but is easily controlled.

Not so my last weed, *Polygonum cuspidatum* 'Variegatum', which is a real problem child. I had this one from Mrs Fish but I have never yet dared to plant it out of its pot, after seeing what it has done in a friend's garden. *Polygonum* is another bogey word in the gardener's ears, and it largely owes its reputation to *P. cuspidatum* itself, a rampant 6 ft. perennial with heart-shaped leaves, that makes vast colonies, especially on damp soil (it is striking near water, especially when carrying its panicles of white blossom in September: there is a hedge of it on the far side of the canal in Hampton Court gardens where it is quite safe) and is, short of the most devastating methods imaginable, practically ineradicable. The variegated version is not so vigorous, admittedly, but don't let that fool you. Before long a piece of it will revert to the plain green type-plant and away it goes. All the same, I have a love-hate relationship with this plant and must explain the love side of it. Not only is the cream-and-green leaf variegation pleasant, but when the young shoots first appear in spring they are brilliant carmine pink and, instinct with burgeoning vitality, they look immensely exciting. If you grow tired of their comparatively mundane summer dress, you can cut your plants down, half way through the growing season, and make them start all over again with a repeat performance of pristine brilliance.

Variegation. A few more variegateds, now we're on the subject, but no more weeds (although I am tempted by the variegated ground elder).

The history of *Phlox paniculata* 'Norah Leigh' is a little sad. It first appeared (with great éclat) in Bloom's wholesale list of 1963–4, but has since been dropped; one by one the retail nurserymen have dropped it also, and so have I. It is a border phlox whose leaf is usually two thirds of pale primrose colouring, only a small central area, green. It was a marvellous sight as I first saw it in Alan Bloom's garden, where a large patch was a picture in every way, health included. I should think it must have been planted on a vast couch of animal manure, because I have never seen it like that since. Its constitution is lamentably weak. The flowers are small and a wan shade of mauve, but I find them entirely appropriate to the serried ranks of subtending foliage. There is now a variegated variety on tap called Harlequin, said to be more robust, but I have not seen this.

Another failure in my garden that I had better get off my chest is the variegated Solomon's Seal, *Polygonatum hybridum* 'Striatum'. With their leaves in two ranks along an arching stem, Solomon's

Seals are always of distinctive appearance but this one has the additional merit of stripy cream-coloured variegation. Naturally it is less vigorous than the type. After I planted mine, it pushed through promisingly: then disappeared. I'm afraid I jumped to the mean conclusion that a predatory visitor had swiped it and I was upset. Further investigation, however, led me to discover that slugs were the executioners. This was even more upsetting; I had only myself to blame.

Lilies-of-the-Valley associate so effectively with Solomon's Seal that the story has got around of their actually benefiting from one another's company. On the whole I dislike 'improvements' to the common Lily-of-the-Valley; there seems no point in the extra-large flowers of Fortin's Giant or the doubling of Plena, while the pink version is dreadfully grubby. But *C. majalis* 'Variegata' is a beauty, especially at its first unfurling in spring. Each of the main longitudinal leaf veins is picked out in bright yellow. The colour later fades, somewhat, but not altogether. The flowers are not large but perfectly serviceable and scented as they should be. I see that Perry's are offering this at £1.25 per plant, but I can assure the reader that one crown will soon multiply to many and that he is unlikely to have a loss on his hands; so long as he can grow lilies-of-the-valley at all. Damp, humus-rich soil and shade are the principal ingredients for success. Lilies grow wild on limestone soils; you needn't add lime expressly but it's nice to know they won't resent it.

Three more variegated shade lovers (and remember that variegation shows up wonderfully well in shade). *Brunnera macrophylla* is a perennial relative of the forget-me-not's and likewise carries blue flowers in spring. Its large, heart-shaped leaves have a

31. ABOVE, *Lonicera nitida* 'Baggesen's Golden' makes a corner-piece where the main line of my Long Border is intersected by a cross-path (not visible). In front of it the foliage of *Bergenia* 'Ballawley' is in its glossy green summer state, but it takes on a variety of fiery and lurid shades in autumn and winter. BELOW, two rodgersias. The platter-like foliage of *Rodgersia tabularis* is brilliant green, when young, in marked contrast to the purple of R. *podophylla*, whose leaves are divided into leaflets shaped like a webbed foot. Both enjoy moisture.

wide outer band of cream variegation in Variegata (from Treasures
of Tenbury). It is boldly handsome in spring but inclined to become coarse and tatty later on. You must not punish this plant
with dry soil (as I have); moisture and sunshine would be better
for it than dry shade. And in the same family of *Boraginaceae* is a
variegated comfrey which I think should be called *Symphitum
asperum* 'Aureo-variegatum' but if you get any variegated comfrey
(none too easily located) of whatever name, it is likely to be the
one I am talking about. A beautiful plant with the usual elongated
comfrey leaf but, again, broadly margined in cream. It rises to
3 ft. to flower (blue, tubular) and retains its attraction until then,
but subsequently goes to pieces for a time and should be cut to
the ground. After this treatment, fresh basal foliage is produced
and the plant's greatest foliar triumphs follow, surprisingly, in late
summer. It is not as vigorous as one would wish and needs well
enriched soil.

Honesty, *Lunaria annua*, is a biennial. Because of its stupid

32. ABOVE LEFT, effective and beautiful evergreen ground cover is
made by mixing the large, leathery-leaved *Bergenia cordifolia* and the
glossy, trailing bramble, *Rubus tricolor*. Both take on purplish tints in
winter. RIGHT, a superb foliage plant, but alas, tender; the woody-
stemmed *Geranium palmatum* hails from Madeira. It grows quickly
from seed or cuttings. The picture shows how old leaf stems bend
back to the ground and form a support for the plant's trunk. MIDDLE,
two ferns in the wild that take well to garden life. *Left*, the beech fern,
Thelipteris (*Gymnocarpium*) *phegopteris*, is a runner, never more than a
foot tall. *Right*, *Cryptogramma crispa*, the parsley fern, is always found
in loose scree, where it is one of the earlier plant colonisers. It has no
special requirements in the garden, apart from acid soil. BELOW
LEFT, *Salix lanata*, the woolly willow, is a rare native in Scotland and
flourishes best in the north. Here seen at Perceval Hall, in Yorkshire,
with *Chamaecyparis lawsoniana* 'Erecta Aurea' (a cypress that I do not
recommend) and squat pygmy specimens of *Picea glauca albertiana*
'Conida'; also *Primula florindae*, a giant yellow cowslip that self-sows
abundantly. RIGHT, maidenhair spleenworts, *Asplenium trichomanes*,
colonising the risers in garden steps, here at Dixter, where we also
have the black spleenwort, *A. adiantumnigrum*. Both are evergreen and
very endearing plants.

specific epithet, the fact has to be rubbed in. Variegated Honesty, *L.a.* 'Variegata' is liberally splashed and mottled with cream over the whole leaf, in spring and summer, especially nearest the margins and it makes striking under-cover to a large and boring shrub like a lilac (as I have it). In winter, the variegation amounts to no more than anaemic intimations. It comes true from seed, as long as kept apart from other kinds of honesty. But as the other kinds are many of them interesting, in respect of their flowers (this one is just mauve, but suitably) and as they do get around without much encouragement, the proviso is not always easily regarded.

There I shall leave you and there I shall leave my subject. If I have succeeded in nothing else, I have at least managed to convince myself, in the course of my rangings, that the world of foliage is a pleasant place to dwell in. I can only hope that a few converts will come to feel the same way. A subject is, largely, what you make of it. If I have failed, the fault is mine, but a small voice whispers that I must surely have communicated something of my sentiments to those readers who have managed to stay the course and reach

THE END

The two main reference works that I have consulted and constantly mentioned herein, are:

The Royal Horticultural Society's Dictionary of Gardening in 4 volumes, published in 1951 and its latest Supplement of 1969.

W. J. Bean's *Trees and Shrubs Hardy in the British Isles* (Murray), frequently referred to *tout court* as Bean. First published in 1914, in 2 volumes, this is now in painfully slow process of republication in extensively revised form, in 4 volumes, only the first of which is out as I write.

Nurseries

*

The following nurseries have been mentioned in the
text as (possible) suppliers of particular plants or seeds:

Bodnant Garden Nursery, Tal-y-Cafn, Colwyn Bay,
Denbighshire.

Thomas Butcher, 60 Wickham Road, Shirley, Croydon,
Surrey.

Samuel Dobie and Son, Chester.

Four Winds Nursery, Holt Pound, Wrecclesham,
Surrey.

Hillier and Sons, Winchester.

Perry's Hardy Plant Farm, Enfield, Middlesex.

The Plantsmen, Buckshaw Gardens, Holwell, Sher-
borne, Dorset.

Robert Poland, Brook House, Nursery Ardingly,
Haywards Heath, Sussex.

G. Reuthe, Fox Hill Nurseries, Keston, Kent.

Thompson & Morgan, London Rd., Ipswich.

Treasures of Tenbury, Tenbury Wells, Worcestershire.

Treseder's Nurseries, Truro, Cornwall.

W. J. Unwin, Histon, Cambridge.

Washfield Nurseries, Hawkhurst, Kent.

Glossary

*

A.G.M. Award of Garden Merit made by the R.H.S. to plants of proven general garden-worthiness.

bipinnate. When the divisions of a pinnate leaf are themselves pinnate.

bipinnatifid. When the divisions of a pinnatifid leaf are themselves pinnatifid.

calcicole. Lime-loving.

calcifuge. Lime-hating.

clone. The vegetatively produced progeny of a single individual.

corymb (adj. corymbose). An inflorescence of stalked flowers springing from different levels but making a flat head e.g. *Sambucus nigra*, Common Elder.

crenate. With rounded marginal teeth (usually of a leaf).

cultivar. Omnibus word for Cultivated Variety: a plant which has originated in cultivation not normally to be given a name of Latin form. Triomphe de Boskoop is a cultivar of *Chamaecyparis lawsoniana* (Lawson's Cypress). So is Allumii, but this dates from the bad old days when cv's (short for cultivars) *were* given names of Latin form.

distal. Away from centre or point of attachment; terminal (opposite of proximal).

fastigiate. Of upright, columnar habit, occupying little lateral space.

glaucous. Bluish.

indumentum. The hairy covering of any plant or part of a plant.

inflorescence. Flowering branch or portion of the stem above the last stem leaves, including its branches, bracts and flowers.

palmate (of a leaf). Lobed, the midribs arising at one point, as in a sycamore and many other maples.

panicle (adg. paniculate). A branched raceme e.g. *Ligustrum* (privet).

petiole. The stalk of a leaf.

pinna (pl. pinnae). Primary division of a pinnate leaf.

pinnate (of a leaf). Having leaflets arranged on either side of a common axis like a feather (e.g. *Fraxinus*, *Ailanthus*).

pinnatifid. Almost but not quite pinnate, not divided to the midrib, e.g. polypody (*Polypodium vulgare*).

pinnatisect. Like pinnatifid but some of the lower divisions reaching very nearly or quite to the midrib.

pinnule. The secondary division in a bipinnate leaf or frond, the division reaching to the pinna midrib.

raceme (adj. racemose). A collection of distinctly stalked flowers arranged at intervals along a stem.

rachis. The axis of a leaf (usually used of fern fronds).

reniform. Kidney-shaped.

rhizome (adj. rhizomatous). An underground stem.

R.H.S. The Royal Horticultural Society.

species. A group of individuals which have the same constant and distinctive characters. The name of a species is, in designating a plant, placed second and has a small initial letter, e.g. *Viburnum tinus*. Tinus is here the specific epithet.

stratification (verb: stratify). A method for preserving seed, often making it germinate easily and freely through exposure to cold under moist conditions. It also separates seeds from the pulpy coating (which contains hormones inhibiting germination) in which they are sometimes enclosed, e.g. rose hips. The seed is generally spread in layers between layers of moist sand.

zygomorphic. Describing an irregular flower, capable of division into two similar halves along one vertical axis only.

Index

*